Deliberative Democracy between Theory and Practice

Deliberative democrats seek to link political choices more closely to the deliberations of common citizens, rather than consigning them to speak only in the desiccated language of checks on a ballot. Sober thinkers from Plato to today, however, have argued that if we want to make good decisions, we cannot entrust them to the deliberations of common citizens. Critics argue that deliberative democracy is wildly unworkable in practice.

Deliberative Democracy between Theory and Practice cuts across this debate by clarifying the structure of a deliberative democratic system, and goes on to reevaluate the main empirical challenges to deliberative democracy in light of this new frame. It simultaneously reclaims the wider theory of deliberative democracy and meets the empirical critics squarely on terms that advance, rather than evade, the debate. Doing so has important implications for institutional design, the normative theory of democracy, and priorities for future research and practice.

Michael A. Neblo is an associate professor in the departments of Political Science and (by courtesy) Philosophy at the Ohio State University.

Deliberative Democracy between Theory and Practice

MICHAEL A. NEBLO
Ohio State University

CAMBRIDGE
UNIVERSITY PRESS

CAMBRIDGE
UNIVERSITY PRESS

University Printing House, Cambridge CB2 8BS, United Kingdom

One Liberty Plaza, 20th Floor, New York, NY 10006, USA

477 Williamstown Road, Port Melbourne, VIC 3207, Australia

4843/24, 2nd Floor, Ansari Road, Daryaganj, Delhi - 110002, India

79 Anson Road, #06-04/06, Singapore 079906

Cambridge University Press is part of the University of Cambridge.

It furthers the University's mission by disseminating knowledge in the pursuit of education, learning and research at the highest international levels of excellence.

www.cambridge.org
Information on this title: www.cambridge.org/9781316649169

© Michael A. Neblo 2015

First published 2015
First paperback edition 2017

A catalogue record for this publication is available from the British Library

Library of Congress Cataloging in Publication data
Neblo, Michael A.
Deliberative democracy between theory and practice / Michael A. Neblo.
pages cm
Includes bibliographical references and index.
ISBN 978-1-107-02767-1 (Hardback)
1. Deliberative democracy–Philosophy. I. Title.
JC423.N386 2015
321.8–dc23   2015027423

ISBN 978-1-107-02767-1 Hardback
ISBN 978-1-316-64916-9 Paperback

For my parents, my wife, and my daughters
Respice, adspice, prospice.

. . .

And so I appeal to a voice, to something shadowy,
a remote important region in all who talk:
though we could fool each other, we should consider –
lest the parade of our mutual life get lost in the dark.

For it is important that awake people be awake,
or a breaking line may discourage them back to sleep;
the signals we give – yes or no, or maybe –
should be clear: the darkness around us is deep.

William Stafford, from "A Ritual to Read to Each Other"

Contents

Tables

Figures

Acknowledgments

Psychologists have found that expressing gratitude makes us happy. I have incurred so many debts of gratitude over years of work on this project that making a final account of them has been one of the happiest tasks of my professional life.

My teacher, Lynn Sanders, inspired and supported this project, starting with its distant ancestor in my first year of graduate school at the University of Chicago. Her critique of deliberative democracy structured the challenge that I have been trying to meet ever since. Mark Hansen and Charles Larmore were magnificent co-chairs for a dissertation that constantly threatened to split apart; they provided the kind of intellectual, professional, and personal support that allowed me to take risks. Michael Dawson was particularly helpful in guiding me to link the empirical and normative dimensions of the dissertation. Jürgen Habermas was extremely generous with his time, encouragement, and advice, especially as it relates to his own work.

Several friends and colleagues at Chicago read, commented on, and argued about the ideas that I developed in my thesis. First among them was Adam Maze, who twice stayed up all night with me to see a chapter through. Scott Blinder, Jake Gersen, Chris Rohrbacher, David Mandell, Chad Cyrenne, Andrew Rehfeld, Fonna Forman, and Eric Schliesser all read one or more chapters and provided valuable feedback as well as the kind of intellectual and personal friendship that make graduate school fun. Though we only overlapped one year at Chicago, Mattias Iser has remained a dear friend and valued colleague ever since.

I was fortunate to spend a very stimulating year teaching in Yale's Ethics, Politics, and Economics Program. The students in my deliberative democracy seminar helped me to begin the process of transforming a technical dissertation into a more broadly engaging book. The late Robert Dahl was wonderfully insightful in criticizing my work over two of the most enjoyable lunches of my life. Many thanks also to Ian Shapiro, Geoffrey Garrett, and John McCormick for their hospitality and intellectual engagement during my stay.

My two years at the University of Michigan as a Robert Wood Johnson Scholar in Health Policy Research were enormously generative. I am grateful to the foundation for its support, and the host faculty at Michigan, especially Skip Lupia who, ever since, has been the best mentor one could hope for. More recently, I have been fortunate to spend the last two years as a visiting Fellow at Northwestern University's Institute for Policy Research. Many thanks to Jamie Druckman, David Figlio, Dan Galvin, Bonnie Honig, Fay Lomax Cook, and Jackie Stevens for their support and hospitality during my stay. In between, I spent a very productive month as a scholar in residence at the Kettering Foundation. Thanks to Derek Barker, Connie Crockett, John Dedrick, Alice Diebel, Libby Kingseed, Mindy LaBreck, David Matthews, Noëlle McAfee, David McIvor, Marie Sims, and Hal Sounders for their kindness and support.

At Ohio State University, I am fortunate to have had a series of supportive chairs: Paul Beck, Kathleen McGraw, Herb Weisberg, and Rick Herrmann have all fostered my growth as a scholar in ways big and small. My current and former colleagues at Ohio State have been a constant source of stimulation over the years. Many thanks to Sonja Amadae, Greg Caldeira, Clarissa Hayward, Don Hubin, Ben McKean, Jennifer Mitzen, Tom Nelson, Irfan Noroodin, John Parrish, Piers Turner, Inés Valdez, Craig Volden, Alex Wendt, Alan Wiseman, and Jack Wright. I have been fortunate to have the support of several terrific research assistants. I am grateful to Michael Dunkin, Deirdre McMahon, Boris Krupa, Daniel Davis, Daniel Blake, Bobby Gulotty, Christina Xydias, Nick Felts, Danny Lempert, and Cameron DeHart. The graduate students in two seminars in which we read portions of this manuscript also provided stimulating feedback for which I am grateful.

Two current colleagues at Ohio State stand out for special thanks. Eric MacGilvray and William Minozzi read multiple drafts of the whole manuscript and provided invaluable comments as well as friendship and moral support. If it is true that an argument is not really an argument until it is rendered clearly, then William and Eric are nigh unto coauthors of this book. I have become so dependent on their advice that I was tempted to ask them to edit these very sentences.

Speaking of coauthors: Chapter 5 draws substantially on an article I wrote with David Lazer, Kevin Esterling, Ryan Kennedy, and Anand Sokhey. Collaborating on that paper and the broader project of which it is a part has been one of the real highlights of my career so far, and I am grateful to all of them for their continuing collegiality and friendship.

Several colleagues beyond Ohio State commented on one or more chapters and provided enormously valuable feedback. Sincere thanks to André Bächtiger, Jim Bohman, Lisa Disch, John Dryzek, JimFishkin, Chad Flanders, Chris Karpowitz, Jim Johnson, George Marcus, Marco Steenbergen, Jurg Steiner, Dennis Thompson, Mark Warren, and especially Jenny Mansbridge for helping to make often clumsy and mistaken arguments better. They are all, of course, innocent of the clumsiness and errors that remain.

Thanks also to the folks at Cambridge University Press. Lew Bateman and Eric Crahan (then at Cambridge) took an early interest in my manuscript, and Debbie Gershenowitz, Dana Bricken, and Elizabeth Shand had the patience and professionalism to see it through. Portions of Chapters 2, 5, and 6 draw on work originally published, respectively, in the *Swiss Political Science Review*, the *American Political Science Review*, and the *Critical Review*. Thanks to Wiley-Blackwell, Cambridge University Press, and Jeffrey Friedman for permission to reprint that work. I am happy to acknowledge the Evans Scholars Foundation, the National Science Foundation, the Mellon Foundation, and the Kettering Foundation for financial and material support at different points throughout my career. Thanks also to all those who participated in my surveys and recruited others to do so (especially Bernie Goss and Jack Scanlon).

When people make the ubiquitous snide joke about in-laws, I simply have no frame of reference (despite having an extra seventeen brothers and sisters, thirteen nieces and nephews, and two parents by marriage). I am grateful to the McMahons, who have never been anything but loving and kind to me. John Neblo and Laura McNabney, my own brother and sister, and their families have supported me with love and good humor over the (too) many years that it has taken to complete this book.

My parents, Joanne and John Neblo, were my first and best teachers. They may not have always understood why I decided to leave a good job to go back to graduate school, but their love and support never depended on what I did in any case. I hope that they know how much anything worthwhile that I have managed to do depended on their love.

Finally, my deepest thanks to Eileen McMahon. As years of loving patience with this project justly gave way to years of loving impatience, the love somehow managed to grow. Thank you for that miracle, and for the even greater miracles of Anna and Kate, who came late in this process, but made it infinitely more joyful.

I

Introduction: Common Voices

My grandfathers had six years of schooling between them, and that includes one of them going through the sixth grade. Despite never learning to read or write in either his native Italian or his adopted English, my father's father voted dutifully and discussed political issues with relatives, friends, neighbors, and co-workers. Even without any formal schooling, he thought that he had things to say about politics that others should hear, and in turn, that he needed to hear what they had to say.

My first memory of being included (such as it was) in an adult conversation about politics took place at the tavern my father frequented with his fellow Teamsters. They were debating the merits of President Carter's deregulation of the trucking industry, whether it constituted a betrayal, and warranted the union endorsing Governor Reagan for president.[1] I knew that important things were at stake in their discussion, and the experience sparked a life-long engagement with such conversations, first as a participant, and eventually as a student of them.

The transition from the citizen's perspective to the scholar's, however, proved to be jarring for my childhood vision of citizen deliberation. I soon learned that the prevailing opinion among social scientists was that most citizens did not – and did not *want* – to deliberate much about politics and that modern democracies had grown too large for what little deliberation there was among the masses to be effectual. Moreover, I learned that

---

[1] If the depiction here of my family's political discussions seems notably gendered, that is because those discussions *were* notably gendered. My grandmothers, both more educated than their husbands, nevertheless deferred to them on political matters. I do not intend to valorize everyday political talk uncritically, and return to this theme later on in this book.

the academic perspective was that this was probably a good thing since people's deliberations proceeded on the basis of appalling ignorance and a questionable commitment to constitutional principles. It is not hard, then, to guess how those scholars would have regarded the political ramblings of a handful of half-drunk truck drivers who knew nothing of microeconomics – never mind those of an illiterate immigrant from authoritarian Italy.

From this scientific perspective, what had seemed like ordinary, sensible, even essential activities appeared strangely unintelligible – epiphenomenal and self-deluding at least, and perhaps dangerous if they could be harnessed by a populist demagogue. The evidence for these factual propositions seemed – indeed, in one sense *is* – overwhelming. Any theory of democracy that does not face it squarely is utopian in the pejorative sense, not worth taking seriously for guiding political practice.

The response, in many circles, has been to make the normative standards of democracy less ambitious so as to narrow the gap between our aspirations and our achievements. Such "realist" theories of democracy, I will show, are unwarranted on good intellectual grounds, not merely out of a sentimental commitment to civics textbook portraits of democracy. We present such portraits in our children's textbooks because they reflect our deepest normative aspirations. We should be slow to set such aspirations aside, even as we frankly engage the daunting gauntlet of challenges that threaten normatively ambitious accounts of democracy.

Deliberative democrats seek to ease the tension between our ideals and the exigencies of modern mass democracy. Deliberative democracy is a form of government that tries to make good political decisions by systematically connecting them to the reasons that equal citizens give each other for and against those decisions. Sober political thinkers from Plato to the present, however, have argued that if we want to make good decisions, we cannot entrust them to the deliberations of common citizens. So I will have to explain why modern mass democracy's empirical record does not preclude having it both ways.

The ambiguity of my title, *Common Voices*, reflects this dual aspiration for popular inclusion in political deliberation and sound political decision making. The account of deliberative democracy that I develop does not concede that the scale and complexity of modern democracy necessarily rule out a meaningful role for the deliberations – the voices – of common citizens. Elites will have important specialized deliberative roles; but common citizens will have a real voice, rather than being consigned to speaking only in the desiccated, if still essential, language of checks on a ballot.

The second sense of "common voices" captures the notion that at least one purpose of such deliberation is to help us, insofar as possible and appropriate, to reach agreements and understandings – colloquially, to "speak with a common voice." This second sense requires a bit more explanation because it is controversial, even as an aspiration, and even among proponents of deliberative democracy. For now I will only note that I deliberately use the plural, "voices," and that commonality admits of degrees. Thus, there is no metaphysically dubious and morally leveling collective will here; just the mundane reality that our understandings and intentions can be more or less aligned, and that there are consequences that typically follow on the "more" and the "less." My defense of deliberative democracy links the two meanings of "common" internally: The deliberations of ordinary citizens provide the raw materials for and help outline our common choices and the reasons behind them; and to the extent that average citizens take those up as their own, they can recognize themselves in that common endeavor. Thus, against the realists, governance can be both genuinely democratic and robustly deliberative.

WHY DELIBERATIVE DEMOCRACY?

Given the apparently grim empirical record, one may wonder why it is worth trying to reconstruct a defensible notion of deliberative democracy. One of the great attractions even of realist democracy is that it gives citizens a reason to abide by decisions by distributing decision-making power equally, at least in a formal sense. If I had an equal chance to influence a decision, then I have at least one reason to regard it as legitimate – that is, there is nothing unfair about it from the standpoint of formal equality. Put this starkly, such a thin notion of equality may seem like a modest claim to legitimacy. But this is to take the short view. Taking the long view of political history, an equal chance to have one's vote "count" appears as no small accomplishment.

Yet most deliberative democrats want to push for a stronger account of legitimacy. They seek to further rationalize the exercise of power by adding a concern for the *quality* of the reasons underwriting democratic decisions. The claim is that doing so will typically produce "better" decisions, and that it promotes our freedom by deepening the sense in which we can consider ourselves people who have to abide by only those laws that we have given to ourselves. Rather than simply having everyone cut their best deal and letting the chips fall where they may, deliberative democrats want to make us accountable to each other in a way that typically goes beyond justifying my choices merely by saying "that is what I want."

Again, put this starkly, the deliberative criterion might seem painfully obvious. But, again, a glance at political history casts a different light. Resistance to democratic reforms was typically justified by appealing to the superior wisdom of some person or group smaller than all adult members of society, whether it was a king, propertied white men, or graduates of Cambridge and Oxford. So, critics have objected that deliberative democrats unwittingly side with elitists and reactionaries by handing them a convenient lever for effectively restoring unequal power. If this accusation turns out to be true, that would indeed be ironic since deliberative democracy was developed in part to expose the ways that merely formal conceptions of democratic equality leave average citizens substantively unequal and unfree.

The full response to this concern will unfold over the course of the book, but it is worth noting that, taken literally, such critics evince more skepticism about the capacities of average citizens than they might intend or coherently invoke. If asking for good reasons is asking too much, then that would seem to grant that the elitists might have a point in worrying about equal power in decision making.[2]

In one sense, requiring a deliberative account from decision makers is anti-elitist and anti-paternalistic on its face. The point of realist theories is that when elites say, in effect, "this is for your own good – you wouldn't understand," they are just acknowledging the prudential limits of mass politics. The point of deliberative theories is to say that citizens are within their rights to reply "try me." Years after the conversation in the tavern about deregulation, while I was in college studying economics, I revisited the topic with my father. I explained how economists could prove that deregulation would create efficiencies that could more than compensate the losers. He understood the argument just fine, and replied flatly, "Then why weren't we ever compensated?" The social critic's reasonable concern over inequalities in the skills of argument too easily devolves into a well-intentioned elitism of its own.

---

[2] One might believe that equality is generally more important than the substantive quality of decisions, but it is far from obvious that the former should completely trump the latter. Alternatively, the critic might be arguing that the criteria for what counts as "good reasons" are arbitrarily restrictive in a way that favors the powerful. I will discuss this line of argument in detail below.

Once we appreciate the logic of asking elites for the reasons behind their decisions, it is easy to see why it is typically reasonable to do the same for our fellow citizens. If deliberative democrats want to create a stronger link between the deliberations of average citizens (common voices) and political outcomes, then those average citizens are effectively moving closer to being decision makers vis-à-vis each other. So a similar rationale would apply. If you are going to use your power to affect my vital interests, then you owe me an explanation that goes beyond a mere assertion of your will. Otherwise, we may subject each other to arbitrary power, which is to say that we could tyrannize each other.

If putting the point this way seems a bit overheated, perhaps it is because in most democracies, majority power is subject to constitutional constraints that check some of the worst ways that we might exercise arbitrary power over each other. However, routine legislation, regulation, and other forms of mundane state power can nevertheless profoundly affect important parts of our lives. So, it may not be hyperbole to say that a democratic political system risks becoming tyrannical if it pays little regard to how a slow drip of arbitrary power can quietly accumulate.[3]

Thus, deliberation done right should help us to avoid tyranny. More-over, to the extent that we can move beyond merely *recognizing* each other's reasons to actually aligning them (i.e., to *persuade* each other), the more we can recognize political decisions as our own. By helping us to speak in more or less common voices, deliberation affects the extent to which we can realize a kind of freedom.[4] Stated this way, the deliberative account may begin to sound a bit like high theory. However, in another sense, this account merely makes explicit the rationale behind intuitive ideas and practices already embedded in our political culture. Deliberative theory makes sense of folk notions like getting to "have our say" and "calling each other to account." The ordinary, sensible political

---

[3] For similar reasons, deliberative democrats are keen to reflect periodically on the accreted consequences of our previous decisions – that is, the structures and institutions within which we exercise power over each other in the present. If our seemingly free and considered preferences are adapted to the limits of a quietly unjust system, then rationales and choices within that system will only relieve the burden of arbitrary power in a local sense. Thus, deliberative democrats want to promote reflective practices and habits that also promote autonomy in this larger structural sense.

[4] None of this is to say that advocating for your own interests is the same as merely asserting your will. The point is that in advocating my interests, I should put them in terms that appeal beyond me. For example: "Here is why I think that I have not been getting my fair share of the gains to cooperation in society lately...." For an excellent discussion, see Mansbridge et al. (2010).

exchanges among average citizens that became unintelligible in light of the realist critique once again appear ordinary and sensible.

Thus, deliberative democratic procedures open up a way of thinking about how political processes could contribute to freedom or autonomy. Such freedom would be otiose, however, if deliberative procedures were to lead consistently to bad decisions by thwarting our intentions and inefficiently realizing our goals. So deliberative democrats must also show that their procedures can lead to "better" decisions, and for many of the same reasons and mechanisms by which it promotes our autonomy.

One obvious reason why we might be able to make better decisions with robust citizen deliberation is that bringing more people into the process brings more and more kinds of information to the table. (We should understand information very broadly here to include factual information, reasons for and against proposals, perspectives, relevant life experiences, etc.) Moreover, by asking each other to justify our information as relevant and our reasons as compelling, we make it more likely that "good" information and "good" reasons will gain more traction. In subsequent chapters, I will consider many ways that such a process might go wrong, but there is certainly enough surface plausibility to these claims to warrant investigating when and how it is possible to make such deliberation effective.

Scholars have proposed many other desirable consequences that are thought to flow from deliberation. For example, there is evidence that deliberation might make for "better citizens" by increasing a host of desiderata: citizens' political sophistication; their interest and participation in politics; their sense of political efficacy; their trust in their fellow citizens, political officials, and the political system more generally; their awareness of and respect for other points of view; their empathy for others; and their willingness to take on others' interests as their own.[5]

In my view, such goods are generally best regarded as instrumental to promoting deliberative democracy's particular conceptions of freedom and good decisions. For example, trust in political officials is only good if they actually deserve such trust and thereby facilitate making good decisions that, in turn, facilitate the citizenry recognizing that their trust was well placed in the first place. But these instrumental goods bear mentioning because research on them suggests that the prospects for effective democratic deliberation may be positively self-reinforcing over

---

[5] Mansbridge (1999), Gastil et al. (2002), Luskin and Fishkin (2002), Searing et al. (2007), Esterling et al. (2011a, 2011c).

time. That is, if practicing deliberation makes one more interested in politics, more knowledgeable, more empathic, more other-regarding, more trusting, and so forth, then we have another reason for thinking that modest deliberative reforms might change the way that we evaluate the challenges to a workable deliberative democracy over time. Nevertheless, those challenges remain formidable.

CHALLENGES TO DELIBERATIVE DEMOCRACY

Soon after deliberative theory rose to prominence among philosophers and political theorists, it began to attract attention from social scientists as well. One might accurately describe the modal response among social scientists as incredulity. If research suggests that citizens cannot show up to vote every few years and reliably get it right (if they bother to show up), then it seems laughable to think that their voices should be given a more prominent place in democracy. Laughable, perhaps, were it not so dangerous. For, in the critics' view, deliberative theory gets it backward. Rather than trying to find ways to empower common voices, social scientists argue that we need to develop a theory that can accommodate the severe and inexorable limits of democracy's encounter with modern mass politics, while salvaging whichever normative remnants survive the clash.

These critics pressed their attack on multiple fronts, arguing that deliberative democracy is (1) *incoherent*, because peoples' varying reasons for and against policies will never add up to anything consistent; (2) *naïve*, because power and self-interest will always trump idealistic calls for public spiritedness; (3) *paternalistic*, because despite deliberativists' entreaties, most people simply and reasonably do not want to spend more time talking about politics; and (4) *inefficient*, because widespread ignorance among citizens will actually make their decisions worse than those of competent elites.[6] All of these criticisms depend crucially on empirical claims, so the critics brought mountains of social scientific evidence with them.

Faced with these empirical challenges, normative theorists found themselves engaging on relatively unfamiliar and unfavorable terrain. They tended to choose one of two patterns of retreat: Either they pulled back

---

[6] Critics often cite the problem of "scale" as another cardinal challenge to the workability of deliberative democracy. I agree that it is a major challenge but argue that it manifests itself in several forms that are better disaggregated and discussed under the preceding headings.

to the normative high ground, dismissing the social scientists as uninformed and their evidence as largely irrelevant to a normative theory, thereby leaving the theory merely aspirational; or they withdrew into narrow, controlled environments (e.g., deliberative opinion polls, discussed in greater detail in subsequent chapters) fortified against the empirical critique. By largely abandoning the broader political system, however, what started out as a theory of deliberative democracy – a kind of political regime – evolved into a much more modest theory of democratic deliberation – a very particular practice within a much larger system. Moreover, the tactical retreat of normative theorists has done little to appease the critics, most of whom scoff at the idea that "a few days of democracy camp" could overcome the fundamental problems facing any deliberative theory.[7] From this point of view, the recent surge in real-world deliberative reforms (e.g., the British Columbia Citizens Assembly) is little more than academic fashion made recklessly real.

TRANSFORMING THE DEBATE

The key to cutting across this impasse involves distinguishing among the means, ends, and structure of a deliberative democratic system. The main goal of such a system is to secure authentic deliberative buy-in for good political decisions. Deliberative buy-in means that citizens can look at the policies, laws, and rationales produced by the political process and recognize them as reasonable and, better yet, embrace them as their own.[8] From this perspective, all manner of institutions and practices that do not seem deliberative on their face (e.g., elections) may nevertheless serve deliberative ends. And conversely, superficially deliberative practices

---

[7] The quip about "democracy camp" is from Bartels (2003: 15). Chambers (2009) develops the distinction between deliberative democracy and democratic deliberation as I intend it here. Mansbridge (2007) uses the distinction differently, meaning to praise the latter, in a limited way, as a more modest, neo-pluralist theory. Habermas pursues a third line of response to the social scientific critics, by arguing that they ignore "what political power owes specifically to its formal constitution in legal terms" (1996: 330) – that is, the way that democratic presuppositions are not merely regulative ideals, offering an external standard of criticism, but rather partially constitute the legal exercise of political power. I discuss this regulative and constitutive distinction in more detail in Chapter 2.

[8] Buy-in should be understood as operating over time, so remaining satisfied with those policies and rationales after living with them is part of the setup and thus incorporates a notion of "good" decisions as well. "Authentic" as a normative modifier is meant to capture the distinction between the mere fact of buy-in and deserving it. In Chapter 2, I develop criteria for warranting such dessert via measures of deliberative quality.

may fail to embody or promote deliberative goals.[9] Deliberative "quality" is thus properly thought of as a property of the broader political system, rather than of discrete moments of deliberation. Together, these two moves – first, conceptualizing deliberation as a set of normative criteria rather than a set of specific talk-based political innovations, and second, applying those criteria at the system level – completely transform deliberative theory's relationship to empirical social science.

Understood this way, deliberative theory is dramatically more flexible and thus can engage the social sciences not as an adversary but as an ally in the search for better ways to realize democratic goals. The key question is no longer whether some institution or practice looks deliberative on its face, but rather whether it contributes to deliberative legitimacy at the level of the larger political system. If so, then one risks making a category mistake by applying standard deliberative criteria like equality or reasonableness directly to every site in the political system.

For example, it is no secret that much naturally occurring political talk among non-elites proceeds on a thin factual basis and in relatively cloistered social situations. However, the main function of such casual political talk is akin to "brainstorming" – simply generating large numbers of ideas, reactions, considerations, feelings, arguments, fragments of arguments, and so forth. The main goal of such talk is to get the contents of people's political thoughts, concerns, and experiences onto the table, without worrying much, for the time being, about their quality, priority, or practicality. Indeed, for brainstorming to work right, ideas must *not* be subjected immediately to substantial criticism and filtering. Thus, what might be a vice at another point in the system – for example, political talk in relatively homogeneous circles or among people with little technical knowledge – can actually serve important purposes, such as giving legitimate minority perspectives time to develop without being assimilated by dominant perspectives, or clarifying key values and interests before subjecting them to technical criticism.

Rather than asking whether deliberative democracy is "realistic," this approach allows us to shift to more interesting and productive questions about how best to realize deliberative ideals. We are not concerned primarily with the absolute distance between reality and the ideal, but rather with whether we can adjust our institutions and practices to help average citizens recognize their contributions and interests in the results

---

[9] My discussion here draws on and develops elements from Habermas (1996), Bohman (1996), Goodin (2003), and Warren (2007).

of an improved policy process. Criticizing the deliberative ideal on the basis of its supposed remoteness is simply beside the point, akin to arguing that measuring a basketball player's shooting percentage is inappropriate because perfection on that scale is "unrealistic." Should we therefore switch to a measure that only requires that the ball gets near the basket, since it would be more realistic in the sense of narrowing the gap between the ideal and the actual? Doing so would not be sensible because the new standard does a poorer job of validly tracking how we value a player's contribution to a team. Those who perseverate on what they take to be the normative over-ambition of deliberative democracy make a similar mistake.

Thus, one of the major goals of this book is to develop the outlines of this transformed relationship between deliberative theory and empirical social science, and to show how doing so opens the door to a vastly more constructive interaction between the two. First, we can respond to the challenges regarding deliberation's workability on their own terms rather than evading them. That is, we can explain why we need not set aside the aspirations from our children's civics textbooks even as we struggle honestly with the messy realities of modern mass governance. But the value of the new relationship goes beyond mere apologetics for deliberative theory. Many findings from social science that had appeared as threats to a brittle conception of deliberation will now appear as valuable guides to improving deliberative practices. Moreover, clarifying the proper relationship between theory, research, and practice allows us to plan further research in a cooperative mode that identifies key gaps in our knowledge, creating opportunities to simultaneously improve normative theory, social scientific inquiry, and democratic practice.

PLAN FOR THE BOOK

In this spirit, then, Chapter 2 develops an account of the components of the deliberative system, and how they interact to secure deliberative goals. From the most local, internal to each individual's mind, to the macrostructures of the state, I describe each site of deliberation as it functions in this system. Only such a unified account will allow us to trace the relevant standards of deliberation through the entire system. In the second half of the chapter, I develop these standards theoretically, introducing a so-called *inferentialist* account of political justification and linking it to more operationally proximate criteria of deliberative quality.

With the goals and structure of the deliberative system clarified, Chapters 3 to 6 systematically re-evaluate, in light of this new frame, the four main empirical challenges to deliberative democracy. The aim of these chapters is to simultaneously reclaim the larger theory of deliberative democracy and meet the empirical critics squarely on terms that advance, rather than evade, the relevant social scientific findings.

Chapter 3 analyzes claims that citizens simply do not have the capacity to form meaningful preferences that could serve as a basis for democratic accountability. The problem is more radical than the familiar notion that the masses are insufficiently informed and sophisticated about politics. Rather than "having" preferences in any antecedent sense, average citizens appear to have only a churning set of attitudes and considerations that can produce wildly divergent *reports* of their preferences, depending on when and how they are asked to report them. Such context dependency appears to be an irreducible feature of our cognitive architecture. Thus, without some implausible notion of a neutral or correct method for eliciting preferences, we are left with no way of knowing whether democratic decisions reflect anything but the arbitrary or power-laden vagaries of political contestation. In response, I begin by noting that this argument proves too much, since it is implausible to believe that elites and average citizens have fundamentally different cognitive architectures. If elites are capable of forming meaningful preferences, the putative problem with citizens must be remediable, at least in principle. This observation also indicates that the issue must be a matter of degree, rather than presenting an either/or choice. Indeed, on the inferentialist account that I develop in Chapter 2 (and extend in subsequent chapters), we should expect and embrace preferences and judgments being responsive to a wide variety of endogenous influences. Finally, I argue that even if it is implausible to think that there is a single correct method of eliciting preferences, that in no way means that we cannot identify some as better or worse than others according to various deliberative criteria.

Just because average citizens are capable of forming democratically meaningful preferences, however, does not mean that they will add up to anything *collectively* meaningful. Thus, Chapter 4 addresses the claim that no amount of deliberation can obviate the need for voting and other forms of democratic aggregation. If deliberative democratic systems will need recourse to voting, then they will be subject to the well-known problems of instability, ambiguity, and manipulability of voting outcomes emerging from social choice theory, game theory, and implementation theory. Moreover, any attempt to invoke notions of the "general will" or cognate concepts as a way to avoid such critiques would commit deliberative democrats to implausible entities and potentially illiberal notions of consensus. In response, I develop an alternative inferentialist model of aggregation that explains how deliberation can go a long way toward reducing the force of the aggregative critique without invoking metaphysically or morally suspect crutches. Each individual has a complex web of beliefs, judgments, and commitments that allows him or her to make novel inferences by reflecting on those beliefs and their implications. Since people are highly social creatures, there will be a significant degree of overlap between those webs of belief. Deliberation, then, can be thought of as a process by which groups of people reflect on the overlapping and nonoverlapping portions of their webs of belief, recombining elements from each by searching through the space of arguments for a more satisfying and consistent set of beliefs and a more common path to public choices. If the process is working well, it should generally increase people's ability to recognize others as reasonable and enable a degree of convergence upon choices and rationales that will, ceteris paribus, reduce the force of the formal critique. Thus, the seemingly nondeliberative practice of voting becomes a key mechanism by which average citizens transmit the authority of their deliberation on to formal political institutions, making it possible to recognize the echo of their voice in the laws those institutions ultimately produce.

Chapter 5 addresses the criticism that most Americans want nothing to do with a more deliberative democracy and that such reticence is reasonable. If this criticism is on the mark, bullying citizens into more deliberative participation would be grossly paternalistic. From the system perspective, however, most citizens already engage in important political talk within their informal political networks. Pointing out that much of that informal talk looks like a far cry from the "ideal speech situation" is not to the point, because talk in informal political networks generally serves a different function. As I have suggested, such deliberation is akin to brainstorming, wherein the main goal is to simply generate ideas, rationales, concerns, and perspectives on an issue, whatever their source and content. Different sites and moments in the process are charged with filtering, refining, and evaluating what gets produced at this stage. Directly applying the normative criteria of deliberative theory to such processes would actually subvert their main function in the same way that immediately criticizing and evaluating ideas defeats the intention of brainstorming. Moreover, extent research has focused on "who deliberates?" rather than "who wants to deliberate?" But if deliberative democrats are right that much nonparticipation is rooted in disaffection with status quo politics, then current patterns of deliberation would not reflect how citizens would participate given more attractive opportunities. I demonstrate that the profile of those willing to deliberate is markedly different from those who participate in standard partisan politics and interest group liberalism. This profile suggests that average citizens do not regard deliberative opportunities as filigree on "real" politics or as an indulgence meant only for political activists and intellectuals.

Even if citizens are more motivated to deliberate than critics assume, it is not clear that they can overcome the formidable hurdles to informed participation. All of us are utterly dependent on experts for nearly all complex matters that fall outside of our narrow range of competence. Chapter 6 addresses this concern with special reference to so-called mini-publics (e.g., deliberative opinion polls, citizen juries). I argue that if mini-publics are made to bear the main weight of deliberative democratic reform, then critics provide strong reasons to doubt that they can appreciably alter the quality of democratic processes. If, however, we assign mini-publics more limited roles in the larger deliberative system, ample evidence suggests that they have significant potential for contributing. After reinterpreting the concept of public opinion in inferentialist terms, I discuss two such roles. First, mini-publics can span what in network theory are called "structural holes" between elected representatives and their constituents. That is, they create direct connections between actors that reduce the distortion that comes from mediating communication through highly interested, nonrepresentative actors. Second, mini-publics can help correct for the biases that accrue from ceding decisions to experts and elites who have more technical knowledge, but who may tend to map that knowledge onto policy decisions in a systematically different way. In the concluding chapter, I summarize and assess the way that the foregoing discussions transform the relationship between democratic theory and empirical research, and I sketch a more cooperative path going forward.

In some ways, the goals for the book are fairly modest. For example, I will *not* attempt to show that citizens in modern democracies come close to any ideal conception of deliberative democracy. Instead I *will* show that posing the question this way is ill-conceived. If deliberative democracy is an ideal worth embracing – indeed, one that we implicitly embrace much of already – then whatever the distance between the ideal and the real, we need only establish that deliberative standards are not perverse on their own terms. Similarly, I will *not* argue generally that the formal and empirical literatures on deliberation are somehow incorrect on their own terms or irrelevant to deliberative democracy. Instead I argue that these literatures do not show that deliberative standards are perverse, but rather only that democratic reforms will have to take account of them in attempting to better embody those deliberative standards.

This book will not work out the details of exactly *how* to take account of this broader literature in reform and implementation. Assessing the full set of conditions under which elements of the deliberative system do and do not serve the functions assigned to them constitutes an enormous, open-ended research agenda. But it will be no small accomplishment if I can remove the dismissive presumptions that have confused and hindered such a research agenda and reorganize the relationship between normative and empirical research going forward.

2

Form Follows Function

President Carter's decision to deregulate the trucking industry lost him my mother's vote, but my father ended up voting for Carter again, judging that this one issue should not overwhelm his typical support for Democratic candidates. He was able to persuade a couple of his friends to his view that day in the tavern, though many had turned decisively against Carter. The larger debate of which theirs was a part was also mixed; the media widely publicized the Teamsters' eventual decision to endorse Governor Reagan, as well as the ensuing controversy among their rank and file, between the national union and its locals, and within the larger labor movement. Contrary to many people's recollection, Reagan never signed further legislation deregulating the industry (though he did pre-empt some state standards). Indeed, against the advice of many economists, his appointee to the Interstate Commerce Commission interpreted the 1980 statute so narrowly that aspects of the interpretation were overturned by the Supreme Court.[1]

I offer this brief anecdote neither as a family memoir nor political history, but rather to illustrate one of the main points of Chapter 1: That any adequate theory of deliberative democracy must be able to make sense

---

[1] *Maislin Industries, U.S., Inc. v. Primary Steel, Inc.,* 497 U.S. 116. The *Surface Transportation Assistance Act of 1982* could be construed as indirect deregulation since its uniform weight and length standards were weaker than those of many states. Reagan actually helped defeat the *Trucking Competition Act* (1983) which would have ended all economic regulation of trucking within sixty days. Late in his second term, though, he supported the similar *Trucking Productivity Act* (1987), which ultimately failed. See Madar (2000) and Belzer (2000).

of the surprisingly diverse kinds of deliberation that occur throughout the political system and how they work together (or fail) to produce legitimate decisions. In this short, simple example, more than a dozen distinct sites of deliberation make cameo appearances: My parents discussed their differing views in *private* conversations over the dinner table. My father and his friends and co-workers, his *informal social network*, debated in their pub (i.e., "public house"). My father's local union was a formal, but not primarily political, *civic organization* geared toward fostering local economic solidarity. The national union (actually the "International" Brotherhood of Teamsters) functioned primarily as the political arm of the confederated locals – that is, a *special interest group* signaling its endorsement in the context of a *campaign and election*. The larger, informal labor movement is classic *subpublic*. Scientific and policy *experts* debate the import of specialized technical (in this case, economic) knowledge. The main *political parties* in the United States help connect these elements of civil society to the deliberations of the formal, political sphere with complex interactions between state entities: The *executive, legislature, bureaucracy*, and *judiciary* at both the *national* and *subnational* levels. The *media* interpret and publicize the deliberations and actions of these various actors. And ultimately all of this interpersonal deliberation depends on the intrapersonal process of *deliberation within* by which individuals weigh matters in their own heads.

A full theory of deliberative democracy must integrate all of these sites of the deliberative system. I begin, therefore, by simply describing the main sites of the deliberative system (Section 2.1), and basic considerations about the roles that they play in the larger system. Many of those sites (e.g., elections or interest groups), however, appear to function in ways that do not seem "deliberative" on their face. I develop and justify the argument (Section 2.2) for conceptualizing deliberation as a set of normative criteria rather than a set of specific talk-based political innovations. In order to give those normative criteria more content, I sketch a so-called "inferentialist" theory (Section 2.3) of meaning that will serve as the master criterion for specific operational criteria of good deliberation. In order for those normative criteria to link up with social scientific research, however, they need to be made more concrete than highly abstract notions of "good decisions" and "authentic buy-in." I therefore (Section 2.4) canvass a number of general strategies for decomposing those highly abstract goals into components of deliberative quality that are more amenable to being operationalized for purposes of social scientific research. With this proliferation of sites of deliberation, activities that might serve deliberative functions, and criteria on which to evaluate them, though, one might worry that deliberative theory has become so expansive as to render it unfalsifiable. I conclude (Section 2.5) by showing that such worries are misguided, and that, taken together, these moves actually allow normative theory and empirical research on deliberation to speak to each other in much more productive ways.

A SYSTEM OF DEMOCRATIC DELIBERATION

Consider Figure 2.1 for a visual representation of the larger deliberative system, and the ways its constituent parts relate to each other.[2] The first thing that one might note is that the diagram might well be labeled "The Political System" rather than "The Deliberative System." That is, this notion of deliberative democracy may not seem so distinctive vis-à-vis standing representations of democratic systems. With a few significant exceptions, that observation is true, and indeed, tracking recognizable institutional forms is part of the point of claiming that deliberative theory attempts to reconstruct implicit normative standards already at work in modern democracy. Beyond an emphasis on political talk and a few institutional innovations, the main difference is that rather than conceiving of these various sites in purely descriptive terms as loci of blind power, they are organized to help us understand how the various elements of the deliberative system might contribute to rationalizing political power via *good* deliberative practices tailored to their proper function within the larger democratic system.

Before proceeding, I should also note that this diagram, despite its complexity, is radically simplified. To capture the full complexity of the system would require bi-directional arrows connecting every site. For example, citizens write thousands of letters directly to the President every day, and most presidents respond directly to at least a few of them. That said, such a saturated diagram would prove unwieldy, so I have tried to capture the modal relationships, and the key channels of communication between the various sites of deliberation.

---

[2] Mansbridge was the first person to use the term "deliberative system." Dryzek, Goodin, Warren, Kramer-Walsh, Krause, and Disch have all made similar suggestions. Habermas' theory is the most worked-out, though it is cast at a fairly high level of abstraction. See chapter 8 of *Between Facts and Norms* (1996). See also Lazer et al. (2011).

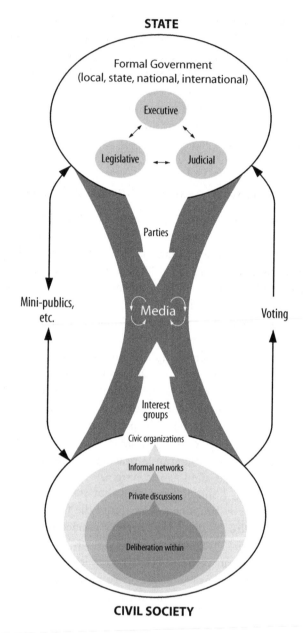

FIGURE 2.1 The Deliberative System.

Deliberation within: Starting with the innermost oval toward the bottom of the diagram, we begin with "deliberation within," by which I mean weighing reasons for and against some action as it occurs within each of our heads.[3] It is important to distinguish from the outset between two aspects of "deliberation within." The first is the obvious notion that, even as we participate in public deliberation of various kinds, those processes operate in and through the psychological operations of individuals. For example, in order for a fellow citizen to affect me, I must first choose to pay attention to what he or she is saying, interpret the point that he or she is trying to make, evaluate its cogency, and so forth. Call this first sense of deliberation within "personal uptake."

In contrast, the second aspect of "deliberation within" is meant to convey individual imagination and cogitation *in lieu of* deliberation with others. That is, sometimes we must emulate intersubjective processes via subjective processes. For example, if I am unable to discuss immigration reform with undocumented immigrants openly, as a fallback, I may try to imagine how an undocumented immigrant might react to a given policy proposal. Call this second sense of deliberation within "personal reflection." The distinction is not perfectly sharp. We never have direct access to one another's minds, so even in interpersonal deliberation, we must engage in countless acts of imaginative identification to interpret one another. The difference is nevertheless clear and important enough to warrant distinct treatment.

The main systemic function of personal uptake, of basic psychological mediation, should be fairly uncontroversial. If individuals do not pay attention to each other, expend some effort to understand and interpret others, and process new information, considerations, and perspectives, there is little point to deliberation at any of the other sites in the system. None of the various "transfer" points within the larger deliberative system can function without a minimal quality of psychological processing at the individual level, among elites and non-elites alike.

Less obviously, personal reflection is essential to fill in unavoidable gaps driven by the natural limits on our time, ability to communicate, and institutional capacity. Typically, we cannot talk to everyone affected by a common decision, and often not even someone representing the main perspectives and interests involved. So our familiar exhortations to imagine

---

[3] My discussion is indebted to Goodin (2000) who coined the term and analyzed many of the issues here.

"what it would feel like to be in their shoes" are not only essential, but may actually be the most common form of ordinary deliberative activity.

Private discussion: With private discussion we move outside of people's heads, but not out into public per se. To some extent, the concepts of private discussion and deliberation in an informal network bleed into each other. Two loose criteria, however, distinguish the concepts: The intimacy and intensity of the relationship, and the degree to which the exchanges are, in principle, public. So, private discussion designates discussion among people in primary relationships: Spouses and partners, parents and children, other relatives, and our closest friends. Such relationships are typically prior to and trump politics. They are among the most common sources of political influence for at least three reasons: First, they are the most common and intense relationships for most of us; second, their intimacy often creates pressure to resolve potential sources of conflict within the relationship; and third, they are often characterized by degrees of trust and shared background that facilitate persuasion. That said, significant political differences both exist and persist within intimate relationships (Huckfeldt 2007).

Informal networks: Our informal networks consist of casual and work friends, neighbors, acquaintances, and more generally, those whom we know personally, but are outside of our circle of intimates.[4] So my parents' political discussions over the dinner table are different from those my father had with his co-workers in their tavern. Such cases are worth analyzing separately because they often differ on several criteria of relevance to deliberative theory: Congruence of interests, differences in background and ideologies, trust, social conformity pressures, repetition and duration of the interactions, and the "public-ness" of their normal locations (e.g., bedrooms and dinner tables versus pubs and water coolers). Studies of political behavior, however, find that both are quite important (Levine 2005: 132; Mutz 2006).

Civic organizations: Here, we move from informal social structures into more or less formal institutions. Religious congregations, clubs, service organizations, bowling leagues, community groups, (local) unions, identity groups, and the like differ from informal networks in being

---

[4] These categories, of course, blend and overlap somewhat. For example, I may be casual friends with people from my church, etc. Theoretically, we could still distinguish between discussion and public interaction qua co-congregationists and those qua casual friends. In practice, though, it will be difficult to cleanly separate them, and in many cases, it may not be very important to do so.

groups with bounded rosters and an identity that members demarcate explicitly. In addition to serving directly as sites of deliberation, recent work in political sociology (Putnam 2000) suggests that civic organizations are important to democratic systems via the notion of "social capital."

In a more specifically deliberative key, we might also think of "communicative capital" as a species of "social capital" more broadly. Communicative capital can serve important functions in the deliberative system: First, by creating enough of a sense of common identity or linked fate to encourage people to deliberate and act in a public spirit; second, by developing a broader base of common understanding and shared background; third, by serving as richer material for imaginative and empathic projection when circumstances force us to have recourse to "deliberation within;" fourth, by fostering greater trust so that others will reciprocate these three functions here; and, fifth in giving credence to another even when deliberation does not yield personal insight (i.e., I trust that "I couldn't understand" and that you will not abuse my willingness to trust you nevertheless).[5]

Interest groups: The term "interest group" carries a generally negative connotation in ordinary language, and perhaps even more so in the context of deliberative democracy. That said, we should be slow to dismiss the notion of interest groups in a system of deliberative democracy. Not all interest groups are "special" interests. Public interest groups abound and historically have played important roles in arguing successfully for social reform. One might worry that the distinction between a public and a special interest group lies in the eye of the beholder, and this worry is surely well founded. But it is not hard to discern useful points of distinction. It is one thing to express special interest claims in public and general terms: "What is good for General Motors is good for America" – that is,

---

[5] As with social capital more broadly, we might further distinguish between "bonding" communicative capital and "bridging" communicative capital. Bonding consists of networks of trust and efficient interaction between like-minded and similarly situated people, whereas bridging spans across differences in situation and thinking. This distinction, in turn, gestures at the notion (not represented in Figure 2.1) of a "subpublic' – i.e., a relatively clustered and autonomous portion of civil society that replicates the structure of the general public sphere. The accreted experiences of living as a member of a minority group can create sufficiently similar group experiences that are sufficiently distinct from the broader culture that it may be useful to think in terms of distinct consciousness. For example, the phrase, "It's a black thing – you wouldn't understand," suggests that a white person attempting personal reflection on behalf of African Americans (*deliberation within*) may find it difficult to muster the necessary imaginative and empathic projection.

we serve a crucial function and have a legitimate claim to represent the public good. And it is quite another to claim to be providing a public good – for example, that everyone has an interest in clean air or clean elections. This conceptual distinction holds even when there is legitimate controversy about whether the claimed public good really does benefit everyone.[6]

Similarly there is the familiar, if operationally tricky, distinction between "grass roots" movements and "astro-turf" – that is, pseudo-popular movements that serve as fronts for organized special interests precisely in order to muddy the public perception of them as organized special interests. Habermas has described this difference as "emerging from" versus "appearing before" the public, though one might refine the idea by noting that a group that authentically emerged from the public might, over time, be captured by special interests in such a way that it evolves into a kind of special interest itself.

Yet such a development need not be bad for deliberative democracy, since being a public interest group does not guarantee that one actually serves the public interest, just as being a special interest group need not guarantee that one harms the public interest. This latter claim may seem less obvious since one might reasonably argue that what makes a special interest special is precisely that it is not general – that is, it is not in the public interest. But the public interest is composed of genuinely public goods and a fair and legitimate distribution of private goods. So on a deliberative conception, special interest groups may serve an essential function in the system if they frame their activities as pressing *legitimate* claims on the distribution of benefits and burdens in society.

Now the problem, of course, is that nearly everyone presses their claims as legitimate. So, just as with a partially adversarial legal system, we will need both norms and enforceable rules to govern interest group behavior, as well as multiple mechanisms to weigh and judge the competing claims. The burden of showing that improvements in this direction can be made will fall on subsequent chapters.

Political parties: The main division in Figure 2.1 is organized around the familiar distinction between the state and civil society. These are sometimes referred to as the "strong" and "weak" public spheres respectively.

---

[6] For example, in this setup, neither pro-life nor pro-choice groups should be thought of as special interests. If one or the other is right in pressing their plausible and sincere claims, then we all have an interest, respectively, in preserving innocent human life or protecting the bodily integrity and equal freedoms of half the population.

Deliberative theory envisions a partial division of labor between the two. In most cases, civil society is charged with identifying and prioritizing social problems: Where the shoe pinches, whom it pinches, and how badly. The state is typically charged with determining whose shoes get fixed and how. As a practical matter, however, the boundary between the state and civil society is rather blurry (Knoke et al. 1996: 122). Political parties function as the brackish estuaries linking interest groups and other elements of civil society to the formal apparatus of the state.

From a deliberative point of view, one might be tempted to treat parties as structurally similar to special interest groups in that the word "party" shares the same root as "partial" (i.e., as opposed to general). As a matter of practice, however, most parties typically present their arguments, policies, and platforms as rival interpretations of the public good and how to achieve it, rather than openly presenting themselves as a faction (White and Ypi 2011). So both intraparty deliberation and public presentations of platforms are more promising sources of deliberation about the public good than it might appear at first.

Formal government: Many people are likely to be skeptical about getting high quality deliberation (at least in public) out of formal state actors (except, perhaps, for the judiciary). Take, for example, the U.S. Senate, which once arrogated to itself the title of "the world's greatest deliberative body." It has now become a cliché for others to use the epithet ironically – as a term of abuse, contrasting the current state of debate in the Senate with a supposed golden age of oratory and statesmanship. Of course, that golden age also included countless instances of deliberative encounters ending in spitting, slander, assault, and all manner of incivility unbecoming even the world's minimally deliberative bodies. For now, I am not so concerned to sort out whether the quality of deliberation in the Senate is or ever was deserving of accolades, but rather to note something that should be obvious, but has been occluded by certain habits of thought: The Senate, along with many other formal governmental bodies, really are deliberative institutions in the simple descriptive sense of spending much of their time engaged in reasoning and political talk on the merits of law and policy.

I hasten to admit that much of the talk may be insincere and much of the reasoning may be epiphenomenal to power. But in the words of the old maxim, hypocrisy is the tribute that vice pays to virtue. Note, though, that "tribute" is a kind of tax, so the norms and forms of public reasoning help limit hypocrisy by making it costly. Given the ubiquity of being called to account in formal deliberative institutions – members of legislatures live under the constant threat of having votes and their attendant rationales come back to haunt them (Arnold 1990) – such tribute can end up constituting a severe tax indeed. Looked at this way, it seems implausible that so many people could sustain so much hypocrisy so consistently for deliberation not to matter greatly, at least, relative to a system that did not require such accounts. In this light, it does not seem so naïve to think that one crucial way for officials to succeed is by reasoning soundly in preparation for enacting good public policy. One could develop a similar argument for most of the other sites of formal governmental deliberation (e.g., courts), shifting the emphasis from regarding them as loci of brute power to bringing out the deliberative dimensions already at work in them.

Media: In Figure 2.1, I represent the mass media as a background space because they serve four theoretically distinct deliberative functions: (1) As a mechanism to subsidize the average citizens' lack of expertise about politics; (2) as a channel, guiding representations of deliberative activity in civil society up to state actors (Herbst 1998), as well as out to other actors within civil society (Mutz1998); (3) as the main channel by which state actors attempt to persuade the public on policy ex ante or justify it post hoc; and (4) as a relatively autonomous forum of debate (e.g., via editorials) between media actors (represented by the cycling arrows), but in view of both the strong and weak publics.

The main threat to the media's ability to serve those functions well is that they may get co-opted by the various constituencies between whom they mediate. For example, government officials reward and punish journalists (e.g., with access) depending on the favorability of coverage. Similarly, market forces create incentives to attract mass viewership and readership by any available means, and to segment into market niches that can create echo-chamber effects among subgroups within the public.

Mini-publics: The recent surge of interest in new deliberative fora is rooted in the notion that standard politics is often inadequate to the task of promoting and preserving good deliberative decision making. Deliberative opinion polls, citizen juries, consensus conferences, and so on, attempt, inter alia, to cut out the middle man (especially the media, parties, and interest groups). The claim is that many of the pathologies of mediated mass democracy hinge on the way that public reasoning gets structured, censored, and transformed by the peculiar concerns and incentives of interest groups, media outlets, and political parties. While a theory of deliberative democracy (as opposed to democratic deliberation) cannot

For Habermas, no practices or institutions can be ruled in a priori – that is, without practical knowledge about the vagaries of implementation. Even more striking, very little can be ruled *out* a priori either – Habermas explicitly countenances Schumpeterian practices as compatible with deliberative standards, even though Schumpeter anchors the minimalist, elitist end of the spectrum of theories that can reasonably be called democratic. Far from displaying naïve utopianism, one might wonder whether Habermas gives away the store to empiricist skeptics here. If deliberative democracy is compatible with everything from radical democracy to elitist minimalism, then it is hard to see how the theory is doing much normative work.

In fact, the theory does not do much work in itself. Deliberative democracy is *theoretically* compatible with a wide range of practical forms – that is to say, it is compatible *a priori*. Fortunately, though, we have a lot of empirical knowledge and practical experience relevant to living in democracies, so we are not limited to assessing proposals a priori. And when we take this knowledge into account, deliberative democratic theory can do a lot of work in helping us to answer the important "organizational questions." Indeed, the bulk of this book is devoted to doing just that.[8]

If this distinction between deliberation as a standard and as a concrete practice was put forth clearly from the beginning, then how did the relationship between the normative theory and social science research become so confused? First, we might note that in the quote mentioned earlier, Habermas relegates all of the relevant empirical research to "organizational questions" in a rather off-handed way. It took twenty years before he addressed himself to those organizational questions in much conceptual detail. Even then, his discussion in *Between Facts and*

---

understanding do not involve any kind of correspondence or comparison between idea and reality.' On the other hand, it is legitimate to use such a projection for a thought experiment. The essentialist misunderstanding is replaced by a methodological fiction in order to obtain a foil against which the substratum of unavoidable societal complexity becomes visible. In this harmless sense, the ideal communication community presents itself as a model of 'pure' communicative sociation" (1996: 323). Similarly, Habermas is clear that we cannot *completely* replace discursive practices with functional analogues (1993: 56).

[8] In this sense, I simply disagree with Owen and Smith's (2013) argument that what they call the "stronger" form of the deliberative systems claim runs into "dilemmas" that threaten to undermine the deliberative thrust of the theory. They are surely right to claim that more theoretical and empirical work needs to be done to fully flesh out a systemic theory, but I see no principled impediments to doing so, and believe – as evidenced by nearly all of what follows – that we already have more material to work with than they allow for.

Norms was cast at a level of abstraction that did not readily translate into the terms of mainstream social science. In the interim, Habermas developed his social and moral theory in even more abstract terms that have tempted readers to apply them inflexibly and directly to politics (e.g., literally requiring unanimity for every political decision), despite his explicit objections to doing so.

In the meantime, most Anglo-American social scientists first encountered deliberative democracy through the work of James Fishkin, and his signature practical proposal, the deliberative opinion poll (DOP). Fishkin's philosophical work is more accessible than Habermas's, and he has done an enormous amount of important empirical research as well. So it should come as no surprise that he is the best known deliberative theorist among empirically oriented researchers, and that his approach should be taken as paradigmatic in their eyes.

Fishkin is, indeed, a major deliberative theorist, and DOPs are among the most important institutional innovations in deliberative democracy to date. However, among major deliberative theorists he is fairly distinctive. One might interpret his theory as primarily aiming at correcting for the low information base and statistical unrepresentativeness of most citizen input to mass democratic politics: "[W]e go to great lengths not to push consensus, to measure the attitude changes in confidential questionnaires (secret ballots if you will), and then to aggregate them statistically" (2005: 72). This approach places less emphasis on mutual justification and accountability, and more importantly, by design, blocks those criteria from being publicly linked to the final judgments of the deliberators.[9]

---

[9] I should note that Fishkin has plausible reasons for setting DOPs up this way (e.g., to avoid mere conformity). And his later work (2009) now includes "conscientiousness" and "equal consideration" in the definition of good deliberation. His gloss on these terms still admits of an individualist, preference-aggregation reading, however, and so run afoul of the same arguments given earlier. There is a trade-off between de-emphasizing the "commonality" of voices and mutual accountability, on the one hand, and not treating individual preferences as sovereign. In contrast, classical deliberative theory emphasizes that if I am going to use the coercive power of the state to affect your vital interests, I owe you a public explanation that cannot be a mere formality – i.e., cheap talk followed by me merely reasserting my personal preferences. One might argue that Fishkin's deliberators are not engaging in binding decisions, and thus not directly using the coercive power of the state. In my view, though, precisely to the extent that discussion is influential on outcomes, it incurs moral burdens. To use a statistical analogy, the combined effect, rather than the direct effect, is the relevant criterion. Fishkin's vision clearly hinges on making DOPs highly effective, even if indirectly. Thus, on my account, his deliberators should incur the burden of public reasoning in forming their final judgments.

In addition, it seems that Fishkin's particular institutional form of deliberative opinion polls serves as the lynchpin to his theory. One's assessment of the theory will accordingly track one's assessment of the empirical research on DOPs. Indeed, many theorists who have a broader notion of deliberation still tend to retreat into controlled deliberative environments when pressed for institutional responses to the empirical critique because, without the deliberative standards / organizational questions distinction, they are stuck on the horns of a dilemma. It is easy to see, then, why many empirically oriented scholars have come to believe that the viability of deliberative theory more generally depends largely on getting "good" empirical results from research on facially deliberative institutions and practices.

I do not argue that we should conceive of things differently because I am hostile to DOPs. In Chapter 6, I develop an argument that gives DOPs and other mini-publics an important role to play in the larger political system. Rather, I think that the vision that Fishkin develops in his earlier, more philosophical works is better served by a more flexible, systemic model that distinguishes between deliberative means and ends. If so, there is no reason to focus so tightly on controlled deliberative environments, and keep fighting the debate with empiricists on this terrain.

In addition to research on facially deliberative practices, we need to study when and how facially non-deliberative practices and institutions might serve deliberative ends, how deliberative functions can be realized in various institutions and practices, and when and how these various "sites" of deliberation manage to hand-off their accomplishments to other sites as communicative processes circulate through society and the state. Such a conception makes deliberative theory much more dynamic and flexible, but it also dramatically expands and complicates research on deliberative politics.

INFERENTIALISM AND SUBSTANTIVE RATIONALITY

If we are to be able to get traction on "organizational questions" surrounding potential deliberative reforms, then we will need some bridge between deliberation's notion of substantive rationality and more concrete categories of deliberative desiderata. Following Brandom (1998), I term this notion of substantive rationality an *inferentialist* perspective, and I will make recurring use of it throughout the rest of the book. Inferentialist semantics is a theory in which the meaning of some term or expression is determined by its inferential relationships to other terms and expressions – for example, how it can be used as a premise or a conclusion in some larger pattern of inferences.

To get an intuitive sense of how this account works imagine that each of us as individuals has a large web of beliefs. These beliefs are inter-related in various ways that allow us to make novel inferences to expand our larger set of beliefs and increase their coherence. For example, if I believe that snow is frozen water, there is a practical sense in which I am committed to the belief that if I bring snow into a warm room, it will melt back into water. The practical meanings of "snow," "frozen," "water," and "warm" hang together in a way that implies certain further inferences. I may not have thought about bringing snow into my house, and so might not "have" this belief about melting in the sense of it pre-existing as a conscious thought. But there is another sense in which I am committed to it nonetheless and in the typical case can be brought to recognize such connections explicitly (or to alter some of my other beliefs, if I want to resist some conclusion). Similarly, take an even clearer example: There are an infinite number of simple arithmetic assertions, very few of which (beyond learning times tables by rote) I will have ever consciously considered. Yet there is a sense in which I know and am committed to some specific answer to, for example, the expression $859 \times 493 = X$ and any number of others like it.

On an inferentialist account, intrapersonal deliberation is merely the process of examining some problematic region of our webs of belief in an effort to resolve the problem. In the math example, I might just get a paper and pencil or a calculator and work out the solution. In a more political context, I might come to realize that some of my beliefs are incompatible – for example, thinking that tax rates are too high, but that we should increase defense and domestic spending, while reducing the deficit – and start a process by which I adjust various beliefs and commitments to make them more coherent.

The inferentialist account of interpersonal deliberation is a bit more complicated, but proceeds along similar lines. Brandom introduces the concept of *deontic score-keeping* as a way of explaining how our normative obligations emerge out of the way our empirical discursive practices help us make sense of the physical and social worlds. The idea here is that each of us implicitly (and sometimes explicitly) keeps track of an ever changing set of commitments and entitlements that we and others take on in virtue of our previous moves in what he calls "the game of giving and asking for reasons." If I assert that I want to bring some snow into my warm house, my interlocutors might reasonably infer that I am OK with allowing that snow to melt. If it appears that I am not OK with the snow melting, they might inquire as to my apparent inconsistency. I then might report that I intend to put the snow in my freezer in order to make snow cones for my children after dinner.

When we run into problems of common concern and there is a discrepancy in our assessment of each other's "scores," we have a practical disagreement that we can try to solve via deliberation. Using the background agreement typically afforded by our common culture, we attempt to isolate the local regions of our webs of belief that are causing the disagreement, and assess whether there are ways of resolving the impasse. In Brandom's terms, we "make explicit" what was previously implicit. For example, I may simply not have realized that I had an inconsistency in my set of beliefs (e.g., because my freezer is broken). Or you might have made an unreliable inference because you did not know some detail of my web of beliefs that render them sensible and coherent (e.g., that I own a freezer, or insist on homemade desserts). This joint process of discursive search and clarification is called *inferential articulation*.

One of the attractive features of such an account is that it opens up the possibility that we can make better and worse arguments in the game of giving and asking for reasons – that is, that we can be right or wrong about some proposition in a way that goes beyond any given instance of deliberation. For example, given our normative commitments to rightness of various scientific and mathematical operations, there may be an implicit right answer to a scientific question *even if no one has ever correctly worked out the right answer*. Indeed, much scholarship is just a systematic version of the folk psychology of inferential "articulation" – making heretofore implicit connections explicit. Controversial political questions are not likely to afford quite the same scope and specificity for working out right answers (on which, more in Chapter 4), but the inferential framework at least gives us a setup to move beyond a merely descriptive account of deliberative dynamics.

Though I will further develop the implications of the inferentialist framework at various points below, it is worth pointing out here that from an inferentialist perspective, it is no more surprising or intrinsically problematic to find that citizens do not have fixed, pre-existing, and highly stable preferences or judgments – that is, antecedent to and independent of democratic politics – than noting that they do not have pre-existing and infallible answers to complicated math problems.

Indeed, in many cases, we would be concerned if their antecedently expressed preferences and judgments were *too* stable, since that might indicate a lack of responsiveness to the needs, wants, interests, and arguments of their fellow citizens. The effort, in so far as political problems allow, to speak with a common voice proceeds on the basis of holding each other to account (via deontic score-keeping) in the game of giving and asking for reasons. To be reasonable is to play by the rules of that game in our joint project of realizing our political freedom and making good decisions in the process. With this brief sketch of a notion of substantive rationality, we can now turn to the task of inventorying more operationally proximate concepts of good deliberative practice.

WAYS TO MEASURE DELIBERATION

The surge in empirical work on deliberation has led to a proliferation of research designs, measurement strategies, operational criteria, and even definitions of the phenomenon. Some of this diversity reflects corresponding diversity in the theoretical roots of the deliberative project. Some of it reflects natural diversity in what is being studied, and some of it stems from the motivations and training of the various researchers. Whatever the sources and merits of such diversity, its magnitude has become sufficiently great that it is necessary to step back and take stock, lest the expanding deliberative research community dissipate its energies in an ironic lack of effective communication across theoretical and methodological approaches.

Is there such a Thing as Really Bad Deliberation?: By trying to measure deliberation and its effects, we implicitly assume that there are better and worse examples of the phenomenon. Without meaningful variation, there is no point to measurement. However, many scholars use the term in a way that precludes there being any such thing as really bad deliberation in an absolute sense. If some communicative exchange were utterly perverse on key deliberative criteria, we would be tempted to say that it is not a case of deliberation at all, rather than a case of really bad deliberation. For example, if a single member of a jury were to completely dominate the discussion, aggressively manipulating the information as well as the fears and prejudices of the other jurors, we are in the realm of strategic domination, rather than deliberation. Deliberation is thus like "courage," which describes a range of phenomena, but does so in a way that is intrinsically approbative. There may be degrees of courage, but we need a different phrase, "utter cowardice," to describe a complete lack of courage. Similarly, political talk that falls below a certain threshold is no longer deliberation. Both political theorists and some empirical researchers have been eager to maintain this distinction, worrying that doing otherwise would extend the concept to the point of vacuity. If deliberation and deliberative theory are to have any cutting power, they must be contrasted with other forms of political interaction.[10]

The danger of "concept stretching," however, has a twin that imperils scientific work on deliberation at least as gravely. If it is reasonable to limit the concept of deliberation to those phenomena that meet its minimal criteria, it might also seem reasonable to limit empirical research on deliberation to deliberative phenomena. Such limits, however, would be a serious mistake. If I were interested in studying the causes and consequences of courageous behavior, I would be ill served by analyzing only instances varying from moderately courageous behavior to very courageous behavior. Much more interesting and important would be the causes and consequences distinguishing courageous behavior from cowardly behavior. Similarly, in our effort to protect the conceptual integrity of deliberation, we might easily fall into selecting on (indeed, censoring) the key variables of interest.

There are two terminological strategies that we might pursue. The first is to preserve deliberation as an evaluative–descriptive concept. In a sense, then, the larger phenomenon that we are interested in might be called "political communication" and "deliberation" proper would be the subset meeting various minimal normative criteria. For the second strategy, the term "deliberation" would cover the full range of cases, and we would use approbative adjectives such as "good" or "high quality" to distinguish their relative status according to normative theory. Depending on one's substantive theory of deliberation, one or the other terminological strategy might work better. For purposes of this study facially "deliberative" (i.e., talk-based) democratic practices can, emphatically, be good or bad answers to organizational questions. But deliberative standards understood as normative criteria are obviously approbative by definition.

---

[10] Skinner (1974) develops the idea of evaluative–descriptive concepts. Thompson (2008: 6) notes that "a discussion does not count as deliberation at all if one person completely dominates." Similarly, Steiner (2008) criticizes Austen-Smith and Feddersen's (2006) description of a purely strategic model of deliberation, calling it an example of "concept stretching."

Unity and Diversity in Deliberative Theory: As deliberative theory has developed, it has become internally differentiated, with potentially important consequences for measuring deliberation. It can be misleading now to speak of "deliberative theory" in monolithic terms, as if all the major questions in the theory were settled. That being said, some alleged distinctions are more apparent than real. Many of the differences do not run particularly deep, and thus do not pose particularly complicated problems for measuring deliberation. For example, deliberative democracy has been repeatedly attacked for its alleged hyper-rationalism. The pre-occupation with reason, so the criticism goes, makes no room for emotion, requiring us to be affectless Vulcans in our approach to politics. For the deliberative democrat, though, the opposite of reason is not emotion, but rather unlegitimated power. Thus there is nothing incoherent about having a theory of rationality that gives emotion an important role.[11]

One can tell a similar story with respect to allegedly deep differences in deliberative theory over the role of rhetoric and story-telling. If by rhetoric we mean the sophistic tradition of winning an argument by any means, then deliberative theory should indeed be wary of rhetoric. If, however, we mean rhetoric as presenting arguments in their most compelling forms, then there is no contradiction at all. The key test is whether we are willing to cooperate in presenting all relevant arguments in this way. Similarly, if the way that we incorporate story-telling and alternate communicative forms into deliberation can be linked back to the goals of deliberation and its preconditions, then there is no problem. Critics add, however, that the criteria for what counts as "good reasons" are arbitrarily restrictive in a way that favors the powerful. But if those criteria really are arbitrarily restrictive, then, on a system conception, deliberative democrats can easily – indeed, on pain of inconsistency, must – broaden those criteria so that they more validly track the theory's larger goals. Moreover, such critics assume that the ability to use rhetoric effectively, for example, is more equally distributed in the population than the capacity to engage in canonical forms of argument. This point needs to be argued rather than assumed. To return to our earlier example, the Teamsters in my father's tavern pride themselves on being "plain spoken," but would not be overly deferent on matters of fact and logic. I suspect that critics underestimate the disadvantage that less educated

---

[11] See Neblo (2003, 2005b, and 2007c) for expanded discussions.

citizens face in a rhetorical battle with the educated and powerful, and overestimate their disadvantage in relatively unadorned argument.

Despite the room for mutual accommodation among deliberative theorists on questions of emotion, rhetoric, and so on, there are at least three points on which there are more serious theoretical divisions: The role of consensus, whether sincerity is an important deliberative criterion, and the extent to which the theory should be purely procedural. Rather than analyzing the merits of each position at length, I take an expansive approach and discuss strategies and indicators encompassing all of the major approaches. Though I will not make extensive use of these indicators in subsequent chapters, sketching them is important to the goal of providing a cooperative framework for the larger research agenda centered on "organizational questions."

Procedural: The procedural approach to measuring deliberative quality is perhaps the most obvious and well-known. Most of the variables here track terms used in any normative discussion of deliberation: For example, participation, equality, justification, respect, reciprocity, sincerity, and so on.[12] Two of these terms deserve brief comment because of particular problems with measuring them. First, sincerity or truthfulness is notoriously difficult to get a handle on for measurement purposes. I suspect that many social scientists, in addition to concerns over reliability, avoid trying to measure sincerity because to do so seems intrinsically moralistic in a way that would compromise scientific objectivity. However it need not, and it may not, be the case that inter-rater reliability is no more difficult to achieve in this case than with other difficult and complex social concepts.

Similarly, "justification" is a complex and multifaceted concept. Most coding schemes for deliberative quality attempt to measure relatively formal aspects of justification.[13] Assessing the formal properties of such arguments is important and valuable. And refraining from assessing the substantive force of arguments is understandable for many of the same reasons as for sincerity. However, doing so comes at significant cost because "the force of the better argument" is not a purely formal property.

---

[12] Steenbergen et al. (2003), Neblo (2000), Dahlberg (2005), Jensen (2003) among others all begin from a basically Habermasian proceduralism and attempt to map the theory's key concepts into operational form. On sincerity in deliberation, see Neblo (2009a).

[13] Steiner et al. (2004), for example, note that they "do not judge how good an argument for a demand is or whether we agree with it. We only judge to what extent a speech gives complete justification for demands" (171).

Negative Strategies: The negative approach is basically a strategy of ruling out alternative hypotheses in the face of lingering doubts about procedural measures. Deliberation is such a complex social process, and the threat of power is so ubiquitous, that ruling out known patterns of power is practically constitutive of deliberative quality.

Substantive: Some deliberative democrats argue that the theory must go "beyond process" to cover cases where we think that the majority is wrong, even after high quality deliberation (e.g., Gutmann and Thompson 2004). The worry here is similar to that behind the negative strategy, but it proposes non-procedural criteria (e.g., equal *outcomes*), rather than appealing to indirect indicators of the procedures going wrong. I think that such criteria should actually be understood as procedural in a larger sense – that is, criteria like constitutional rights that have been deliberatively validated in meta-discourses governing routine discourse. But as a matter of measurement, such criteria clearly go beyond our so far modest operational ability to capture the full normative force of proceduralism.

Progressive Vanguardism: One particularly strong (and controversial) variant of a substantive measurement strategy might be called "progressive vanguardism." On this understanding, deliberative democracy is intrinsically and primarily an emancipatory project with strong substantive content, more or less tracking leftist political concerns. On this conception, outcomes that result in progressive goals sought by such theorists become at least indirect indicators of deliberative quality, and perhaps necessary conditions. Similarly, deliberative outcomes that frustrate such goals indicate poor deliberative quality.

Elite Ratification: Elite ratification is similar to progressive vanguardism but differs in that the results that high quality deliberation are presumed to track do not correspond with any specific ideological agenda, but rather function to ratify the putatively superior technical judgment of elites. The idea here is that the core problem of democracy is not identifying good policy, but rather getting the public to support it. That is, there is little hope that mass opinion could ever prove superior to elite judgments about how to manage the increasingly complex and technical problems of modern societies. However, the demands of such complex management have opened up a gap in that the public cannot understand elite decision processes. So the main contribution of a deliberative democracy is to close the gap in judgment between elite and mass opinion, thereby relieving the corresponding legitimation gap.

Participatory: Diametrically opposed to elite ratification criteria, participatory measurement strategies emphasize the fact that political theorists and empirical researchers trying to operationalize their concepts may do so in a way that is biased. In that case, deliberative theory would be in the rather ironic position of claiming to be radically democratic, but insisting on elite criteria of measurement. Participatory measurement strategies try to incorporate subjects into the measurement process itself, and check measurement criteria against the considered judgments of those who are not professionally invested. At the very least, one would want to count perceived legitimacy and attitudes toward the deliberative process as relevant toward any full measure of deliberative quality.

Structuralist: Some scholars of deliberation have pursued a middle way between pure proceduralism and frankly substantive measures by rejuvenating the structuralist paradigm: Measuring the sophistication of arguments, rather than their substance. Semi-formal criteria are deemed superior in a developmental or hierarchical sense (e.g., Kohlberg 1971).

Rationalist: In a similar move, one could imagine establishing deliberative criteria according to how well such procedures conform to less controversial matters of rationality. For example, behavioral decision-making literature has identified a whole host of deviations from canonical rationality. Deliberation that lessens sensitivity to various defeating conditions for canonical rationality might count as promoting rationality, and thus be an indicator of quality deliberation, *ceteris paribus*. Similarly, deliberation that reduces collective forms of irrationality, such as voting cycles or perverse social choice functions would seem to offer evidence for the salutary effects of deliberation, again, at least *ceteris paribus*.

Consequentialist: Mark Warren proposes, in effect, to completely invert deliberation's typical measurement strategy away from procedures to a purely substantive assessment. In effect, he proposes to remove the *ceteris paribus* conditions mentioned earlier, and generalize them to a whole host of substantive criteria of "good outcomes," defining deliberative features that causally promote such outcomes as constitutive of good deliberation. He argues that "Deliberation should therefore be defined not only broadly, but even counter-intuitively to include *all activities that function as communicative influence under conditions of conflict.* Thus, deliberation may include rational argument, but also [...] strategic communications, lies and half-truths, demonstration, dialogue, and angry discussion, since each can advance deliberative outcomes under some conditions" (2007: 10). Thus, like the expansive strategy that Steiner (2007) criticizes, Warren's definition includes nearly any form of communication in principle. (Indeed, it is unclear why he rules out any given that the criterion is advancing deliberative outcomes, not modally, but under "some conditions".) However, unlike the expansive strategy, he maintains deliberation as an evaluative concept in so far as it is intrinsically approbative.

This combination is genuinely attractive, and in certain respects comports well with the distinction that we have developed between deliberation as a standard and as a discrete practice. However, we should pause to consider a few points of potential difference, depending on how Warren would implement his general conceptual move. First, as presented, this move is resolutely substantive in that approbation is meted out according to the criteria of "deliberative outcomes" that are independent of procedure, and thus presumably knowable by the social theorist ahead of time. Rather than testing scientific propositions prospectively, we only backwards engineer the set of deliberative instances according to the way that they map onto these substantive principles.

Second, it is highly local in that each instance is to be judged by its contribution to a specific instance of deliberative opinion change. The problem with this approach is that it disables prospective judgments. That is, we could only know if some mechanism contributed to deliberative opinion change after the fact. But this criterion cannot guide practice going forward. So even if there are no unambiguous, infallible, operational indicators for good deliberation (except perhaps negative ones – e.g., incitement to violence) both empirical research and institutional practice would have to proceed as if there were nonetheless fairly stable patterns.

Finally, it is difficult to see how lies, half-truths, and other "accidental" forms of deliberation could express respect in any straightforward way. This approach, then, would seem to be maximally effective in linking theory to various deliberative desiderata such as increased knowledge, internal and external efficacy, equal outcomes judged by external standards, and so on. However, it buys all of this at the potentially steep price of breaking deliberation's epistemic link, its internal standards of justification (e.g., for what counts as an equal and fair outcome), and because of these, its ability to express respect. That said, a more circumscribed version of this approach is essential to my call for tracking deliberative functions at the "system level," rather than applying directly to each instance of deliberation.

Instrumental: Finally, we can imagine a variation on the causal strategy in which we do not require that "good deliberative outcomes" be judged with reference to the polity as a whole, and that the criteria could even vary between individuals. The most obvious version of this approach would conceive of deliberation as a means of improving more traditional notions of aggregative democracy. Deliberation is not judged by promoting some abstract and elusive notion of the public good. Rather, deliberation is high quality if it helps individuals better understand how various policy proposals are likely to affect their interests, and to more effectively link them to their elected representatives. On this view, the problems of aggregative democracy are not so much that it lacks respect-generating properties, but rather that it is an inefficient market. Measurement strategies here might follow proposals for determining the extent to which deliberation helps citizens vote "correctly" according to their own lights (Bartels 1996; Lau and Redlawsk 1997). Similarly, one could measure the effectiveness of the larger deliberative process by gauging the extent to which such individual-level phenomena aggregate up to representation and policy that tracks the counterfactual of the full-information views of a given constituency.

In the last four sections, I have differentiated the deliberative system into its main constituent elements, argued for expanding our focus beyond new facially deliberative practices, introduced the inferentialist account of political rationality, and canvassed a large set of measurement strategies rooted in competing normative theories of deliberation. Doing so allows deliberative theory to engage empirical research in a much more open-ended and cooperative mode. However, we might also worry that it renders deliberative theory unmanageable and unfalsifiable as an empirical research program.

IS DELIBERATIVE DEMOCRACY A FALSIFIABLE THEORY?

Diana Mutz poses this question in her important and influential 2008 *Annual Review of Political Science* paper of the same name. She answers it in the negative, and as a consequence proposes to fundamentally reorganize the empirical research agenda on deliberation. I address myself to the same question, both because it is important to my purposes, and because I fear that some of Mutz's proposals, despite their evident attractions, may actually damage the valuable and urgent goal that she seeks to promote (and that I share with her) – that is, fostering productive interaction between the normative theory of deliberative democracy and empirical research on it.

Mutz speaks eloquently for many other empiricists when she articulates the reasons behind her frustration with how normative political theorists introduce pathologies into the empirical study of deliberation. She argues that political theorists leave their concepts ill defined, the logical relationships among them vague, and their operational indicators underspecified – and that is when they can agree on key points. Complicating matters, there is so much diversity in defining and measuring deliberation that it is often unclear how any given finding really bears on the theory. As a result, post hoc adjustments and evasions are easy to come by, and such a "moving target" theory becomes unfalsifiable as a matter of practice (2008: 527). Finally, the whole process is aggravated by theorists' already meager scientific integrity being blinded by their devotion not only to "a pet theory" but "a social cause" – Mutz goes so far as to compare deliberative democrats to drug companies who suppress unfavorable data to promote their products and profits (536).

Many of Mutz's specifically scientific criticisms have merit, and the bulk of the concrete recommendations in the article will benefit normative theory, social science, and democratic practice if taken to heart. For example, her suggestions for how to sequence progressively more complex research designs that move beyond additive models of deliberative outcomes should be required reading for both empiricists and theorists (532).That said, at a few key points, the arguments are unjustly dismissive and distort what theorists are doing beyond recognition. If the problem were just rhetorical, there would be limited value in merely setting the record straight. Unfortunately, these distortions underwrite arguments that, if taken to heart, would damage fruitful interaction between theory and empirical research even more than the specifically scientific suggestions would help.

For example, Mutz sharply criticizes theorists' attempts to distinguish between deliberation per se (i.e., facially deliberative practices) and the larger deliberative processes of which it is a part: "Empirical researchers attempting to test deliberative theory can be forgiven for wanting to bang their collective heads against a wall...What does it mean to say that something is not part of deliberation but is part of the larger deliberative process" (526)? I do not believe that this idea should be so maddening. Indeed, I do not see why it should not be regarded as routine and necessary for exactly the kind of conceptual clarity that Mutz rightly calls for. Complex relationships between a concept understood strictly and its penumbra show up everywhere. For example, conducting international diplomacy typically requires securing interpreters, but it would be scientifically unhelpful to insist that recruiting competent interpreters must be either part of diplomacy per se, or completely irrelevant to analyzing instances of diplomatic failure. Similarly, it is entirely sensible to argue that when citizens read the newspaper or discuss politics over the dinner table, they contribute to the deliberative process, while not categorizing such activities as public deliberation per se. Far from hindering progress, this sensible distinction between deliberation as a discrete practice and the larger system in which deliberation as a normative standard is met or thwarted is essential for fostering fruitful exchange between theory and practice. Though it complicates the empirical study of deliberation somewhat, the trade-offs are well worth it in better capturing what the normative theory is really trying to get at.

Mutz takes this hostility toward the complications of deliberative theory pretty far, arguing that "it is widely recognized as a senseless and unproductive exercise to haggle about what qualifies as true deliberation" (525). This claim is quite extraordinary since it would seem to wave away, without argument, a lot of what political theorists do while thinking themselves sensible and productive. Moreover, it should seem problematic for empiricists as well, since without a detailed account that maps their results back into normative theory, it is not clear why the research questions that are being answered matter for that theory. (Nor could those results help to adjudicate between rival theories of deliberation.) The attitude revealed in Mutz's critique inverts Habermas' remark relegating empirical work to the realm of mere organizational questions. Here there are *only* organizational questions, but no debate about the larger theory concerning what we are organizing and why. Such an attitude would make fruitful interaction between normative and empirical inquiry impossible.

Mutz presses her attack, expressing incredulity that theorists would call for research into the conditions under which deliberative democracy might work best, arguing that such a move violates scientific norms by presuming that deliberative democracy is worth promoting: "At this juncture, the traditions of normative theory begin to befuddle the empiricist. This is because deliberative democratic theory is unabashedly a social movement as well as a theory. Its advocates promote it not only as a pet theory but also as a social cause" (529). I suspect that many theorists, in turn, find this objection befuddling. If it was not clear from the beginning that normative theory should be unembarrassed about making normative arguments, then the misunderstandings between theorists and empiricists do indeed run deep. Moreover, it is not clear why the traditions of science should generate any prejudice against the kind of implementation research that theorists propose.

In the face of this mutual befuddlement, we should search for sources of misunderstanding between theorists and empiricists, rather than dismissing each other as hopelessly benighted. Let me suggest two such points of misunderstanding: First, that deliberative theory must be primarily about promoting talk-centered political innovations like deliberative opinion polls; and second, that deliberative quality is, in itself, normatively empty and thus irrelevant to the central empirical research questions on deliberative theory. Let's take a closer look at both.

Mutz complains that "In practice, good deliberation is often defined as deliberation that produces the desired consequences outlined in the theory," (527) and adds the corollary that deliberation is defined so broadly, for example, to include emotional appeals, that "it is not clear how deliberative theory can be differentiated from any of dozens of other theories" (526). This argument takes for granted that the apparent circularity here should trouble normative theorists. But the circularity is only a problem if we conflate deliberation as a normative standard with scientific questions about how best to realize that standard. As I argued before, conflating the two fundamentally distorts what many deliberative theorists aspire to do with their theories, even if they are sometimes vague about how to handle the empirical critique beyond controlled deliberative environments. Deliberative theory differentiates itself from the dozens of other empirical theories by being a normative theory, whereas, for scientific purposes, it need not differentiate itself – if any of those dozens of other theories help answer relevant organizational questions, they can be interpreted as part of deliberative theory in that limited sense.[14]

Ironically, Mutz ends up calling for an empirical research agenda that is similar to what Habermas called for over thirty years ago. She suggests that we build up causal knowledge about how and when facially deliberative practices contribute to deliberative desiderata like citizen knowledge, trust, participation, efficacy, and public-spiritedness, while "leaving open the possibility that these ends might be better achieved another way" (529). As noted before, Habermas makes a similar move by setting up his normative standard, and then leaving wide open whether institutional arrangements from minimalist elitism to radical democracy will best promote that standard as an empirical matter.

---

[14] When Mutz refers to "dozens of other theories", it is not entirely clear whether she means empirical or normative theories. I read her as objecting to the proliferation of potentially relevant empirical theories when we do not restrict ourselves to testing the causal virtues of a small number of talk-based political practices. If she meant normative theories, then deliberative theory differentiates itself by the normative criteria used to judge political outcomes – e.g., vs. Pareto efficiency, interpersonally compared utility, freedom understood as pure non-interference, etc.

Despite such flexibility about how best to achieve deliberative ends, the situation gets a bit more complex because many deliberative theorists do suggest that facially deliberative processes should also play a more direct role. For example, Joshua Cohen argues that, "The virtues of the *deliberative* view are also *more intrinsic*" (1999: 403). Jumping on this claim, Mutz argues, "The key difference is that, in normative political theory, the activity described as deliberation is *assumed* to have certain beneficial outcomes, and in empirical research, it is *hypothesized* to have those same desirable outcomes. Hypotheses often turn out to be wrong, but assumptions, by their very nature, cannot be" (524). This uncharacteristically tendentious way of putting things is, in part, simply false. Many normative theorists have explicitly framed parts of their theories in hypothetical terms amenable to standard hypothesis testing.[15] Nevertheless, for some purposes, Mutz's accusation has a grain of truth to it that requires some explanation.

Even when theorists do assign deliberation a more intrinsic role, it is subtly incorrect to say that they assume that it has beneficial outcomes. A more accurate formulation would read something like this: In normative political theory, the activity described as high quality deliberation often constitutes a direct indicator of legitimacy. It is not a matter of assuming causal consequences, but rather of stipulating an operational definition. This clarification might seem even more alarming to empiricists since it would appear to make causal analysis superfluous, rather than merely covert. Mutz is dismissive of the theorists' approach, and research on deliberative quality more specifically: "[W]hether an instance of discourse meets a set of criteria to qualify as [good] deliberation is irrelevant...Knowing what a given instance of deliberation is like simply cannot tell us anything about its consequences" (529). Strictly speaking, of course, this statement is true. But to see why it mostly misses the point, consider a closely related case.

Imagine that we are trying to do research to understand and improve a country's judicial system. We gather extensive data on the quality of the court's proceedings: Whether judges and juries are independent, or subject to payoffs and political pressure; whether the court has access to high quality information like reliable forensic evidence or independent expert testimony; whether laws and procedures are applied consistently and

---

[15] For example, Habermas (1996: 287–302), Fishkin and Luskin (2005), Mansbridge et al. (2006), Warren (2004), Bächtiger et al. (2010), Esterling et al. (2011b), Neblo (2005), Esterling et al. (2013), Burden et al. (2007).

equally regardless of the social or economic status of the parties involved; whether those parties have roughly equal access to resources like quality lawyers, and so on. There would be something very strange about saying that these indicators of procedural quality are "irrelevant" on the grounds that they simply cannot tell us anything about their consequences for a given case. These indicators of procedural quality are typically a big part of the legal definition of whether "justice was served," and not simply on the grounds of their typical empirical consequences. Indeed, in many cases, it is hard to imagine what scientific evidence for good consequences completely independent of fair procedures would even look like.[16]

In this light, it seems strange that Mutz criticizes theorists for advocating research on how we "might mitigate inequality" in deliberation, arguing that "Before we set a goal of equality...[or] any other deliberative standard, we should first have evidence that the theory works as advertised and that these particular standards are crucial to its beneficial outcomes" (528). To many deliberative theorists that is akin to saying, "Before we set a goal of equality in voting, we should first have evidence that doing so is crucial to electing the best candidates." Today, such a call for empirical proof for the franchise sounds obtuse. During debates over the nineteenth amendment to the U.S. constitution, however, critics did make arguments along these lines: That extending the franchise to women would either (1) not make a difference, since husbands and fathers could serve as adequate proxies, or worse, (2) that women's "emotional" nature meant that they would degrade the quality of the electorate.

The main response, though, was not to rebut the argument against suffrage by undermining the empirical premises supporting it, but rather to question the relevance of those empirical premises in the first place. Empirical evidence on voting patterns might be interesting for some ancillary purposes, but the argument misses much more important points about why we value equality in voting. First, that equality expresses a

---

[16] Except in a negative sense, and then only presumptively, e.g., if we found that black defendants got longer sentences on average, controlling for other relevant factors, we would have a presumption of injustice, but would not be able to define justice more positively in any given case. Similarly, in some cases (e.g., murder), we could imagine the occasional example of decisive factual evidence emerging post hoc, but even here we know that there was a lack of crucial evidence available in the initial deliberations. Finally, we could also imagine some legally non-germane "good" consequences. For example, locking up lots of people with criminal histories regardless of their guilt in the present case might lead to a reduction in subsequent crime. But such an argument would be otiose to say the least. See Neblo (2007) for further discussion of these issues.

kind of respect and embodies a kind of freedom both of which are central, or intrinsically valuable, to democracy. Thus, the correlation between women's votes and their husbands' and fathers' and whether it would change many election outcomes is irrelevant. Moreover, in a democracy, the concept of "electing the best candidates" cannot be operationalized in a normatively satisfying way without at least some reference to what equal citizens would decide under sufficiently good conditions.[17] The concept of "degrading the quality of the electorate" presumes that researchers have access to sufficient indicators of good democratic outcomes that do not have to refer back to what free, equal, well-informed citizens in a democracy want when the system is running well.[18]

Now it cannot be that Mutz has an objection to the concept of intrinsic values per se. She lists several "outcomes" that she implies require no preliminary research to justify their utility. Strangely, though, several of the "outcomes" that she claims "are consensually valued by theorists and empiricists alike" seem like instrumental values in need of more empirical justification than something like equality. For example, she cites "more informed citizens" as a consensually valued "outcome" that can serve as a reasonable independent variable in research on deliberation (523). But reams of political science research dispute whether highly informed citizens are really all that crucial for good democratic results, especially given the opportunity costs. And more information, truly for its own sake, would seem to have modest intrinsic value compared to something like equality.[19]

---

[17] Certainly in the past J. S. Mill and others did not require universal and equal franchise, but it would be hard to think of a contemporary democratic theorist who would give up on equality entirely; nor does the use of such a counterfactual put us outside the realm of social science. Presumably the substantial literature on "correct voting" is motivated by something like the present logic. See, for example, Bartels (1996) and Lau and Redlawsk (1997).

[18] It is not that researchers could not come up with some such indicators – indeed the critical theoretic notion of false consciousness is apposite here. But the idea is that the expression of competent adults has a presumption in its favor, and that researchers, especially those, like Mutz, who are concerned about encumbering their scientific work too heavily with controversial normative assumptions should have no problem with procedural indicators like this, especially if they are among others, and defeasible.

[19] Lupia and McCubbins (1998) among many other dispute the necessity of large amounts of political knowledge. There is a counter-literature, to be sure (e.g., Delli Carpini and Keeter 1996), and I am sympathetic to the notion that a more informed citizenry *is* a good thing, but largely on instrumental grounds. Alternatively, we could think of informed citizens as a kind of procedural indicator for what it means to have good democratic outcomes: What highly informed citizens decide under various other conditions (e.g., equality, etc.) has a ceteris paribus presumption of rational legitimacy. That

There is nothing more or less scientific about research on the conditions that promote equality in deliberation than there is about research on whether deliberation is one of the conditions that promotes more informed citizens. Surely science in itself is agnostic about their relative value as research questions. So why might one advocate the latter and scorn the former? I see no good reason for the difference. Indeed, equality actually has the stronger case for being intrinsic to democracy. So research on how to promote equality is at least as justified as research on whether deliberation produces informed citizens.

The mutual befuddlement between empiricists and normative theorists turns out to have nothing to do with the traditions of science versus philosophy. The real, but unstated, distinction here is between procedural and consequentialist criteria for a well-functioning democracy. The consequentialist stipulates more or less directly observable good "outcomes," and then inquires as to whether political talk or some other set of practices best promotes them. For the proceduralist, the standard for good or right, "legitimacy," is a latent concept that a set of procedural and substantive indicators warrants us in claiming as more or less realized. There are legitimate debates within political theory as to which approach is better, but they do not hinge on the number of causal steps before one hits normative bedrock.

The more direct outcome structure of consequentialist theories, however, creates the illusion that its normative commitments are more scientifically grounded, less dependent on extra-scientific values. A tempting illusion, perhaps, but an illusion nonetheless. Science per se is not doing any of the normative work, and in either case, one eventually gets to the kind of implementation questions that critics advocate in one case and scorn in the other. Thus, procedural criteria are no less the subject of reasonable scientific research than consequentialist criteria, and provide no less reasonable a basis for a normative theory of democracy that aspires to take questions of practice seriously.

Deliberative democrats offer a theory of political legitimacy. Equality and other procedural criteria serve as (ceteris paribus) indicators of legitimacy in the same way that "outcome" measures like citizens' self-reports of perceived legitimacy do. Mutz seems to want to deny the relevance of procedural criteria of legitimacy:

> presumption can be defeated, especially in cases that hinge decisively on some factual matter (e.g., whether some proposal for lowering greenhouse gases will in fact accomplish its goal).

The perceived legitimacy of the decision outcome is also argued to be enhanced through deliberation, though some theorists suggest that regardless of how it is perceived the process is inherently legitimizing. Still, it is difficult to conceive of inherent legitimacy benefiting a democratic society without also being perceived as such by its citizens. Moreover, inherent legitimacy is not observable; empirical researchers must, of necessity, study perceptions or some other manifestation of legitimacy. (524)

The first claim about perception mediating all forms of inherent legitimacy is almost certainly false. Abolishing Jim Crow practices in the American South made politics there more legitimate, even before the bulk of the white population continued the process by coming to perceive it as such. Or take the case of transitions from a one-party democracy to more competitive systems: It is easy to imagine that distaste for the increased conflict among elites in multiparty democracies might permanently lower survey measures of perceived legitimacy while enhancing all kinds of other reasonable indicators of legitimacy (e.g., competitive elections) to the benefit of democratic societies.[20] In this light, the attacks on research into deliberative quality are all the more problematic because such indicators are precisely the "observable manifestations" that many theorists claim make the process inherently legitimizing. Defining away this route out of the dilemma posed to theorists simply will not do. Just as the process of meeting criteria for conducting free and fair elections typically creates a presumption of legitimacy, so does the process of conducting free and fair deliberation.

In sum, Mutz suggests that we should: (1) Jettison the larger theoretical context as hopelessly muddled, (2) define deliberation narrowly so that research focuses on the "outcomes" of facially deliberative practices, and (3) dismiss questions of deliberative quality as irrelevant. All three of these suggestions will push us in precisely the wrong direction. The first suggestion cuts off the detailed findings of empirical research from the larger theoretical debate that makes them relevant beyond the confines of the particular study at hand. Instead, we need to focus on how to connect theories of the middle range to their larger context. The second suggestion, by failing to see that facially deliberative practices are only part of the relevant picture, discourages research on indirectly deliberative

---

[20] Internal support for authoritarian regimes is enough to dispel the notion that perceived legitimacy is a sufficient condition for inherent legitimacy. The case is stronger that it is a necessary condition, though even here, we would want to be careful about assuming linear or even monotonic relationships (e.g., too much perceived legitimacy might be a sign that the regime quashes dissent), and would want to add qualifications like "over time."

practices. Instead, we need to focus on how all the elements of the larger deliberative system work together to serve the larger deliberative standard of legitimacy. And the third suggestion covertly rules out crucial procedural conceptions of deliberation under the pretense of being more scientific. Instead, we need to integrate the various kinds of indicators of legitimacy into a coherent research agenda.

So, returning to the question of falsifiability, Mutz is surely right that deliberative theory understood in its larger, normative guise is not falsifiable in the traditional sense, whereas mid-level theories about the causal effect of various kinds of political talk are. In another sense, though, the normative theory of deliberative democracy *is* falsifiable; one cannot falsify a normative theory of democracy in the same way one might falsify a theory about fluid dynamics. However, most deliberative democrats aspire for the theory to help guide practice. Consequently, it must be able to bear some of the weight of the social world. If many of its implicit empirical premises and causal claims prove false, there is a sense in which it could be rendered *practically* falsified. That is, if the theory's ideal content were sufficiently incongruent with realizable political goals, striving to achieve its ideal could lead to perverse consequences.[21]

However, this criterion is inherently comparative in a way that canonical accounts of falsification are not. In science we can just admit that we have nothing that passes scientific muster – that is, that all of the extent theories have been falsified, and so we remain agnostic. In political practice, however, you cannot beat something with nothing, and so we might say with Churchill that "democracy is the worst form of government except all the others." We often have to act (or do so implicitly by not acting), and so we act on the best supported theory, whether or not any theory is well supported by typical scientific standards. So from now on, in evaluating scientific evidence bearing on normative deliberative theory, we will often recur to the question "compared to what" in a way that is relevant to falsifying the larger theory, even if it would be inappropriate for narrowly tailored scientific hypotheses.

---

[21] For example, Rawls appeals to "the fact of reasonable pluralism" as something that we have learned through historical experience, and Cohen argues that this fact can tutor us as to the "scope and competence of practical reason." If this is so, then in principle, I see no reason why practical reason can afford to forego being tutored by the less grand and certain facts uncovered by modern social science. Indeed, much social scientific inquiry has the considerable advantage of not requiring centuries of bloodshed to warrant its factual claims.

Similarly, a falsification frame is ill-suited to evaluate deliberative democracy in its role as a critical theory. That is, deliberative theory strives to explore whether acting to *change* various empirical realities would positively affect the deliberative system (and whether they are changeable, or under what conditions they might be changeable). So any attempt to falsify the theory must account for whether the theory could work under foreseeably favorable conditions – that is, neither people and institutions just as they are, nor however we may wish them to be, but the way plausible reforms might make them. In a falsificationist framework, such an approach opens the door to troublesome kinds of post hoc pleading and baroque emendation – cardinal sins of testing scientific theories. For purposes of *practically* falsifying the larger theory, however, we must learn to live with such complexity and try to manage it honestly.

CONCLUSION

By distributing deliberative functions and tasks throughout the larger democratic system, we simultaneously reincorporate the broader terrain of politics into the theory and take pressure off of any single site of deliberation. The system conception leads naturally to the distinction between normative standards of deliberative democracy, and the concrete practices that might realize them. Elections may not be deliberative on their face, yet on the system conception, it is easy to make sense of how they may yet serve essential deliberative ends. With this basic distinction in place, we are ready to engage the empirical challenges to deliberative democracy on their own terms. I begin with the claim that particular actors in the deliberative system are incapable of discharging their function – that is, that average citizens do not and cannot form preferences with enough stability and sense to serve as inputs to the larger deliberative process. If true, such a disability would pre-empt the entire deliberative enterprise.

3

Framing the Public: Do Citizens Have "Real" Preferences?

> *In the mind of man, Appetites, and Aversions, Hopes, and Fears, concerning one and the same thing, arise alternately, and...come successively into our thoughts, so that sometimes we have an Appetite to it; sometimes an Aversion...The whole sum of Desires, Aversions, Hopes and Fears, continued till the thing be either done, or thought impossible, is that we call Deliberation...And it is called Deliberation because it is a putting an end to the Liberty we had of doing, or omitting...In Deliberation, the last appetite, or aversion immediately adhering to the action, or to the omission thereof, is that we call the will.*
>
> (*Hobbes*, Leviathan, I:6)

For Hobbes, our individual deliberations are hardly a matter of carefully weighing reasons for and against a choice, but rather a tropistic churn of our appetites and emotions. Far from settling on some reasonable resolution of competing claims, the will issuing from such deliberations is rooted in whatever contingent configuration of our impulses happens to hold sway at the moment of choice. There can be no expression of our rational freedom in this vision; *de-liberation* is just the opposite – a process that ends in our loss of liberty to act differently. Given this definition, Hobbes naturally concludes that "beasts also deliberate" since the process operates in the same way for both us and the brutes, and ends in the same thing – brute will (1991 [1651]: 44).

The picture that Hobbes paints is stark, but hardly surprising. In this section of *Leviathan*, he is trying to overturn the notion, inherited in his day from the medieval Schoolmen (but extending back to Plato), that there is any sense in speaking of "rational appetites" or reasonable preferences. Hobbes's seemingly innocuous definition is actually a dramatic move to demote substantive practical reason, and elevate the looming, primal passion that we share with other animals – fear of violent death.

Major political consequences follow from this inversion. Since our internal deliberations are largely just a blind stir of our passions, we do not really lose freedom or much else worth having when we cede political authority to deliberate and act on our behalf. Beyond ensuring peace, order, and stability, the sovereign cannot represent our will in any more substantive sense, because it does not exist, except as a contingent, shifting bundle of impulses. Crucially, for Hobbes, this claim about the contingency of our deliberation and will is not itself contingent. That is, his claim is *not* the familiar one (e.g., from Plato, Aristotle, and many others up to the present) about the uninformed masses needing to be either educated, led, or ruled by wise elites. Rather, Hobbes's claim is about the kind of creatures we all are. No amount of education can remediate the basic facts of our psychology appreciably, and thus, not even leaders are exempt. Their claims to legitimacy are not grounded in superior wisdom or some preternatural ability to escape the human condition, but merely in their capacity to maintain peace, order, and stability. Striving for anything more in politics is pining after a mirage in the desert, and will raise false hopes that lead us astray, with the same disastrous results.

The grim power of Hobbes's argument continues to be deployed and deplored promiscuously. Yet a puzzling detail about his discussion of deliberation remains largely unexplored. Hobbes was one of the leading Latinists of his day, composing *De Cive* and other major works directly in Latin. Nevertheless, he made a spectacular etymological error in marshaling "deliberation" to designate the supposed "loss of freedom" that ensues when we form a will to act. The English word is not derived from the Latin *liberare* (to grant freedom), but rather from *librare* (to balance or weigh, as with a pair of scales, *libra*) combined with the prefix *de* (to the bottom, completely, methodically). Thus, the real root of the word is not merely different than, but rather actively opposes, Hobbes's point. His argument hinges on denying that we are equipped with anything like the necessary set of scales, or that we can do anything methodical with the parade of appetites, aversions, hopes, and fears that cycle through our minds.

I do not claim to know whether Hobbes merely nodded here or whether he was being slyly polemical.[1] And of course, the etymology

---

[1] One reason to think that he was being polemical comes from the fact that he did not make the same etymological error a few years earlier in *De Cive*: "[D]eliberation is simply

(much less his sincerity in invoking it) can hardly settle the underlying questions about human psychology and the nature of practical reason. But pointing out the mistake does highlight the fact that Hobbes, far from mobilizing common wisdom of ancient provenance, denies a very old and very prominent feature of folk psychology and ordinary experience. Each of us, every day, engages in deliberation that we experience as more like using scales than passively observing billiard balls as they ricochet about. And, again, each of us, every day, manages to interact successfully with others in large part by assuming that they can and do weigh reasons as well. Like modern elitist theories, Hobbes's argument renders much of what we take to be at the core of everyday politics unintelligible and epiphenomenal. Except now, no one is exempt. We are all, elite and mass alike, strangers to ourselves.

Few people today, of course, defend Hobbes's absolutist theory of the state. Yet, I will show later that prominent critics of deliberative democracy avail themselves of arguments that are strikingly similar to Hobbes, and that, taken on their face, have similar, if unacknowledged, normative implications. I begin by sketching the evidence from political psychology (Section 3.1) that purports to show that most citizens do not have and *cannot* typically form stable preferences over a very wide range of political phenomena. I go on to argue (Section 3.2) that we cannot assess the force of this problem for democratic theory without an account of "arbitrary" variation in people's judgments and preferences. That prompts me to revisit the *inferentialist* account of political deliberation (Section 3.3) that helps us refine our notion of "arbitrary" without provoking the problems associated with foundationalism. Using that account, I show (Section 3.4) that, contrary to critics, the problem of unstable judgments and preferences must be remediable, at least in principle, and go on to develop (Section 3.5) a conception of judgments and preferences as a kind of *latent construct*, linking the concept to both social scientific issues of measurement, and their role in democratic theory. With such a concept in place, we are in a much better position to assess (Section 3.6) the scale of the problem as a practical impediment to democracy. I then argue that deliberative conceptions of democracy (Section 3.7) are particularly well suited to handle the problem, and analyze the circumstances under which a certain amount of preference instability may actually be a good thing.

weighing up the advantages and disadvantages of the action we are addressing (as if on a pair of scales)." Thanks to Jenny Mansbridge for bringing this passage to my attention.

I conclude (Section 3.8) with an analysis of how the problem interacts with institutions of representative democracy.

CONTEXT DEPENDENCE, (NON-) ATTITUDES, AND PREFERENCES

Politicians and political scientists have long known that most of their fellow citizens appear not to think about politics quite like politicians and political scientists do. Few people organize their political beliefs into coherent ideologies, so it is difficult to predict how they will respond to new political questions. Their preferences about one issue tell us little about their preferences for another. Some find this pattern distressing in itself. It suggests that citizens do not assess policies by reference to broad principles, but rather, at best, through ad hoc reasoning.

Perhaps more distressing is the fact that citizens not only respond to different political issues ad hoc, they respond to different ways of asking about the *same* political issue ad hoc. That is, if I make a seemingly innocuous change to the way that I ask a question, I may get very different responses. For example, in 1976, 45 percent of the public thought that the government should "not allow" speeches against democracy. However, only 20 percent thought that the government should "forbid" such speeches (Schuman and Presser 1996: 277). A 44 percent reduction in support seems quite out of proportion to any slight connotative difference between "not allowing" and "forbidding." The cumulative weight of such examples led Philip Converse, the great scholar of public opinion, to argue that shockingly large numbers of citizens "do not have meaningful beliefs, even on issues that have formed the basis for intense political controversy among elites for substantial periods of time" (1964: 245). The term *non-attitudes* refers to citizens expressing preferences that are not "real" in the sense of being stable over time and across more or less arbitrary ways of asking questions – they exhibit a high degree of *context dependency*. Like Hobbesian deliberators, people oscillate between appetites for and aversions to the same policy, as various hopes and fears get stimulated by differences in question wording and context. Their responses reflect nothing more than "the last appetite or aversion immediately adhering to the action" of answering the question.

If the public really exhibits irredeemably rampant non-attitudes in this sense, democracy has a problem. Most theories of democracy rely on some connection between policy and the preferences or judgments of the citizenry. One can, and should, put many qualifiers on this basic formulation. For example, most democratic theorists subject democratic majorities to constitutional limits. Similarly, many theorists are not interested in just any democratic majority; the quality of the deliberative process by which the majority becomes a majority is important. And most democratic theorists would concede that mediation through representative institutions is at least pragmatically necessary, if not valuable in itself.

But the basic point remains: If one cannot warrant some robust connection between policies and citizens' judgments and preferences, one cannot warrant the specifically democratic legitimacy of the polity. Without such a justification, so the argument goes, we are thrown back on minimalist conceptions of democracy such as Joseph Schumpeter's, which holds that in large modern democracies, the people are not sovereign in any robust sense.

> If we are to argue that the will of the citizens per se is a political factor entitled to respect, it must first exist. That is to say, it must be something more than an indeterminate bundle of vague impulses loosely playing about given slogans and mistaken impressions. (Schumpeter 1942: 253)

According to this extremely influential view, citizens can, at best, serve as an occasional check on elites, throwing them out of power if they are grossly out of step with public sentiment.

Proposals for applied deliberative democracy emerged precisely as a response to such pessimistic conclusions about democracy. As Fishkin put it, "We seem to face a forced choice between politically equal but relatively incompetent masses and politically unequal but relatively more competent elites" (1991: 2). However, more recent research in political psychology has radicalized the problem of discerning public preferences. According to this new work, instability in our judgments and preferences is rooted in fundamental cognitive processes, rather than stemming from shallow reasoning with little information. These scholars question whether deliberative democracy can do much to remediate democracy's plight. Indeed, they question whether *anything* can do much to remediate democracy's plight.

Consider the famous "Asian disease" example, in which subjects were asked to respond to a question about a policy with fixed outcomes versus a risky policy option (Tversky and Kahneman 1981). The two options were randomly framed either in terms of the number of people who would be saved or the number who would die, though the choices were logically identical across the frames. Yet, under the "saving" frame, 72 percent of subjects chose the fixed outcome policy, while under the "dying" frame, only 22 percent chose the sure thing. This simple, logically irrelevant change caused a whopping 50 percent swing in support for the policy. Scholars have produced a seemingly endless stream of similar results using less contrived examples, across different policy domains, and across different populations. All the evidence points to the idea that framing effects and similar phenomena powerfully and irreducibly influence public opinion. This observation may seem familiar to the point of banality, but it is not clear whether scholars have come to grips with its implications for democracy.

If public opinion toward a given policy is powerfully and irreducibly dependent on how the policy options are framed, then how are we to know the preferences or considered judgments of citizens? And if we cannot know them, then we cannot know whether there is an adequate connection between them and public policy. Thus, democracy loses all sense of direction.

If this conclusion seems overly dramatic, consider that in a case like the Asian disease example, we could believe that we have a solid super-majority in favor of one policy, making it an obvious democratic choice. Yet, we could garner a similar super-majority in the opposite direction with an alternate frame. We are left with two obviously well-supported democratic choices that are just as obviously opposed to one another. Moreover, since so many seemingly innocuous variations can shift opinion, we cannot even know when we are in danger of this kind of incoherence. Framing effects appear to be ubiquitous. And since there will never be an objectively correct or neutral way to describe choices, there will never be an objectively correct or neutral way of assessing public opinion about policy. As Converse quipped, "What needs repair is not the [survey] item[s] but the population" (1963: 176).

Indeed, many have proposed trying to repair the population, believing that citizens would have real preferences if they just had enough information and gave problems enough consideration. But critics argue that framing things this way mischaracterizes the issue. The problem here is different from the familiar ones about democratic competence or rational ignorance. Rather, as with Hobbes, the claim is about the inescapable limits imposed by the way that creatures like us function. Larry Bartels, for example, pre-empts any easy remediation based solutions, arguing that "'It would be naïve to expect psychological laws to be negated by procedural fiddling'...We should, I think, take seriously the possibility that natural language imposes significant restrictions on our ability to describe and deliberate about alternative policy outcomes, either within our own minds or with other people" (2003: 54–5).

Perhaps coincidentally, political theorists have also been engaged in such an immanent critique for some time now. At least since Ludwig Wittgenstein, philosophers have not only taken seriously the idea that natural language irreducibly shapes and frames our thinking, they have also criticized "normal" social science for not taking natural language seriously enough. It is somewhat ironic, then, that political psychology's discovery of linguistic dependence has come full circle, with social scientific research confirming, in a sense, what philosophers have been saying all along. Nevertheless, this scientific restatement of the problem poses it back to democratic theory in sharpened form. I propose trying to sharpen that form even further, pointing out remaining problems in the formulation of the critique, but also trying to give the scope and meaning of the problem a more concrete sense in order to educate our intuitions about how it should affect our views of democracy.

SAME DIFFERENCE

I have distinct memories of being confused as a child by the idiom "it's the same difference." At first, I had no idea what the phrase meant, since it seemed simply contradictory. Then, for a while, I thought that there might be four things being compared in two pairs (e.g., 7 minus 5 and 3 minus 1 come to the same difference), though that never seemed to fit. Finally, perhaps when I was about eleven, I realized (though not in so many words) that the phrase was used to note that some evident difference should be judged as irrelevant for grouping things given the purpose under discussion. Thus, the phrase reflects a mix of the normative with the taxonomic. The speakers were saying that some distinction was a difference that *should* not make a difference. The worry over framing in democratic deliberation has this same character of mixing categorization and normative judgments that seem to follow from how we group things.

For example, in one notable example, 22 percent of citizens believed that the U.S. was spending too little on "welfare," yet about 64 percent thought that we should be spending more on "assistance to the poor" (Raskinski 1989: 391). In one sense, these findings are easy to reconcile. Many Americans resent what they see as wasteful or undeserved spending on "welfare queens," yet they quite genuinely feel that we have a moral responsibility to relieve poverty. In the abstract, the two sentiments are far from logically inconsistent. However, Bartels correctly notes:

[T]hese very different mental images are attached to the same set of programs and policies; any effort to make subtle distinctions of substance between 'welfare' and 'assistance to the poor' seems fruitlessly tendentious. Nevertheless, one frame suggests that a substantial majority of the public supports spending more on those programs and policies, while the other – equally legitimate on its face – suggests that they are deeply unpopular. What can a democratic theory of preference make of this perplexing situation (59)?

A "preference," here, refers to a judgment about the relative desirability of some program or policy *in itself*, whereas an "attitude" can be responsive to contextual features of how the policy is presented, and how opinion is elicited.[2] For an attitude to qualify as a full-blown preference, it must exhibit "invariance" or "extensionality." Both concepts boil down to the idea that preferences must be insensitive to "arbitrary features of the context, formulation, or procedure used to elicit those preferences" (51).

On the one hand, this idea of being robust to arbitrary variation is quite intuitive. After all, "forbidding" and "not allowing" do seem like they refer to the same thing. On the other hand, the notion of "arbitrary" creates a whole set of problems not only in using the term, but in specifying the baseline from which we can measure arbitrary variation. The point is not to deny that some variations should be considered arbitrary. But it is to say that "arbitrary" requires a normative judgment, and that we should like to have a theory that amounts to more than "we know them when we see them" – an arbitrary theory of what counts as arbitrary. In the example given here, Bartels stipulates that both frames are "equally legitimate," and I agree. But we can imagine many others where the judgment would be more controversial. Without a good theory of "extension"– that is, a theory of "same differences" – we do not have a critique of deliberative democracy so much as a series of worrisome anecdotes. That is, we cannot give enough specificity to the claim that citizens do not have "real enough" preferences to even evaluate it.

Thus the distinction between a preference and an attitude is only sharp to the extent that we have a sharp theory of extension. However, there are good reasons to think that a sharp theory of extension will be hard to come by. Ironically, it conflicts with the larger theory that it is being invoked to vindicate. The notion of extension implies that we can specify a policy in some neutral way, but the whole point of the psychological law is that natural language blocks us from doing just that. If so, the search for a true

---

[2] In studies of comparative political behavior, the term "attitude" is sometimes used to designate a basic political orientation, akin to an ideology. Such usage inverts the relationship to context dependence relative to the way that the term is used in psychology and American political behavior, the literatures that I am drawing on here.

theory of extension would appear to be something of a fool's errand, since such a theory amounts to a theory of the "thing-in-itself." This conclusion need not imply any deep relativism. Indeed, it is a very old idea:

The only force of saying that texts do not refer to non-texts is just the old pragmatist chestnut that any specification of a referent is going to be in some vocabulary. Thus one is really comparing two descriptions of a thing rather than a description with the thing-in-itself. This chestnut, in turn, is just an expanded form of Kant's slogan that 'Intuitions without concepts are blind,'...These are all merely misleading ways of saying that we shall not see reality plain, unmasked, naked to our gaze. (Rorty 1982: 154)

FOUNDATIONS, WEBS, AND REALIZING WHAT WE ALREADY KNOW

Now this perspective might seem to just rearticulate the central criticism of democratic decision making at stake here – that is, that the limits of natural language also limit our ability to deliberate about, or even describe, policies and their outcomes. But the real point is both more and less radical. It is more radical in that "policies" cannot even be defined outside of natural language. That is, rather than "seriously limiting" us, natural language actually *enables* us to "describe and deliberate about alternative policy outcomes." Natural language, in itself, only appears as limiting if we insist on a God's eye view of "reality plain, unmasked, naked to our gaze" as a meaningful standard.

Those who would invoke Schumpeter's argument, though, seem to suggest that elites can more or less "see reality plain" when it comes to what those policies are. The problem is that average citizens are moved by differing descriptions, and we have no good account of which of those descriptions are more justifiable, or even of when a given description is properly regarded as covering the same "thing." But if critics have no good account of why some descriptions would be more or less justifiable, or even when a given description designates the same thing, then it is hard to understand why elites would not be subject to the same severe limits imposed by natural language.

This problem is actually less radical than it may seem, however, because a change in our perspective can account for the obvious fact that elites, as a practical matter, *do* seem better able to differentiate between the same and different "things," and to have more stable preferences over descriptions of the same things.

Earlier, I argued that deliberative quality should be thought of as a property of the larger political system, rather than an isolated exchange of political talk. The same applies at the micro-level to our beliefs, desires, and judgments more generally. In the typical case, we make judgments, categorize objects, assess arguments, and so on, not in isolation, but rather in the context of a much larger web of beliefs, desires, judgments, categories, and the like. In order to assess a claim like "that moving light in the sky last night was probably not an alien spacecraft," I have to bring in many other kinds of beliefs. For example: "The laws of physics make interstellar space travel relatively implausible." In turn, my belief in the laws of physics borrows support from their evident usefulness in solving all kinds of technical problems, which, in turn, make me confident that I can safely board an airplane, and so on. There is no single foundational belief here, but rather an interlocking set of beliefs that lend each other credence, and allow me to solve practical problems, and make further inferences.

Recall that on the *inferentialist* account, the meaning of some term or statement is defined by its relation to other propositions in our larger web of beliefs and desires.[3] Just as a chess piece is defined not by its shape or color, but rather by what it can do in a larger system of pieces and rules, so too a given proposition is defined by what it allows us to do (i.e., infer) in a larger system of beliefs, desires, and rules for moving among them. Yet this larger system and its set of implications are vast. So we are not consciously aware of all of the mutual implications, nor the inevitable tensions and contradictions lying about in our heads. When we deliberate, we attempt to consciously resolve tensions and articulate latent implications, rendering the web more coherent, and its full contents more readily apparent for warranting reasonable action.

Notice that I spoke of both beliefs and desires being embedded in this web. It may seem strange to say that our desires are similar to beliefs in the sense of being subject to *articulation* and inference. (By articulation, I mean drawing out implicit or latent connections to a belief or desire that allow us to better appreciate their significance.) In some ways, we experience many of our desires as more "brute" than this discussion would seem to allow for. However, it should be obvious that at least some of our desires are related thus. If I have a strong desire to lose weight, then *ceteris paribus*, a desire to avoid the temptation of high calorie foods should

---

[3] My account here and later on draws on Brandom (1994, 2000), Heath (2008), and Wanderer (2008).

follow upon reflection. Indeed, there are good reasons to think that our ability to articulate desires runs even deeper, encompassing them all, at least in principle. For example, I have had health problems related to my weight for much of my life. In the course of treatment for these problems, I learned that research has shown that heavy people have difficulty accurately distinguishing hunger from other bodily sensations. That is, we think that we are hungry, but misidentify thirst as hunger, for example, and then, unsurprisingly, remain unsatisfied after we have eaten in response to being "hungry." Yet people can also learn to more accurately identify hunger by consciously reflecting on their bodily sensations in the context of other information. Thus, hunger and the desire to eat are subject to criticism *as* desires, not merely in light of other, weightier, desires. For example, if I say that I am hungry, my wife might remind me that we have just eaten, and that I have been sweating from our walk, and thus am more likely to be thirsty than hungry. The fact that I can update my desires shows that they can be functionally similar to beliefs on an inferentialist account.

None of this is to deny that some of our beliefs and desires seem to be rather centrally located in our web, and thus we find it difficult to do without them relative to more peripheral elements – that is, that for most practical purposes, we take them as "given" or "real." Nor is it to say that new experiences – interpreted through our existing concepts, beliefs, and desires – cannot help us to update and further articulate our web in a way that allows us to act more successfully in the world. But it is to say that the given-ness of objects or the primitiveness of desires only appear so when we abstract away from their inferential context. In many cases it is harmless (and indeed useful) to do so, but in many others, doing so can cause confusion and lead us seriously astray.

WHY THE PROBLEM MUST BE REMEDIABLE

Bartels, for example, forcefully illustrates the context dependency criticism, wondering whether any amount or kind of deliberation can "make concrete the suffering of 20,000 birds drowning in oil, or synthesize the myriad charms and irritations of New York City? Can better deliberative procedures reconcile conflicting attitudes toward 'welfare' and 'assistance to the poor,' much less 'forbidding' and 'not allowing'" (72)?

To varying extents, I think that the answer to this question must be "yes." The point cannot be that it is impossible to become appropriately sensitive to a disaster on a scale like 20,000 birds – otherwise how could we come to know that there is a problem in the way that people typically deal with such scales? Precisely to the extent that you can convince me that my sensitivity to scale is inappropriate, you must be able to show me that another would be more appropriate. The alleged limit can only be a local limit because if it were universal, we would never know it.[4]

If ordinary language and our cognitive architecture place severe *in principle* limits on our ability to form meaningful preferences and judgments, how is it that elites are not similarly limited by natural language and human cognitive structure? On their own terms, none of these limits can, in principle, be themselves in principle limits in the relevant sense. As Dewey noted:

[O]ccupancy of office may enlarge a man's views and stimulate his social interest so that he exhibits traits foreign to his private life. But since...holding official position does not work a miracle of transubstantiation, there is nothing perplexing nor even discouraging in the spectacle of the stupidities and errors of political behavior. (1927: 68)

But if we accept the updated Hobbesian vision of severe, irremediable limits on our ability to form reasonable judgments and preferences, then the spectacle is indeed discouraging, though in a way that has no institutional implications either way. It is just a counsel of despair. In particular, Schumpeter's theory of competitive elites does not follow, despite the range of scholars who seem to think that it does. On the neo-Hobbesian account, we would not really be choosing those competitive elites on any reliable, substantive, criteria, and they are not really implementing policy based on much more. So democracy has become mere form, good only instrumentally for peace and stability.[5] Moreover, direct democracy, random lot, and all manner of other procedures might be as good or better at producing mere stability and decisiveness. Indeed, Hobbes explicitly allowed for a democratic sovereign – not out of a concern for freedom or good decisions, but only if it could show promise "in the difference of convenience or aptitude to produce the peace" (131).

---

[4] One might object that this is a fallacy: For example, we can know that people have cognitive limits to their ability to manipulate complex mathematical problems in their head without being committed to the proposition that the investigators who determine this fact are able to do such manipulations in their head. But the point is that we must be able to identify the correct answers via *some* method, perhaps using paper and pencil, or a computer. This point is what I mean to designate by "local" versus "universal."

[5] We must not confuse constitutional or liberal rights with democracy per se. That is, constitutional democracies might give us something worth having in the current scenario, but it is the "constitutional" part that is doing all of the work.

So critics in this vein are on the horns of a dilemma: Either they must explain how political elites "work a miracle of transubstantiation" in escaping natural language and the cognitive architecture of our species, or they must admit that neither minimalist democracy nor anything else follows from their argument – that it proves too much. I offer a third possibility that flows rather directly out of the account of inferentialism sketched here. On this account, it is not natural language that places limits on our ability to deliberate, since such a claim presumes that we can characterize reality in itself, beyond natural language. Rather, on the inferentialist account, we are all limited in our ability to resolve the tensions in our webs of belief and to draw out all of the latent inferences available to us, if for no other reason than that they are infinite. For example, I can infer the solution to just about *any* simple problem of arithmetic given my current beliefs, but that does not mean that I could infer *all* of them, much less that I "have" them as beliefs ex ante.

From this perspective, it is easy to understand why elites should be more robust to framing and context: They have spent much more time adding content to, articulating, and rendering coherent the portion of their web pertaining to politics. Question wording variations that seem properly irrelevant to a policy choice (e.g., "welfare" versus "assistance to the poor") are more likely to be recognized as irrelevant with minimal additional effort, since the expert will have made many similar inferences before. Less experienced citizens will have a smaller and less developed framework to evaluate the question, and will be more likely to have to work out the relevant inferences on the fly. So they will be more responsive to the peculiarities of the specific problem at hand, and less able to see how they may be led astray by attending to unimportant criteria.

With this setup, we now have a ready first definition for what "irrelevant" or "arbitrary" variations might mean: Something that upon developing a well-articulated web on the topic, people would reliably deem irrelevant. As a corollary, a usable definition of extension emerges, trading on insensitivity with respect to arbitrary variation, rather than appeal to something beyond language. And we can even discern the outlines of a normative account of "better" frames and contexts based on facilitating inferences that people would arrive at under very well-articulated corners of their webs. If so, then it is no longer obvious why elitist democracy should follow so naturally or obviously, never mind a Hobbesian interpretation of it. Elites are doing something different from average citizens as a matter of degree, rather than a matter of kind, and the gap between them must be remediable, at least in principle. None of these insights might seem earth moving. But on the neo-Hobbesian account, none of these simple explanations and conceptual moves are available to us.

INFERENTIALISM AS ESTIMATING A LATENT CONSTRUCT

As we saw in the previous section, the radical critique of deliberation based on context dependence found itself in an ironic paradox, undermined by the same phenomena that it tried to use as the basis of its critique. With the move to an inferentialist framework, however, we are in a position to both reconstruct the valid intuition behind the critique, and to see how a deliberative theorist might respond. Basically the idea is to approach the problem of extension as a measurement problem for a latent construct – something that we cannot observe directly, but that we can characterize via its observable manifestations. With this strategy, the set of relevant considerations would be analogous to standard validity criteria, and irrelevant variations could be identified and controlled for via statistical techniques that work on something very much like an inferentialist basis, positing a latent and moving back and forth between items and raters to reconstruct an interpretation that can coherently account for as much of the data as possible. In some cases, we may not be able to warrant that there is a stable construct worth the name, in others, there may be more than one way, or ambiguity about how to interpret them, while in others, we may be able to "measure" it with only moderate precision. As in the statistical case, positing the latent is a kind of methodological or procedural device, whose value is cashed out in terms of the usefulness of doing so after we have seen how much we can account for using the premise.

For "invariance" to hold, a true preference must not be driven by arbitrary features of the context in which the preference is elicited or the procedure used to elicit them. However, relying on vague (if not arbitrary) judgments of what should count as "arbitrary" already threatens the theoretical precision that promised to make preferences more useful than attitudes. As a result of interpretive ambiguity, the concept of invariance will have to come in degrees. If invariance is understood in strictly binary terms, then the argument that almost no one has preferences about almost anything controversial is very easy to make – and precisely to that extent, it is not very interesting. The real question is whether a given set of preferences typically has enough stability to serve some purpose well enough. So I want to acknowledge the issue in the abstract, but try to evaluate how serious it is in practice.[6] The points is, emphatically, not to deny the validity of research on framing nor the ubiquity of the phenomenon in practice, but rather to call in to question its democracy damaging implications.

Part of what inferentialism brings to the framing literature is a way to talk about good and bad frames (and by extension, manipulation versus persuasion) that goes beyond the bare facts of what works and does not work. On an inferentialist interpretation, frames should be evaluated as implicit (or highly compressed) argument proffers – for example, "we should evaluate issue X using criterion A rather than criterion B." Some such arguments will cohere better than others given our other discursive commitments, and so we have at least some leverage for criticizing and evaluating competing frames from a normative point of view. With such leverage, we are in a position to investigate the conditions under which better frames are also more factually effective frames, and vice versa.[7]

THE SCALE OF FRAMING PROBLEMS IN PRACTICE

There are good reasons to think that major normative problems arising from contextual indeterminacy in real political applications are less frequent than one might suppose given some of the disheartening examples discussed so far. Some of people's sensitivity to framing effects actually *is* remediable with better (and plausible) procedures, and political theory can offer significant guidance on how to distinguish among democratically preferable frames. Moreover, democratic theory can tolerate – and even embrace – more ambiguity in people's preferences and judgments than it might appear at first blush.

For example, Kühberger (1998) conducted a meta-analysis of 230 framing studies and found an average effect size of 0.3, expressed in terms of Cohen's d – the difference between the control and treatment

---

[6] For example, I doubt that strict invariance holds for most economic phenomena – the hold field of advertising psychology suggests that it does not – but this fact does not prevent the concept from being useful in a host of economic applications.

[7] Indeed, I see the inferentialist interpretation of framing as *an extension* of the Druckman program rather than a critique of it. The extension is that now in addition to strong and weak frames, we can also get at least some traction on normatively better and worse frames. Juxtaposing the two, opens up the possibility for a whole new line of research on the conditions under which better frames are also strong frames and vice versa. It is easy to see how such research would be extraordinarily valuable for purposes of deliberative reform.

group as a fraction of the standard deviation in the response. Cohen's *d*, however, is a very unintuitive statistic for getting a feel for the seriousness of the political problem posed by framing effects. To render the import of average effect sizes more intuitive, we can define a *reversibility threshold* as the margin of victory in a binary choice within which an effect size *d* could reverse the outcome.[8] If we start with an upper bound for the average *d* of about 0.3, majorities of less than 57.4 percent are within the reversibility threshold.

Since a very sizable proportion of votes and polls fall inside this range, it would seem that democracies might frequently be making decisions without a strong warrant for believing that they have real majorities in favor of the policy. Moreover, it would appear that over a huge range of issues, we have no good way to determine what the public thinks. If so, then it is difficult, even in a heuristic sense, to assess whether any given democratic institution is functioning well – that is, that there is some robust mapping between policy and the preferences of its citizens. On its face, then, this issue does seem important to address.

Reversibility thresholds shrink as the effect sizes shrink. For example, if *d* = 0.2, one needs a margin of 54.9 percent, and if *d* = 0.1, only those under 52.5 percent are ambiguous. Recall that an effect size *d* of 0.3 is an *upper bound* on average effect sizes. The 230 studies that were used to obtain this estimate were nearly all designed to elicit framing effects. Thus, the kind of variation that we are likely to find among good faith efforts at choosing language for opinion questions is likely to generate substantially smaller effects sizes. (I will discuss attempts at political manipulation later.) And the sample of 230 published studies almost certainly overestimates even experimental effect sizes, since there is a bias in favor of publishing statistically significant results (Scargle 2000).

Moreover, in his meta-analysis, Kühberger found that the average *d* was much smaller (0.12) in cases where the two choices were between a risky option and a less risky option (rather than risky versus a sure thing).

---

[8] So to derive the reversibility threshold, let *p* be the proportion of people supporting policy A, and $1-p$ the proportion opposing policy A (or supporting the alternative policy in a binary choice). Hence, the margin in support of policy A can be expressed as the difference between those supporting and those opposing: $p - (1 - p)$, or $2p - 1$. Since binary choices follow a Bernoulli distribution, their standard deviation can be expressed as $\sqrt{(p \times (1-p))}$. Thus, the effect size in terms of the margin of victory is $d \times \sqrt{(p - p^2)}$. Setting the margin of support and the effect size equal to each other and rearranging terms, we get $d = (2p - 1)/\sqrt{(p - p^2)}$ as the largest non-reversible effect size given *p*. As it happens, this function is very nearly linear over the relevant range such that $p \approx 0.5 + 0.245(d)$.

Since almost no real political decisions present us with truly riskless options, there is reason to believe that real effect sizes will be smaller than the experimental examples would suggest. Similarly, Druckman (2004) found that subjects who were exposed to a counter-frame realized a dramatic 80 percent reduction in the size of the original framing effect. Since real political issues are almost always presented in terms of competing frames by competing political elites, policies with a single frame will be almost as rare as policies without risk. If one were to judge from the examples offered in the critical literature, we might be tempted to think that applied framing effects were *larger* in the experimental studies. However, findings like those given here should give us pause to consider that disturbing examples, like a 25 percent swing between "forbidding" versus "not allowing," were chosen precisely to dramatize how big framing effects *can* be. Thus, they are a highly selected sample of framing issues, and serve as a poor tutor for our intuitions about what a typical framing effect is likely to be in practice.

Similarly, experiments that manipulated the frame of a single event (e.g., a surgical procedure having a 90 percent survival rate versus a 10 percent death rate) saw similarly dramatic reductions in average effect size ($d = 0.11$). And perhaps most importantly, framing effects shrink even further when subjects are asked to rate or judge various options rather than choose between them ($d = 0.08$; within 50.02 percent would be reversible). This finding suggests that various forms of approval voting or support ratings (which could still be converted into a social choice function) might help provide a format for public input that is much less subject to the uncertainty that the framing effects literature argues induces a crisis in democratic theory.

THE DELIBERATIVE FRAME

Thus the experimental literature does not provide compelling evidence to believe that framing effects will routinely reverse democratic majorities, even if we remain within the genre of standard opinion polling and voting procedures. However, if we broaden our understanding of democratic preferences, and our tools for measuring them, there are also good reasons to think that we can tame the problem even further. The first thing to note in this regard is that "democracy" and "preference," as used in the literature connecting democratic theory and the psychology of choice, are rather more specific than the full range of their ordinary language meanings. For example, David Miller claims that "democracy is predominantly understood as involving the aggregation of independently formed preferences" (1992: 55). Similarly, a "preference" is implicitly restricted to an ordered valuation over: (i) A set of states-of-affairs in the world, (ii) measured via standard opinion polls, (iii) where the valuation is stable over time and across contexts. From a deliberative democratic perspective, all three of these criteria are potentially problematic.

Quite the opposite of merely "aggregating independently formed preferences," deliberative democratic theorists endorse something like Dewey's description of the normative essence of democracy:

> What is more significant is that counting of heads compels prior recourse to methods of discussion, consultation and persuasion ...*Majority rule, just as majority rule, is as foolish as its critics charge it with being.* But it is never *merely* majority rule ... 'The means by which a majority comes to be a majority is the important thing'... The essential need, in other words, is the improvement of the methods and conditions of debate, discussion, and persuasion. That is *the* problem of the public. (1927: 207)

From Dewey's perspective, then, Miller's formulation that "democracy is predominantly understood as involving the aggregation of independently formed preferences" makes three mistakes: The preferences themselves are secondary to the way they are formed, the aggregation is tertiary, and independently formed preferences works *against* democratic legitimacy rather than for it. None of this is to say that people do not have to form preferences or judgments in the end, that they do not have to be aggregated, or that many issues can be resolved via full consensus.

Dewey's argument is obviously normative, but it is also meant to be partly descriptive. He is not so naïve as to think that counting heads always, in fact, compels a satisfactory debate, nor that majority rule is never merely majority rule in practice. Neither does he believe that reformed deliberative procedures will cure all of the problems of the public. Rather, he is claiming that majority rule, in itself, has only indirect and conditional value.

From this perspective, it is not clear how much of the apparently overwhelming evidence that political psychologists bring to bear is germane to the real question. Almost all of the evidence is taken from mass opinion polls or experiments that mimic their conditions. Such off-the-cuff, socially isolated opinions are simply not what deliberative democratic theorists have in mind, so showing that such opinion has significant limits for democratic theory carries limited force. Put another way, mere preferences, *as operationalized*, are *not* a "centrally important strand of liberal democratic theory." Paraphrasing Dewey, we can admit that majority rule, just as majority rule, is as foolish (or incoherent) as charged, but it is not at all clear that critics have thereby induced anything like the kind of crisis in deliberative democratic theory that they suggest exists.

For example, the assumption that preferences must be over "states-of-affairs" in the world is crucially misleading. As we saw in the discussion of Mutz earlier, one cannot stipulate away non-consequentialist criteria of legitimacy, and then be surprised to find that a proceduralist theory does not work as advertised. What the standard approach would describe as problematic response instability is often a *good* thing from a deliberative perspective. Consider the following three ways of asking if someone supports: (a) "military action against Iraq," versus (b) "military action against Iraq to redress aggression against a peaceful and sovereign neighbor," versus (c) "military action against Iraq to protect U.S. oil interests." On the strict extensional reading, all three versions involve the same underlying choice among actions, and thus we are left with the implausible implication that responses should not vary.

However, on the deliberative reading, different response patterns would indicate sensitivity to reason giving, something that really is normatively foundational. It is completely consistent to say that military action might be justified to protect oil interests but not to redress aggression (or vice versa), and thus to answer the questions differently. In politics, reasons, motives, and process should, and do, matter. It simply will not do to define such sensitivity as a problem to be overcome. As we have noted, the phrase "the underlying substantive issues" can also be fruitlessly tendentious. "Public reason" is perhaps the central concept in contemporary democratic theory. The neo-Hobbesian set up leaves out both the "public" and the "reason." Thus, if someone can be persuaded to change his or her mind on an issue, that hardly implies that he or she does not have a real preference. Far from making an attempt at a theoretical distinction, this literature systematically misdescribes the problem, and portrays the public as more fickle than the evidence warrants. Many examples of response instability should not only not be counted *against* democracy; they might serve as evidence that deliberation is working as it should, as citizens further develop and articulate the basis of their political judgments and preferences.

But critics argue that no amount of articulation can overcome the problem. Kahneman et al., for example, claim that "the context dependency of preferences is an unavoidable consequence of the basic cognitive and evaluative processes. It is not a result of defective procedures"(1999: 221). This claim runs into a dilemma similar to the one described before: Either analysts can cleanly demarcate arbitrary and non-arbitrary context dependence or they cannot. If they cannot, then the claim cannot be evaluated. If analysts *can* cleanly separate what is arbitrary, then it would be possible to define the set of relevant considerations. But then most of the alleged context dependency could be attributed to under-specification of the question – that is, a lack of inferential articulation – rather than being "an unavoidable consequence of basic cognitive and evaluative processes." Since none of the evidence on offer even attempts to evaluate approximations to this standard, there is no relevant evidence to support the claim.

Indeed, it is not clear that one *could* get a reasonable approximation within the genre of mass opinion surveys. In that sense, the problem, again, is indeed not with the individual "items" exactly. But neither is it with the "population." Rather, part of the problem lies in the idea that one can typically capture all of the relevant considerations in short, close-ended survey questions.

One might object that since full specification of the set of potentially relevant considerations is an imprecise goal which can only be approached asymptotically, at best, this admission would be tantamount to conceding irresolvable context dependency. However, if under-specification is the main problem, then there *is* reason to think that better procedures, more information, more careful thought and deliberation would help. And if the issue is always a matter of degree, then we will need more and more differentiated arguments as to when, how, and at what cost, average citizens could act competently in the deliberative system. Chapter 6 will address such arguments in depth, so here I will only cite one particularly dramatic demonstration that even minimal deliberation can help to overcome framing effects. Druckman (2004) shows that a mere five minutes of discussion reduces the typical framing effect by about 50 percent. Thus, there are good prima facie reasons to suppose that deliberative norms and institutions promise reasonable returns on investments in them.

But then we are thrown back onto the question of how much stability is enough to underwrite democratic legitimacy. An account requiring "complete and coherent preferences of the sort required by conventional liberal democratic theory" does not accord with any reasonable description of what the most prominent liberal democratic theorists, much less deliberative theorists, expect (Bartels 2003: 65). Unfortunately, deliberative democratic theorists have not been quick in offering many operational criteria with the simplicity, scope, and precision available in standard opinion polling. In fact, comparable levels of those particular virtues may simply be unavailable. However, if all you have is a power saw and a screwdriver, it does not do any good to insist on using the power saw to bind two boards. The system conception of deliberative democracy requires a more complicated set of indicators and maps than a simple, aggregative, majoritarian theory, but moving us beyond Hobbesian pseudo-paradoxes is abundant recompense. In Chapter 6, in particular, I will return to this issue, and argue that, in fact, the situation is not as convoluted as we might think. Fishkin's deliberative opinion polls, along with various other innovations in "mini-publics," offer an adjunct to standard polling that can help us to situate familiar evidence about democratic judgments and preferences into a larger systemic frame.

Perhaps more to the point, though, a certain amount of ambiguity in people's preferences is not necessarily bad at all. It should not surprise us if many people are effectively indifferent about a wide range of issues, even with good information and upon reflection. The matter may simply not engage them powerfully, they may be genuinely conflicted, or they may be genuinely open to a range of outcomes. Indeed, they may come closer to one of these conditions *after* deliberation. The worry over instability and ambiguity in people's judgments and preferences is only compelling if we think that its main sources are ignorance and manipulation, and that with more articulation, they would have clear and stable judgments and preferences instead. If not, expressions of their judgments and preferences *should* reflect their ambivalence or indifference.

Stated more generally, then, democratic theory can tolerate ambiguity as long as: (a) Citizens perceive there to be a sufficient mapping between their judgments, preferences, or interests, and public policy, so as to underwrite a prevailing sense of legitimacy; and (b) there is a reasonable basis for thinking that such perceived legitimacy is not illusory. Given: (i) The level of perceived legitimacy in the developed democracies; (ii) arguments for such perceptions not being simply a matter of ignorance or hegemonic domination; and (iii) the arguments presented here to blunt the force of framing examples, the burden shifts to critics to show much more concretely that some relevant "minimum" to underwrite an adequate level of democratic legitimacy is not met, and is not ever likely to be met through plausible reforms.[9]

DELIBERATION, MOBILIZATION, AND REPRESENTATION

Lisa Disch's (2011) account of democratic representation is the most sophisticated attempt so far to develop a theory of democratic representation that can account for the recursive nature of democratic public opinion discussed in the previous sections. Her account starts from an analysis in many ways very similar to the one offered here. We agree on a remarkably wide range of issues, and yet end up with very different conclusions. Disch's account starts from the premise that context dependence is real and ubiquitous. And she argues that average citizens, nonetheless, can and do form genuine opinions and register preferences that can serve as suitable subjects of democratic representation. Thus, she also rejects Schumpetarianism. The key fact for Disch is that:

The reasoning process by which they form these preferences depends on communications put forward by political elites in their bids to forge a winning majority in an election or policy contest. Elites educate constituents as they recruit them to positions that work to elites' own advantage in an interparty struggle for power, typically without avowing the dual motive. (100)

I agree that this finding means that most citizens do not have well-articulated opinions and preferences just waiting to be elicited, in which case "promissory" notions of democratic representation (and their relatives) cannot function as advertised. Thus, influence between elites and citizens cannot, indeed *should not*, be a one-way street. Elected officials and other elites have necessary and legitimate roles to play in the larger deliberative system. Disch develops her notion of "reflexivity" (a distant cousin to my notion of articulation) as the proper measure of democratic legitimacy, and like me, argues that it should be evaluated at the system level, rather than in discrete, dyadic cases. We also agree that political representation is constitutive – that is, inescapably procedural and emergent. As a result, we both embrace non-foundationalist theories of

---

[9] Kelly (2012) proposes an interesting "behavioral" approach to democratic theory on the grounds in the face of framing effects. His discussion of the institutional implications of his approach is especially helpful. Yet on my account, he confuses the issue of normative standards and organizational questions, and thus sets up more stringent requirements for the perversity of some account of democratic legitimacy given a stipulated level of framing reversals and the like.

political rationality. Finally, Disch and I agree that it is not possible or necessary for political parties and candidates to completely eschew their "dual motives," that rhetoric arises from the confluence of those motives, and that it is "not easy to operationalize" the distinction between persuasion and manipulation.[10]

Despite this extensive range of agreement, Disch's theory ends up at quite a distance from the conception of deliberative democracy developed here. In her account, citizens cannot be said to have meaningful preferences independent of strategic conflict between political elites, and that there is no adequate way to judge whether such conflict conduces toward normatively adequate preference formation. For example, she concludes that, in the face of difficulties in distinguishing between persuasion and manipulation, Jane Mansbridge (2003) falls back onto individualistic foundationalism and gives up on the system conception of deliberation. As a result, Disch appears to give mostly on identifying criteria for distinguishing between persuasion and manipulation, turning to Derrida and other rhetorical theories of deliberative politics instead. In the end, though, she seems to conclude that these do not provide sturdy enough normative criteria. Instead, her theory proposes "reflexivity" as the normative standard:

> [Reflexivity] is not purely descriptive...Nor is it normative in the strong sense...It is, instead, the measure according to which a representation process can be judged as more or less democratic insofar as it does more or less to mobilize both express and implicit objections from the represented...[It] means more than the mere fact of contestation...[and] would require provision for a formal response. (111)

Disch goes on to illustrate the idea by drawing on Condorcet's proposal for the French constitution, in which he provides for a remarkable proliferation of checks and balances. For example, his "design would permit voting majorities of the Assemblies in just 1 of 85 national departments to call the legitimacy of a national law into question" (112). And the sites and modes of contestation go on extensively from there.

Thus, Disch's normative vision rests largely on a kind of political version of falsificationism. We can never say much confirming about a given policy or process representing anything in the positive sense, but we can expose proposals to a gauntlet of falsifying criticism, and see what

---

[10] Disch is actually quoting Mansbridge (2003) on the difficulty in operationalizing the distinction between manipulation and education (or what I prefer here to call persuasion). However, it is clear that Disch agrees with Mansbridge, and actually thinks that her way of putting it is a severe understatement.

survives. Despite its apparent attractions, the first problem with this proposal is that it seems quite certain that almost nothing will survive. Brady and Volden (2005), among others (Krehbiel 1998), have shown that a much less extensive set of points for contestation produce "revolving gridlock." Anything remotely resembling Condorcet's proposal would not even revolve. It is not clear that simple falsificationism is even the best model for science. But at least scientists can remain agnostic about a given question, and take the long view. Such standards are much less appropriate to what C. S. Peirce called "vital questions" of choice wherein nonaction is itself a substantive choice. Thus, when we move from theory to practice, proponents of this kind of reflexivity will face a direct trade-off between impotence and an inadvertent (yet extreme) form of status quo conservatism, rather than the dynamic, generative contestation that they hope for.

Moreover, the implicit appeal to falsificationism gets stretched even further when we consider that reflexivity "cannot guarantee that objections that make it through the process will be reasonable" (112). Citizens, interest groups, and other actors will also have "dual motives." If so, then either reflexivity really is just a descriptive concept with no normative bite, or attempts to assess its normative content will run into the same problems that supposedly make the distinction between manipulation and persuasion otiose. It is not just that we cannot effectively control the free play of power; we cannot even conceptualize what it would mean to do so. The normative content of the falsificationist strategy relies implicitly on versions of the same cognitive and procedural assumptions that were rejected in representational theories.[11] So it would seem that Disch's constructive project – contrary to its intentions – is stuck in the same Hobbesian logic discussed here. Thus, if her critical project holds, we are all stuck.

The concept of reflexivity, taken on its own terms, cannot serve its normative function. If we can get any leverage on the distinction between persuasion and manipulation, however, it could be a very useful part of a larger repertoire for assessing democratic legitimacy at the system level. In pressing the argument from elite political contestation against Habermas, Disch writes: "Thus, communication that discourse theory regards as

---

[11] For example, scientific falsificationism would be meaningless if we had no reason to think that scientists had not manipulated their data, avoided difficult tests, or otherwise aggressively put their own careers and interests above the norms and standards of good scientific procedure.

manipulative turns out to be intrinsic to the learning process" (101). This need not present a particular problem once we make the distinction between a systemic normative standard and discrete applications at one site within the system.

But what is more, the cited studies emphatically do *not* show that manipulation is intrinsic to the learning process. Imagine that we had a campaign between two extraordinarily punctilious candidates who were unwilling to strategically distort their opponents' records, pander to popular prejudice, and so on. They both want to win, and press their differing qualifications, policy positions, and the rationales behind them vigorously, but transparently. The political psychology literature provides no reason to think that citizens would not be as, or better, able to learn from the campaign and form preferences capable of being represented. All of the evidence is equally consistent with the notion that citizens learn *in spite of*, rather than because of, elites' "second" motive.[12]

Moreover, even in the unlikely event that manipulation is a necessary ingredient for learning via mobilization, none of the relevant studies show that partisan mobilization is the *only* path to learning. The applied wing of the deliberative reform movement, for example, has developed a range of alternative environments in which the organizers have a much lower stake in the outcomes than candidates for office. Several studies suggest that citizens learn at least as well in such environments.[13] It is true that political campaigns and other partisan activity reach many more citizens than various mini-publics and their like. The whole point of deliberative reform, however, is to intervene to improve the system. So claims about manipulation being "intrinsic" in this sense threaten to become question-begging and ideological.

Talk of improving the system brings us back around to the question of how to distinguish between persuasion and manipulation. At the beginning of this section, I conceded that the distinction was "not easy to operationalize." That said, I do not think that the evident difficulties in

---

[12] There is some disagreement in the literature on negative campaigning as to whether there is something about negativity itself that promotes learning. I will only note: (1) The literature is not settled; (2) "negative," as operationalized, is not at all the same thing as manipulation (i.e., neither is a subset of the other); and (3) even if the effects are real, they are effects on the margin, and hardly warrant the claim that manipulation is "intrinsic" to learning.

[13] Fishkin and Luskin (2005). Esterling, Neblo, and Lazer (2011a) reports on a hybrid case, wherein elected representatives interact with average citizens on terms that mirror mini-publics more than the open conflict of campaigns or even standard town hall formats.

doing so should stop us from trying. Disch, however, marshals powerful arguments for thinking that operationalizing the distinction is not only difficult but that it is impossible to do so without covertly appealing to a kind of foundationalist, representational theory that I have already rejected, and agree is untenable. If so, then perhaps we are both stuck in Hobbes's trap.

However the inferentialist account attempts to reconstruct representational intuitions in pragmatic terms, rather than dispensing with them outright. So I admit that I am trying to have it both ways, but argue that this is a feature, not a bug. There is a reason that representationalist thinking has such a pull on us in ordinary life. Non-foundationalist webs of belief still have a certain amount of structure, and moreover there are degrees of similarity among webs of belief as a result of their origins in language and socialization. Thus, even if language is a social practice rather than a tool for representing things-in-themselves, that does not mean that instances of those social practices cannot be better or worse at representing things-as-we-use-them.[14] The figurative and constructive moments in political deliberation need not disable our everyday normative notions completely. Disch acknowledges that "The idea is not that political elites create constituencies arbitrarily and in words alone" (108), and that "Rhetors who want to persuade cannot invent frames out of whole cloth" (110).

I will develop why I think that Disch's concessions here are both understated and underappreciated throughout the rest of the book (especially in Chapters 4, 6, and 7). Here I will only note that most of us, in practice, more or less know what it feels like to manipulate and be manipulated, and can often distinguish it from persuasion. We can make the distinction in the third, second, and especially the first person, and think it important in all three roles. And, we can often secure a high degree of agreement about the distinction in practice. So it is important not to get captured by abstractions. Disch invokes Hannah Pitkin to help make her point, arguing that Pitkin came up to the line, but ultimately passed on the radical implications of her own analysis out of a dogmatic commitment to an abstract principle that citizens should influence only elites, and not vice versa. My own reading of Pitkin runs in the other direction. I think that she tried to establish a kind of reflective equilibrium, preventing her conceptual explorations from leading her too far

---

[14] Moreover, that function is a prominent feature of the linguistic practice of argument (Mercier and Sperber 2011).

away from the kind of basic normative intuitions that any adequate theory must accommodate. Referring to the distinction between manipulation and leadership, Pitkin writes:

> Again, these are not just verbal games, but the right terms for naming a distinction in reality: the difference between democratic and dictatorial relationships between ruler and ruled. Only if it seems right to attribute governmental action to the people in the substantive sense do we speak of representative government. But all this makes the notion of representative government seem far more impressionistic, intuitive, and temporary than it really is when we use it. Judging a government to be representative is not merely a matter of a sort of over-all esthetic impression one has formed; though there may be difficult borderline cases, not all cases are borderline. (1967: 233–234)

At points, Disch seems ambivalent about her larger claim, and admits that we can get *some* leverage on manipulation, at least in cases that are far from the borderline – that is, that Pitkin's broad distinction between democratic and dictatorial relations is valid. If so, then the claim cannot be that attempts to measure the distinction are confused and nonsensical in themselves, but rather that we can only hope to have a very coarse, ordinal scale. As we shall see in Chapter 6, I think that there are reasons to be more sanguine on the measurement issue. But in one sense, such discussions occlude the more important issue: If the distinction between manipulation and leadership is a valid normative construct, then we just have to live with whatever coarseness and noise that we run up against in our criteria for measurement. And if the distinction really cannot be reconstructed in a normatively adequate way, then the putative coarseness and noise are not apposite. Pitkin insists that her analysis rests on more than "just verbal games," but Disch nevertheless accuses her of using "a linguistic sleight of hand [to] fuse representation to democracy" (109). Perhaps. But if so, Disch risks inadvertently deploying a methodological red herring that threatens to tear asunder the long-standing normative relationship between representation and democracy.

CONCLUSION

Since Hobbes was no democrat, he did not bother running his argument out to its conclusion for democratic deliberation understood in collective terms. But it is easy to see the implications. His argument about intrapersonal deliberation would apply *a fortiori* in the case of interpersonal deliberation, since harmonizing the churning impulses between separate people, rather than simply within them, can only compound the problem dramatically. If the psychology of the fear of violent death makes anarchy intolerable, its sociology makes sovereignty possible – though on terms that should give cold comfort to theorists of democracy. In this chapter, I have argued that we are in a better position to know our own minds for purposes of democratic citizenship than is commonly thought. Yet, if our contending judgments and preferences cannot by expressed in terms of a reasonable set of common voices, knowing our minds could just as easily end up being the source of arbitrariness and oppression as its remedy.

4

How Deliberation Counts: Talking, Voting, and Strategy in Democratic Choice

Rule #20 Unethical Play: Poker is an individual game. Any action or chat intended to help another player is unethical and is prohibited.
(Tournament Rules of Poker)

[I]n poker the interest of the player lies in preventing "signaling" – i.e., the spreading of information to the opponent. This is usually achieved by irregular and seemingly illogical behavior. . .signaling lead[s] to a delicate problem of balancing in actual playing, i.e., in the process of trying to define "good," "rational" playing.
(von Neumann and Morgenstern, 1944: 54)[1]

President Harry Truman was an avid poker player most of his adult life, though he knew that the game was considered unseemly and antisocial by many, especially for a respectable, public man like himself. Truman was unbowed, however. He wrote to his future wife Bess, explaining that though he considered himself religious, "I like to play cards. . .but I don't feel badly about it. I go when I feel like it and the good church members are glad to hear what it's like" (Truman 1983: 23). Though part of the attraction was fraternal, Truman took the game very seriously on its own terms, and was an able player by all accounts. In March of 1946, he rode the train with Winston Churchill from Washington to Missouri, where Churchill delivered his legendary "Iron Curtain" speech. The night

---

[1] The original quotation contained a fair bit of mathematical notation that would have been distracting in the present context, so I have edited without ellipses in a few places, without changing the meaning materially.

before the speech, the two played poker in Truman's train car, along with some of their aides and a few journalists. David Brinkley, then a young reporter sent to cover the speech, recounts that "[A]fter we'd been playing for a while, it was evident Churchill didn't know the game very well . . . When Churchill excused himself to go to the bathroom, Truman said to the rest of us: 'This man saved the free world. Lose.' So the rest of the night, we were folding with flushes and three of a kind" (Brinkley 1996).

Strictly on poker terms, the rationale for Truman's order is unintelligible, if not "unethical." Like other social practices, poker has its own norms and standards. But they are very peculiar norms and standards. A big part of what makes the game distinctive and enjoyable is that many of the norms that regulate most social interaction are not only relaxed, they are positively inverted. Truman's moralistic critics struck upon a grain of truth – in a certain sense, the game *is* antisocial. In tournament play, it is considered unethical, not merely imprudent, to try to help another player. Similarly, telling the truth about one's cards can be punished, while lying is protected. And similar social inversions emerge in friendly pick-up games as well. Had Churchill known that the other players were trying to assist him, rather than manipulate and defeat him, he would not have felt grateful, but rather embarrassed or insulted.[2]

Indeed, if mundane human beneficence is a prominent factor in the game, you may be *teaching* someone to play poker or trying to help an honored guest save face. But when players are intentionally folding with flushes and three of a kind, there is an important sense in which they have ceased playing poker, no matter what they seem to be doing with their hands, and cards, and chips. And they have ceased playing poker precisely

---

[2] I happen to enjoy poker myself, and consider the peculiar sense in which it is antisocial harmless in most cases. On the point about lying and truth telling: Consider the following reply (from a poker discussion board) to a post expressing incredulity about the way this rule was applied in a particular tournament: DCJ001: "If you sincerely don't understand how a player can lie about his holding, but if he tells the truth he is violating a Tournament Directors' Association rule, you are either new to poker, or . . . you have not read and made an effort to understand the TDA rules. . .If a player truthfully announces the cards that he holds, it's the same as showing his cards, which is against the rules. And, if he is lying, he has not shown his cards. Not showing one's hand is not against the rules." www.pokertda. com/forum/index.php?topic=219.15 In my view, the real oddity about this rule is that, on the grounds in the epigraph from von Neumann and Morgenstern, enforcing it ends up conveying more information when a player speaks, since the other players can confidently infer the negation of the speech. I should also note that part of the injunction against helping other players is to prevent collusion. But that is only a part of the rationale. One need not intend to benefit, actually benefit, or potentially benefit personally to run afoul of the rule.

in virtue of substituting some other set of norms and goals for the norms and goals of poker – that is, trying to maximize one's individual gains, positively excluding regard for others. Without such norms and goals, "trying to define 'good,' 'rational' playing," becomes much more than just "a delicate problem." Without seeing the folded cards and knowing a fair bit about poker, a third party might have had difficulty even knowing that Truman's game had changed utterly.

Since von Neumann and Morgenstern's 1944 classic, *Theory of Games and Economic Behavior*, poker has served as perhaps the paradigmatic case to motivate intuitions and provide examples for game theoretic concepts. And that makes good sense. It represents something close to unambiguous zero-sum strategic conflict, with well-defined rules, and consistent, knowable motivations under normal circumstances. But, as noted, poker is really quite peculiar vis-à-vis most other forms of social interaction. Nonetheless, poker (along with chess) is forever being dragooned into serving as a metaphor for politics. Indeed, Churchill's "Iron Curtain" speech contains such echoes, and Truman's press release announcing the Hiroshima bombing refers to the technological race against the Germans as having wagered "two billion dollars on the greatest scientific gamble in history — and won."[3]

And yet the comparisons are often inapt in crucial respects. Real political problems are typically not well defined, interpretations of the structure of the game vary across players and change over time, the operative social norms and individual motivations tend to be quite different from poker, besides other dissimilarities. None of this is to say that simple game theoretic models cannot capture important parts of more complex phenomena, nor that rational choice cannot accommodate altruistic preferences, expressive values, inequality aversion, a taste for telling the truth, and the like. But there is an elegance and aptness to the way that game theory captures the heart of poker without ad hoc emendations. In principle, one could represent things like Churchill's vivid appeal to the

---

[3] In fact, Truman gradually informed the press corps about the Manhattan Project and the impending attacks on Japan during a series of poker games aboard the U.S.S. Augusta, while on his voyage to the Potsdam Conference (Ferrell 1994: 204). The press release had been written before he left, but was announced while he was en route home. To my ear (and with the benefit of historical distance), the connection to poker creates a whiff of glibness in the triumphalism that otherwise might have been forgivable given the scale of the conflict that was beginning to wind down. Secretary of State James Byrnes is reported to have had related concerns. A reporter remarked that Truman "was running a straight stud filibuster against his own Secretary of State" (McManus 2009).

shared identity and values of the "English speaking peoples" or Truman's orders to switch from playing poker to playing gracious host. But doing so is not likely to be very enlightening without a partnering theory to help us understand when and how we come to be playing the games that we actually play. Indeed, it may sometimes add to our confusion, rather than resolve it.

As a case in point, game theory, social choice theory, and democratic theory have developed an unnecessarily fraught relationship over the last few decades. Formal theorists have developed an impressive set of results that many believe severely constrain the ambitions of normative theories of democracy. Though there are antecedents, this project got going in earnest with Kenneth Arrow's famous analysis of voting rules. In recent years, this literature has grown to include formal accounts of specifically deliberative theories of democracy as well. Though there are many complications, it is fair to summarize the take-away as generally critical and negative: Normative theorists seem to consistently underestimate the obstacles and limits involved in realizing their normative ambitions. For the most part, deliberative democrats have responded by trying to show that the formal results are largely irrelevant, by lowering their normative standards, or by trying to fortify specific institutions against the brunt of the critique.

In this chapter, I reorganize this debate on terms that can rekindle a generative partnership between deliberative and formal theories of democracy. I begin by briefly assessing the main arc of the debate to date (Section 4.1), with particular emphasis on William Riker's influential attempt to show that social choice theory renders populist notions of democracy meaningless, along with Gerry Mackie's influential response to Riker. I then go on to show how the aftermath of that encounter has left essential questions unresolved (Sections 4.2), and the prospects for fruitful engagement going forward dim. Next, I reprise, develop, and deploy the inferentialist account of deliberation introduced in the previous chapter (Section 4.3), and explain how it can answer many of the unresolved questions, and point the way toward constructive rapprochement between formal theory and deliberative democracy. This rapprochement hinges on the role of reasoning in producing democratic majorities, and so I examine a controversial feature of deliberative accounts, the "one right answer" presumption, and defend a novel version of it (Section 4.4), showing why it does not simply reproduce traditional problems of social choice (Section 4.5), nor fall prey to the so-called "discursive dilemma" (Section 4.6). I then explain how extant game–theoretic models fail to capture key elements of concern to deliberative democrats (Section 4.7), and link the problem to the peculiar force and importance of social norms (Section 4.8) sketching the outlines for a cooperative research agenda going forward.

INSTABILITY, AMBIGUITY, AND MANIPULATION IN DEMOCRATIC CHOICE

William Riker argued that his "confrontation between the theory of democracy and the theory of social choice" ends in a decisive victory for social choice. Popular democracy is at best "meaningless" and at worst leads to "hatreds and oppression" (Riker 1982: 253). All that is left for democracy is the bland and periodic function of throwing elites out of power. Many others agree that social choice theory is fatal to democratic theory's ambitions. And, since the social choice results are formal proofs, some take the conflict as settled permanently. Democratic theorists responded to this challenge from social choice theory, but the early responses tended to take the form of a wholesale rejection of the rational choice paradigm. Yet, given the existence of reasonable disagreement, modern complex democracies will need recourse to voting, and social choice theory has a lot to teach democratic theorists about voting. Social choice theory without democratic theory is normatively blind, but democratic theory without social choice theory is institutionally deaf.

Riker draws upon a large literature with many important results. But three stand out as iconic for the gauntlet of challenges that ambitious theories of democracy face: Arrow (1951), Gibbard-Satterthwaite (1973/ 1975), and McKelvey (1979). In his celebrated proof, Kenneth Arrow demonstrates that no social choice mechanism (meeting fairly minimal normative criteria) exists which can guarantee a rational (i.e., transitive) aggregation of individual preferences.[4] Those minimal criteria are as follows: First, the mechanism must be able to accept as inputs any coherent set of individual preferences (unrestricted domain); second, a mechanism must be Pareto efficient – that is, if you can make someone better off, without making anyone else worse off, then you should make the one person better off; third, a mechanism must not allow any one person to dictate an outcome to all the others; and finally, the aggregation

---

[4] Arrow's seminal version of the proof relies on intransitivity, though other versions weaken the notion to acyclic aggregation.

mechanism should be "independent of irrelevant alternatives." That is, the pairwise ranking produced by a social choice mechanism must be solely a function of the individuals' rankings of the given pair of alternatives.

If we grant these seemingly benign conditions, then indeed it follows that, in a situation with at least three voters assessing at least three alternatives, either a choice mechanism violates one or more conditions, or there are situations where the mechanism does not produce internally consistent results for all possible inputs. Allan Gibbard and Mark Satterthwaite separately showed that the situation is even worse, in that all minimally attractive voting rules are subject to manipulation by the voters, making it difficult to tell whether any given choice – if we can even get a stable choice – reflects the sincere preferences of the voters, or their skill in gaming the system. Worse yet, McKelvey radicalizes the problem by showing that in a large class of cases, with sufficient information, whoever sets the agenda for voting can, in principle, get nearly any result by manipulating the sequence of votes.

Motivated by these findings, Riker makes a structurally similar move to the one that Disch made, as discussed in the previous chapter. Disch concludes that standard interpretations of democratic voting and representation are untenable because people cannot be said to have meaningful preferences independent of strategic conflict between political elites. Riker does the same in asserting the non-existence of any meaningful notion of a collective will independent of the arbitrary (and strategically manipulable) rules used to aggregate individual preferences. As a result, he argues for a similarly negative understanding of democracy's normative content, though in his case, unlike Disch's, one more like Schumpeter's vision of merely chastening elites than Condorcet's proliferation of opportunities for contestation.

There has been a whole host of responses to these conclusions, but none more forceful than Gerry Mackie's exhaustive rebuttal of Riker in *Democracy Defended*. Rather than evading the criticisms, Mackie shows that Riker's conclusions do not follow, largely on their own terms. He concludes that many social choice theorists have systematically misinterpreted the meaning and applicability of the theorems that they have proven.[5]

First, Riker's approach suggests a false dichotomy: That just as a proof is either valid or invalid, a voting scheme can either guarantee

---

[5] This section draws on Mackie (2003) and my own similar, though much less comprehensive, discussion of Riker in Neblo (2000).

rational outcomes or it cannot. Yet just because a given voting rule can go wrong or yield ambiguous results does not mean that it will do so often. And it would be a wild overreaction to declare robust democracy "meaningless" and revert to Schumpeter on the mere possibility of a misfire. Indeed, Riker proves too much. Taken on his own terms, he renders democratic voting meaningless *tout court* since even his preferred "liberal" interpretation would have to establish some reasonably reliable connection between offending voters and losing an election. Thus, Riker either obviates his own theory or holds populism to a much higher standard without adequate motivation for the double standard (i.e., one that is not rooted in a brittle, strawman formulation of the theory he opposes).

If this is so, then the crucial questions begin to swirl around how often and under what conditions democratic choices run into the problems that Riker describes. As a way to get a handle on this issue, consider the "impartial culture assumption" (ICA) which requires that given a number of alternatives, each voter is assigned a random and equal probability over each of the possible preference rankings. The ICA is useful for understanding how important unrestricted domain is in practice by providing a baseline. It is equivalent to assuming that there is nothing about the specific situation that would lead some people to similar judgments. For the overwhelming majority of choice situations, of course, this is wildly implausible. It is not simply that the provision models reasonable disagreement, but rather that it effectively considers *all* disagreement *equally* reasonable. Indeed, every form of disagreement is to be *expected*.

To see how strange this assumption is, consider a vote designed to rank American presidents on their greatness as chief executives. There are an enormous number of possible preference profiles ($43!$ or $\approx 6.04 \times 10^{52}$). Impartial culture would imply that a profile beginning 1 Harding, 2 Grant, 3 Coolidge, 4 Nixon, ... would be just as common as 1 Lincoln, 2 FDR, 3 Washington, 4 Jefferson, ..., which is clearly ridiculous. Yet, even modest deviations from impartial culture result in rapid convergence toward stability (i.e., the existence of Condorcet winners – a choice that can beat each of the others in a pairwise race). For example, in an election with 100 million voters (roughly the turnout in a U.S. Presidential election) and five alternatives, with just a small amount of similarity in preference orders, the likelihood that a Condorcet winner exists (i.e., that a transitive aggregation of preferences is possible) approaches 100 percent (Kuga and Nagatani 1974). In such contexts, impartial culture is at best useless and at worst, positively misleading. Preferences do tend to correlate at least somewhat, and their correlation should mitigate our worries about instability and ambiguity greatly.[6]

I am highly sympathetic to Mackie's arguments, and think that he is largely successful in the task that he sets himself – that is, to show that democratic minimalism does not directly follow from the social choice results. He marshals a remarkably powerful and thorough defense of our folk understanding of voting, and puts the burden squarely back on democracy's critics. And that is no small accomplishment. That said, his arguments offer us little guidance for going forward with respect to either social science, democratic theory, or political reform in practice, beyond suggestions to increase the use of the Borda rule, among a few other ideas.

For many theorists, one of the main attractions of deliberative democracy is that it seems to provide a way to sidestep the whole setup of this debate. Democracy is not primarily about preferences and preference aggregation, so any purported problems in meaningful preference aggregation were moot. As a simple empirical matter, though, real political deliberation over controversial political issues rarely results in anything like a full consensus. Whether because of a deep pluralism of values, differences in our culture and socialization, or because of simple human finitude in our cognitive or volitional capacities, we rarely reach consensus, and have to recur to some other decision rule such as voting. Thus, deliberative theories rapidly found themselves back in the same boat as aggregative theories, trying to withstand the force of the social choice and game theoretic critiques of their coherence and workability. Mackie's arguments would seem to provide significant comfort for deliberative

---

[6] Mackie's most remarkable claim, however, comes in his reply to worries over manipulation. He argues that the case for agenda manipulation rests on a slim empirical base, with fewer than twenty specific cases claimed as examples across all recorded political time and space. He then goes on to examine each one in great detail. Effective agenda manipulation requires an enormous amount of detailed information about everyone's preferences, an enormous amount of structural power, and a willingness to exploit all of it (without provoking backlash). In some cases, it may be difficult to tell either way whether manipulation has occurred, but Mackie makes a strong case against the claim that such instability is endemic to democracy in practice. Though, see Shepsle and Weingast (1984) and the ensuing literature for a contrary view.

democracy on this front, and vice versa – that is, deliberation may be one of the ways that we can induce the similarity in preferences that leads to stability.

Ironically, however, by attending to the specifically deliberative concerns of democratic theorists, it becomes apparent that Mackie's arguments only pass the buck down to "the means by which the majority becomes the majority." Any gains in vindicating the normative meaningfulness of voting are utterly dependent on successfully mounting a similar defense of deliberation per se. Upon reflection, this insight should not be too surprising. But it should alert us to the fact that what was supposed to be an escape route can also serve as a second entrance for the original trouble.

In a more recent wave of research, formal theorists have shown that many of the same incentive and coherence problems that threatened the meaningfulness of voting appear endemic to the process of exchanging, assessing, and aggregating information and reasoning as well (Austen-Smith and Feddersen 2006; Meirowitz 2007).That is, deliberation is not immune to the formal critique. Even if we all want the same thing – to convict the guilty and exonerate the innocent, for example – strategic dynamics can interfere with our ability to reason together productively under a remarkably wide range of circumstances (Landa and Meirowitz 2009). The situation only degenerates further as partially conflicting interests begin to come into play. By the time we reach predominantly conflictual situations, cheap talk abounds (Calvert 2006; Meirowitz 2006).We find ourselves stuck in a democratic Babel of belief.

These results threaten to throw us back into the Hobbesian interpretation of voting. The whole point of the Arrow conditions, of course, is to build modest normative features beyond Hobbesian stability into democratic voting. Pareto efficiency is a kind of minimal welfare condition. Non-dictatorship guards against being subject to arbitrary power. Independence of irrelevant alternatives embodies a kind of respect for the separateness of persons in excluding interpersonal comparisons of utility. And unrestricted domain guarantees extensive room for pluralistic values.

However, if we do not know whether the majority became a majority via passably good deliberation, then there is little reason to think that the outcome promotes even these modest goods. We would have little warrant, for example, to believe that the choice really is Pareto efficient unless we are willing to take any old preference report at face value. As we saw in the previous chapter, however, a significant literature suggests that people do not reliably know their own minds about politics ex ante. So without good deliberation, it would be question begging to appeal to the sovereignty of preferences in establishing the welfare improving properties of democratic votes. Similarly, if my fellow citizens form their preferences in a haphazard or power-laden way, then non-dictatorship hardly protects me from being subject to arbitrary power. Formal equality is cold comfort if my co-equals are coercing me on the basis of vague impulses, or worse. And if Disch is right about the depth of our dependence on the way that elites frame politics, then any goods flowing from the independence of irrelevant alternatives go out the window, since invariance under framing practically defines the criterion. Finally, the prospect of unrestricted domain is positively alarming in the presence of demagogues – radical pluralism becomes a pretext to pander to or draw out the worst in us.

Thus, democratic stability, agreement between voting rules, and the other apparent goods that Mackie shows that we can get with some reliability reduce down to Hobbesian decisiveness, without any evidence of reasonably good deliberation. Or, put differently, these criteria for good democratic choices are interactive, rather than simply additive. Just as the extremely high voter turnout in Saddam Hussein's Iraq flipped its normal significance, bespeaking tyranny rather than democratic legitimacy, the putatively good components of democratic voting can become valueless or even perverse without good deliberative warrants across the system. All of this is to say that, despite his evident accomplishments, Mackie leaves us in need of a positive account of what it is that we think democratic votes are supposed to be tracking. Riker, Schumpeter, and others did not argue that democratic procedures did a bad job of tracking their normative goals, but rather that there was nothing to track in the first place. Mackie shows that democratic procedures are reasonably reliable at tracking something, and thus he successfully rebuts the more radical claim about existence. But reliability is not the same as validity.

Indeed some democratic theorists might want to consider whether Mackie establishes *too much* stability. We might expect a certain amount of cycling and instability in large, pluralistic democracies, either as an extension of Rawls's notion of the fact of reasonable pluralism and the burdens of judgment, or deeper commitments to agonistic pluralism. As a corollary, too much stability would indicate that something might be awry, with arbitrary structures or covert power inducing a false sense of "meta-consensus" if not substantive agreement. Similarly, reasonable contestation over agendas and the terms of debate is just the other side of the normative coin when it comes to manipulation. Parliamentary petitions to separate issues cannot serve as a general solution because many issues are properly non-separable, with our views about one issue hinging on the outcome of another (Lacy 2001). Mackie's brilliant analyses of alleged cases of agenda manipulation therefore analyze the scene *in medias res*. What they might be missing is a larger concern over the antecedent mobilization of bias (Schattschneider 1960). In one sense, an agenda setter cannot manipulate votes that do not occur, but in another sense, non-votes can bespeak a deeper sense of manipulation, or return us to a situation where the baseline is not well defined enough to distinguish manipulation from reasonable ways to pose a problem to a voting body.

So we are left without a theoretically unified account of *why* instability is not ubiquitous, whether the same problems end up re-entering through the back door of deliberative quality, nor much in the way of advice on how to improve. We do get several reasons to think that things are not likely to be *that* bad. Natural human sympathy means that people will take some regard for each other. The civilizing force of hypocrisy will constrain most people's worst motives. A certain degree of cultural similarity will induce concomitant similarity in their preference profiles, and so on. One might think that we should not let a focus on abstract possibilities magnify the problem out of proportion when common sense tells us that things are mostly alright.

As it happens, I do not believe that things are *that* bad. But serious people present arguments that the strategic implications for deliberation *are* that bad, and that an assessment that does not let our hopes tutor our intuitions will reveal it so. Other serious people argue that we do not really know, and so we should like a more general explanation of why things go better (if they go better) than we might think. And in any case, a more integrated theoretical account, beyond its academic value to both social science and normative theory, would be valuable in helping us to do better as a matter of practice, even if we are already doing reasonably well.

Mackie conducted his battle with formal theory as something of a scorched earth campaign, leaving us in a poor position to re-engage in order to assess what the extent theories *can* tell us. None of the original authors of the seminal papers (e.g., Arrow) thought that they were showing that democracy was meaningless, even if some of their epigones interpreted them that way. Indeed, they generally hoped to develop research going forward to help democracies function better. Fortunately, the inferentialist account of deliberation that I introduced in the previous chapter holds out the promise of providing a more integrated theoretical account of how and why voting, deliberation and other democratic processes manage to avoid the dismal implications of rampant instability predicted by some formal critics of democracy.

BUYING INTO THE GAME

In poker, one typically has to "buy in" to a game. In games with a betting limit, the buy-in is substantial, usually ten times the maximum bet. And once in a game, many poker forms require that players "ante up" or make "blind" bets for each individual hand as well. The idea is that players should have a significant stake in the larger game before the local action even gets started. They cannot dip in and out of the game at will, and must pay some cost to do so for individual hands. These sorts of rules are necessary to keep the players meaningfully engaged, induce the right kind of motivations, and reward skillful play by spreading the vagaries of chance over a larger number of hands.

Without trying to push the analogy too far, I want to suggest that something like the concept of a buy-in can illuminate the way that deliberation helps to stabilize political interaction, and invests it with normative content. The philosopher Robert Brandom has described "the core of discursive practice as the game of giving and asking for reasons" (1994: 159). Like other games, the game of giving and asking for reasons has rules (even if, again, like other games, they are sometimes implicit), and requires that we apply and interpret those rules in the course of playing the game. That is to say, discourse is a normative practice. The social meaning of the words that we speak or write and the actions that we take or eschew emerge out of this practice.

The poker analogy operates at both the level of buying-in to the larger game and at the level of making blind bets or antes. That is, except in extreme cases – sociopaths and people with severe autism – all adults have already bought-in to the larger game of giving and asking for reasons. I hasten to add that this claim does not imply that there is no variance in the level of buy-in among adults. It only means that, excepting rare cases, everyone's buy-in to the larger game is well above zero. Children buy-in gradually as they become socialized, and thus exhibit variance as well. Such variation across adults and over-time in children means that there are testable implications of the claim about game-level buy-in. It is not a *deus ex machina* invoked to redeem us from political perdition. Similarly, most particular "hands" of the game of giving and asking for reasons call for an ante or a blind bet. And here, we have much more variation – among individuals, social situations, the interaction between the two, over time, across cultures, "objects" of the reasoning game, and so on.

Though Brandom's ideas developed via paths internal to philosophy, the broad outlines of his approach have received substantial support from a remarkable range of independent sources, including evolutionary anthropology, developmental psychology, and cognitive linguistics. Developmental psychologist Michael Tomasello and his colleagues (2005), for example, show that our ability to understand other people's intentions is not enough to explain our capacity for language, mutual coordination, and a whole range of cultural accomplishments. Contrary to previous assumptions, nonhuman species (e.g., chimpanzees) are quite capable of understanding the intentions of other actors (675).

Similarly, people with autism were once thought to be lacking in such capacities, but it turns out that our previous understanding was subtly mistaken (686). For example, while it is true that children with autism tend not to follow the gaze of other people spontaneously, if they are specifically asked to assess what others are attending to, they are quite able to do so. The difference between children with severe autism and those without lies less in their ability to understand intentional action than in their motivation to and practice with sharing experiences and emotions with others. From a very early developmental stage, most children evince a remarkably strong drive to *share* psychological states with other people – that is, to interpret others' internal states (to understand), to express their own internal states (to be understood), and to bring the two into alignment (to mirror or share experiences and intentions). This process is essential for language acquisition and more generally for successful socialization, which is why children with autism typically experience difficulty with both. And what starts out as a relative lack of drive develops into a lack of skill in managing shared intention in complex social environments.

What such deficits throw into relief, however, is the powerful and pervasive legacy of the developmental path that the vast majority of us take into the social world. Tomasello et al. describe the main achievement of this process as an older child's ability to manage what they call "dialogic cognitive representations" (2005: 675). In effect, the game of giving and asking for reasons is the adult manifestation (and vehicle) of this continuing drive toward shared meaning, experience, and intention.[7]

This is not to say that adults cannot kick the ladder out after they climb up, so to speak. Part of becoming socially competent involves learning how to deploy social meaning for more narrowly strategic purposes. But for most of us, both the medium itself and the legacy of emerging into the social world via this path means that we typically have at least minimal normative buy-in to individual "hands" in the game of giving and asking for reasons. Indeed, one might aptly distinguish sociopaths as people who have completely "kicked the ladder out." That is, they have mastered the social skills surrounding shared intention – they can understand and effectively manipulate social situations – but do not give the typical normative buy-in any intrinsic weight in their individual deliberations, no matter the situation. In particular, sociopaths seem unresponsive to socially articulating emotions. They may understand how various emotions typically map into social situations, but they exhibit no motivation to align them with others (Blair et al. 2005). Since emotions often serve as affective markers of evaluative judgments, sociopaths end up wildly out of alignment regarding norms of feeling remorse, indignation, and other socially evaluative emotions.[8] Happily, though, few of us are sociopaths. So in most situations, we retain strong motivations to coordinate our actions (at least in part) by socially articulating the reasons for and against those actions. That is, we seek to justify ourselves to each other.

DELIBERATION AND THE "ONE" RIGHT ANSWER

Deliberation is just a more organized extension of this basic, common process of trying to understand others, to make ourselves understood, and to bring those understandings into greater alignment when it is possible and helpful to do so. On Habermas' account, the process of alignment, of generating more coherent common understandings is not purely a matter of semantic content – that is, of the shared linguistic meanings in our community. In addition, we have to appeal to the "pragmatic presuppositions

---

[7] These developmental findings comport remarkably well with Habermas' notions of an "orientation toward understanding" and "the weak motivating force of good reasons." Similarly, Habermas anticipated important elements of Brandom's project.

[8] As a clinical matter, the older terms "sociopath" and "psychopath" have been more or less absorbed into the DSM-IV diagnosis of antisocial personality disorder (ASPD). I use the older term both because it is less clumsy, and because I want to evoke a phenomenon that shades out of the clinical into more general experience.

of argumentation" (1996: 229). The idea here is that there are implicit rules for making sense of some activity as really being an example of that activity. For example, we noted earlier that there was an important sense in which the people playing poker with Churchill were no longer really playing poker after Truman ordered them to lose.

Similarly, in order for something to really count as rational argumentation, we have to presuppose certain things about the discussion. Prominent among them is that, at least in principle, we could all agree on the one right answer to the question at hand. That is, for Habermas, we must presume that *moral* questions (as he uses the term) could gain the agreement of all people everywhere, at least in the limit. For what he calls *ethical-political* questions, we must presume we could gain the agreement of all people in our particular community (prominently the nation-state, but many other larger or smaller groups as well). He is quick to admit that for many problems, neither presumption may be reasonable even as a counterfactual, in which case, we shift out of deliberation per se, and into striking "fair bargains" (1996: 165).

This consensus criterion is one of the more controversial features of Habermas' account. Even theorists very sympathetic to his general approach have rejected it, arguing that it either runs afoul of pluralism or inadvertently renders deliberation marginal, as nearly all live questions become matters of fair bargaining. Without something like the one right answer presumption, however, it is not clear what we are deliberating *about*. The inferentialist account that I have sketched, and especially the analogy to estimating a latent construct, do seem to rely on presuming that there is something to which our deliberations refer, at least in the limit and for purposes of discussion. Note, however, that there is an ambiguity in what it means to say that some question has one right answer. The equation $x^2 = 1$ has exactly one right answer, namely the set $\{1, -1\}$. Both elements of the set fully satisfy the equation, and it would be positively a mistake to claim one or the other element as the uniquely correct answer. That is the sense in which it is not merely a verbal trick to claim that the set is the one right answer. In a similar way, it is possible that articulating our common understanding of a situation will yield a single right answer in the sense of a single set, the elements of which we cannot currently presume can be further distinguished, even in the limit.

In more concrete terms, we might say that there may or may not be a uniquely best policy, but there are plenty of bad policies, and we must presume that deliberation can at least rule those out. That is, in order to construe what we are doing as rational argumentation, we have to think that deliberation is either constructive or epistemic at least to a point. However, there may well be a point past which we do not think that further deliberation has an epistemic warrant. In such cases, we may continue to deliberate for non-epistemic reasons (e.g., building trust based on respectful listening in our disagreements), but past this point, our self-understanding about what the process is supposed to accomplish and why it binds us changes.

There is a sense in which it is misleading to characterize such cases as matters of fair bargaining *simpliciter*. Getting down to the one right "set" of answers is a genuine moral (or ethical) accomplishment, and the deliberation leading up to it is genuinely moral or ethical as well. It is true that the final disposition of which unique element to implement out of the one right set is a matter of fair bargaining. But that is no reason to denigrate the rational content of the process that came before, since by delimiting the scope of arbitrariness and power, it contributes greatly to the presumption of rational legitimacy in the outcome.

Critics of this model may think that the line between the first and second phases falls very early in the process. However, it is important to stress the first, because without it, many of deliberation's supposed benefits would have no warrant. For example, it is not clear why we should value deliberation producing things like "meta-consensus" (agreement about the structure of remaining disagreement) unless the first phase of deliberation is *properly* getting people to focus on the relevant dimension of conflict and filtering others out as irrelevant. If not, deliberation is not buying us anything intrinsically valuable. If a choice situation really has two legitimate dimensions of normative conflict, then deliberation might merely distract participants away from one dimension via an arbitrary kind of framing. If so, more stable decisions based upon such a mechanism would be normatively suspect – mere stability, or worse, stability for the wrong reasons. I take this to be one of the important concerns that theorists of agonistic democracy have about deliberation, even when deliberativists emphasize their commitment to pluralism and difference.

If we already have good reason to know that we have identified the elements of the one right set with reasonable confidence, then valuing meta-consensus, single-peaked or single-crossing preferences, and the like are all moot, if not actively misleading (c.f., Farrar et al. 2010). Such considerations would only come into play if they can speak to issues of "fair bargaining" and other second order normative criteria that take over when deliberation has exhausted its rational potential. For example, if we have single-peaked preferences across elements of the one right set, then median voter logic means that simple majoritarian considerations can resolve the residual indeterminacy, which may be attractive in some cases, but should not be mistaken for adding further epistemic justification to the decision. Since it does not, we might also prefer other criteria for certain kinds of questions, such as a status quo bias, or randomization, and so on.

It is just such concerns over misapplication of the consensus criterion that led some critics to reject it. For these critics, the *practical* dangers of implementing deliberation are such that as soon as we move away from the ideal, the potential for consensus to be perverse in practice makes it suspect at best. Clumsy attempts to reason directly from the mere fact of increased agreement to better outcomes gloss over the myriad of ways that groups can induce greater consensus via perverse means (Sanders 1997). Groupthink and social conformity pressures are just two of the most obvious ways in which increased consensus can be an unreliable indicator of good deliberation. Moreover, it is possible that merely having consensus as the group's goal can (ironically) increase the likelihood that such distortions actually obtain.

All of this is more than plausible, but it is also mostly an empirical matter, and so ends up reducing to an organizational question. We can study the circumstances under which explicitly setting consensus as a goal (versus merely acknowledging it as a pragmatic presupposition) leads to social conformity. Similarly, empirical studies of deliberation that carefully control for information cascades and social conformity pressures as the sources of deliberative opinion change may be in a position to claim increased consensus as an indicator of deliberative quality if they can rule out such alternative mechanisms (see my discussion of the "Negative Strategy" in Chapter 2).[9]

Another group of more radical critics reject consensus even as a pragmatic presupposition of rational discourse. If the good is radically plural, then we should not expect deliberation, even on average or in the

---

[9] So this form of the critique of consensus may not run as philosophically deep. One could accept hedges on the use of consensus as an applied criterion as opposed to a pragmatic presupposition. Or perhaps more precisely, such differences do not run philosophically deep if the critique of consensus is based upon observed consensus' potentially non-monotonic empirical relationship to other procedural criteria of deliberative quality. If the critique is that deliberation, though perhaps conducive to epistemic gains, is not internally linked to criteria of epistemic warrant, then the critique of consensus, though deep, reduces to a disagreement about a substantive versus proceduralist conception of deliberation.

long run, to produce more consensus. Even deliberation's more modest role of trying to rule out bad policy, rather than trying to affirm a unique solution, is likely to do more harm than good. Increased consensus from deliberation is *prima facie* suspect as a likely case of disciplinary social power. In such cases, we are more or less out of the realm of deliberative politics and into the realm of agonistic politics.

However, if respect is to emerge out of the nobility of the struggle, it can only do so if we have some (at least partially) common notion of what the struggle is for, and how the rules for success track something that it worthy of respect. To use agonistic theories' nominative analogy, one cannot win the respect of a worthy adversary in athletic *agon* unless both contestants measure excellence and winning by similar standards. Moreover, they must agree that the goal or standard of the struggle marks something that is respect generating. A contest over who can guess a random number generator's output will not do. So whether the rules and norms of the game are more like poker or more like a graduate seminar, we cannot completely evade the way that normative buy-in pervades the game. Any attempt to completely avoid the common, inferential content of deliberation ends up sliding us rapidly back toward the Hobbesian problem. Thus, one can see the outlines for the basis of a rapprochement between such theories and a form of deliberative theory that weakens the one right answer criterion to its set interpretation, and remains vigorously cognizant of consensus as a pragmatic presupposition, rather than a first order goal.

COMING TO BE A MAJORITY

Now it may seem that my move to the "set" interpretation of the one right answer thesis is an unhappy compromise – the worst of both worlds. On the one hand, I have ceded ground to pure power rather than insisting on a more robust notion of consensus. And on the other, someone like Riker might object that I have merely poured old wine into new bottles and slapped a happy label on them. That is, Riker never denied that voting could remove *some* items from the public agenda. My description of the one right set begins to sound a lot like the social choice concept of the "top-cycle" (the set of choices that can win at least one pairwise contest against another item). His point was only that the top-cycle set will often be large, and ruling out a few clear losers is a far cry from being able to reliably determine a concrete democratic will.

There is a grain of truth to this accusation, in that the concept of the one right set is analogous to a sort of epistemic top-cycle. Rather than taking any preference report as sovereign, we examine what choices can be supported via public articulation, without any ex ante guarantee that only one choice can be supported, even in the limit. This difference, however, makes a difference for democratic theory in at least five ways.

First, on the system conception of deliberation, voting outcomes are a major component of democratic legitimacy, but they do not *define* it, unlike on Riker's description of populism. So a certain degree of residual indeterminacy is not necessarily a big problem just so long as voting outcomes are typically indicative of democratic legitimacy.[10] Second, in line with many of Mackie's arguments, if we have reasons to think that the epistemic top-cycles have been generated by reasonably good deliberation, we would then have reasons to think that they will typically be considerably smaller than a more abstract analysis of the major social choice and game theoretic results would suggest, since any common content in social articulation will induce correlated preferences, make it more difficult to manipulate agendas, and so on. The size and frequency of top-cycles is important for making Riker's arguments against ambitious normative theories go through, since his case for political science being "*the* dismal science" rests largely on there being "no fundamental equilibria to predict" (1980: 443).

As I pointed out earlier, though, mere stability is cold comfort to a deliberative democrat. On the deliberative interpretation of the top-cycle, however, we have three crucial warrants that are missing from the standard social choice interpretation. And these additional warrants allow us to infer that the values built into voting rules (e.g., Pareto efficiency) have actually been promoted in a given case. The first warrant is that individual judgments and preferences are based on good information and are otherwise well-formed even on an individualist interpretation. That is, that people basically know their own minds, are not being grossly manipulated, and have a well-articulated sense of their considered private preferences. There are many reasons to think that deliberation in practice might fail to bring this about, and I will address those concerns in Chapter 6.

---

[10] My use of phrases like "reasonably good" and "typically" may seem like I am having overly free recourse to weasel words. However, on the notion of estimating a latent construct as sketched in the previous chapter, I mean these words to indicate that we should expect and explicitly build in "error terms" for each of our indicators of the latent construct.

For the time being, however, it suffices to note that *if* we can warrant deliberation as being of reasonably high quality, then we can also warrant the modest normative goods built into voting criteria – for example, that a stable voting result will in fact be Pareto efficient in a non-tautological sense.

The second warrant is similar, but operates at the social, rather than just the individual level. To the extent that deliberation helps construct, draw out, and articulate latent social meanings, we can start to get some traction on the notion of a common good, or at least social choices that are not inconsistent with viable interpretations of the common good. If deliberation can typically move us closer to the one right set of socially defensible answers, then we have reasons to think that people's individual judgments will better reflect that wider perspective, greater information, and so on, and that they will be better able to articulate these more common perspectives better. In addition to generating a theoretically relevant normative difference here, deliberation also provides plausible methods and mechanisms for getting more of what (in principle) can be recovered via articulation than is plausible from "deliberation within" alone.

Moreover, there are good reasons to think that there will be big differences between this inferentialist account of opinion that is formed *in* public according *to* public criteria, versus merely aggregating privately formed, unaccountable opinions, however well informed and altruistic. In addition to familiar arguments about firsthand information about others, activating pro-social "forum" frames, laundering preferences, and so on, recent research provides a very general framework for believing that social argumentation, properly organized, will outperform private reasoning in a wide range of circumstances. Mercier and Sperber's (2011) argumentative theory of reasoning, for example, shows how we become much more adept at reasoning individually when tasks are embedded in social contexts, and that our individual failures and biases are much more likely to be controlled and corrected when dialogue is real, rather than simulated in our own heads.

The final warrant that a deliberative, but not an aggregative, top-cycle carries is related to the second, but it is more procedural, and concerns the kinds of reasons we use to justify exercising coercive power over each other. It shows me a kind of respect to have things explained to me in terms that I can understand, according to commonly held stand- ards. In addition to respect, such explanations create a presumption that I am not subject to *arbitrary* state power, and provide a basis on which to contest the exercise of state power, should I wish to question the reasoning, and thus to determine whether the presumption of non-arbitrary coercion holds. Both of these conditions are central to securing political freedom as it is understood in republican theories of legitimacy (Pettit 2003).

So, taken together, these five differences between Riker's top-cycles and deliberative top-cycles mean that the one right "set" interpretation places us in a very different position vis-à-vis normative democratic theory. We have reasons to think that the deliberative top-cycle will typically be a smaller, more manageable set. In addition, we have more positive affirmations about the properties of what gets left in the deliberative top-cycle. We can positively affirm that the elements are indistinguishable on deliberative criteria, versus simply not knowing their relationship – analogous to the difference between being ambivalent or indifferent versus having no opinion about some object or question. This distinction can help explain, for example, a norm of losers' consent (and, for that matter, the winners' claim on the losers' consent) that goes beyond merely wanting to preserve the system. If we go through a public process that shows that I do not have decisive public arguments in favor of my preferred outcome over the social choice, then I have a reason to grant legitimacy to a decision that goes beyond the state's raw power to enforce it.

THE DISCURSIVE DILEMMA

These considerations regarding the reasons motivating our choices, however, reveal the way that many of the same formal problems that threatened to plague voting seem to recur in deliberation. Perhaps the most striking is the so-called doctrinal or discursive dilemma (Pettit 2001). Like theories of deliberation, legal decision making is concerned about not only the disposition of a given case, but also the reasons given for the decision. For example, in deciding on a tort case, judges must determine whether the plaintiff suffered harm and whether the defendant had some legal responsibility to protect the plaintiff from harm. The defendant is liable only if both conditions obtain. Now imagine a three judge panel in which one judge holds that both conditions are attained, one that the plaintiff suffered harm but the defendant had no responsibility to protect against it, and one the opposite (that there was responsibility in the relationship, but no harm occurred). The latter two judges, deciding separately, carry the case, voting for the defendant since neither believes that both conditions obtain. Yet, two judges (i.e., a majority) believe that each condition obtains, so there is a sense in which their collective judgment points toward a decision in favor of the plaintiff. The dilemma comes in deciding whether the overall choice should be responsive to the overall judgments of the individual judges, or whether it should emphasize collective consistency in tracking the logical implications of their judgments about the rationales. This particular example is rather stylized, but there is reason to think that various versions of the general issue can arise in a wide variety of situations in which we care about aggregating judgments about both what to do and why we should do it – that is, the modal case for most deliberative democrats.

Pettit (2003) argues that when the two modes of judgment conflict, we should favor collective consistency on the grounds of republican contestation discussed in the previous section. That is, if there is no coherent rationale offered as the basis of the state's coercion, there is nothing for me to contest should I wish to dispute the grounds on which I am coerced. Being subject to such arbitrary power means that I am subject to tyranny, and lose my freedom in this sense. I am sympathetic to Pettit's argument, though I will not dwell upon it because I think that the discursive dilemma is just a species of a more general issue for deliberative democracy, and that focusing on the specifically aggregative dilemma shrinks and segregates the real source of the problem. The worry over contestation arises in any situation in which we do not have an overlapping majority about both what to do and why to do it. Cases of the discursive dilemma are just one species of this larger genus.

For example, a coalition to eliminate agricultural subsidies for growing corn may combine those who support the measure primarily on grounds of economic efficiency and those who support it primarily out of environmental concerns. The reasons are merely heterogeneous, rather than contradictory or paradoxical. Pettit's solution (to prefer collective coherence) cannot serve as a general solution because there may be a class of cases for which no rationale commands a majority (or there is no agreement on the doctrinal criteria for deciding a case). Indeed, it is likely that such cases will be more common than true dilemmas. Full blown discursive inconsistencies are likely to be moderately rare (which is not to say inconsequential) for the same kinds of reasons that Mackie adduces to show that large differences between voting rules or cyclic structures tend to be rare in real democratic politics (e.g., that people's judgments about well-defined questions tend to cluster, even when they do not converge). But otherwise stable majorities regarding *what* to do are often composed of subgroups that diverge about *why* to do it, especially when the set of potential reasons is open-ended.

Precisely out of concerns like these, Habermas formulates his version of the one right answer presumption in terms of both a single right answer *and* a single rationale in support of that answer. To critics, this joint stipulation elevates an already implausible assumption all the way to preposterous. But Pettit's argument clarifies the cost of completely casting off the consensus criterion as a pragmatic presupposition. Pettit only requires a common rationale among the decisive majority, but as a practical matter, Habermas ends up making a similar concession, even if he insists on the theoretical distinction in the limit (1996: 306). Without some version of consensus in the public justification for coercion, both the epistemic and respect (freedom) promoting functions of deliberation are placed in jeopardy. So on my "one right set" interpretation, the elements of the set are really pairs of outcomes and their attendant rationales.

Thus, we would seem to be on the horns of a dilemma. Either we insist on an implausibly stringent (even as a pragmatic presupposition) notion of a single right answer under a single rationale, or nearly all politics becomes a pure matter of fair bargaining, deliberation becomes marginal, and we cede soft tyranny a wide berth in democratic politics. The one right set interpretation strikes a compromise in that it is more plausible as a pragmatic presupposition, and it at least narrows the scope of arbitrary power. But there would seem to be a direct trade-off between the way that it accomplishes these two goals such that it may be a *mere* compromise – that is, it is not clear that it improves all that much over pure position either unless we think that there are "gains from trade" to be had by trying to develop a middle position. As it happens, though, there are indeed potential gains from trade, here, and they are quite substantial.

First, moving from the strong version of the one right answer thesis to the set interpretation effectively moves us from a (local) form of monism to reasonable pluralism, but stops short of an unrestricted domain (i.e., complete sovereignty of preference expressions). Except on strong libertarian grounds, it is not clear that moving all the way to an unrestricted domain is valuable at all, on balance, much less when we face a trade-off with Pettit's concerns. Yet moving from monism to reasonable pluralism is likely to be valuable both theoretically and as a practical matter. Theoretically, any pluralist will find it strange and objectionable to assume a single right answer for a very large range of important questions, even as a pragmatic presupposition. So the range of cases amenable to deliberation shrinks dramatically. Conversely, on the one right set interpretation, deliberation can play an important role on any question that is not a pure matter of taste or preference. And as a practical matter, a pragmatic presupposition that does not require convergence on a unique element may be less likely to squash legitimate difference, induce unmotivated conformity or "spirals of silence," and more.

Now it may seem that the potential gains from trade are less promising on the side of avoiding tyranny. Shrinking the set may not gain us that much as long as the rationales undergirding majoritarian coercion remain heterogeneous. However, upon inspection, the set interpretation creates the potential for very substantial normative gains here too. If deliberation really is working well (again, deferring questions about whether and when it might to Chapters 6 and 7) and we have good reasons to think that we have a reasonable approximation to the one right set, then we also have reason to think that any remaining arbitrariness in our ultimate decision is *unavoidable*. Without a single public justification, we cannot warrant that the minority is not being coerced, but we *can* warrant that there is no alternative to some group being so coerced, because there is no single, majoritarian, public justification to be had. We have reached the (local) limits of republican freedom. And this is a difference that makes a great deal of difference for matters of democratic justice. We may yearn to be free from the tyranny of gravity, but that is hardly the same as yearning to be free from the tyranny of a jailor, or even just an unreflective, capricious, majority. But this analogy to natural versus moral evil is perhaps too glib. We should frankly acknowledge and mourn the unavoidable degree of tragedy in political life, and remain vigilant against mistaking tragedy for complacency. But doing so should not numb us to distinctions in the nature and scope of the non-ideal choices before us, nor to inquiry that may shrink the scope of tragedy going forward.

So the one right set interpretation acknowledges a (potentially large) agonistic moment at the heart of deliberative democratic practice, but the goods attributable to the struggle appear in a different, better warranted light. Once deliberation has (locally) exhausted itself, we shift to second order criteria for fair bargaining, contestation, and political struggle. For example, even if there is no unified public rationale to contest, we can still enjoy a kind of freedom in contestation by trying to destabilize the majority coalition, addressing ourselves to one of the rationales necessary to sustain the majority. Moreover, in the shadow of reasonable warrants for the one right set, weaker democratic goods embodied in various voting rules – for example, Pareto efficiency, anonymity, neutrality, and so on – can once again claim value. And since we avoid mistaking the majority for anything but a heterogeneous coalition, we have positive reasons to prioritize political experimentation designed to help generate new experiences and new knowledge that could update our sense of the one right set, shifting the coalitions or providing for a better articulated democratic majority.

RATIONAL EXPECTATIONS

Discursive dilemmas are not strategic in origin. They can arise even when everyone is arguing in good faith, shares common values and evidentiary standards, and reveals their true preferences, judgments, and rationales candidly. Deliberation runs into a whole new set of potential problems when we cannot make all of these assumptions – that is, when we consider the potential for strategic dynamics in deliberative encounters. Game theorists have developed a substantial literature analyzing such situations, much of it at odds with the setup and claims of normative theorists of deliberation. Landa and Meirowitz (2009) lament the lack of fruitful interaction between the two camps, attributing it to the fact that "game theorists tend to exert little effort toward making their results accessible to a less technical readership ... [and that] the normative literature, with very few exceptions, takes essentially no account of the presence of the game-theoretic work on deliberation and ignores the fundamental incentive problems that surface in nearly all relevant game-theoretic studies" (428). In an important and ambitious project, they aim to summarize and translate this body of results into non-technical terms in order to "make the case for the relevance of the existing game-theoretic analysis of deliberation to the development of deliberative democratic theory" (428).

Landa and Meirowitz motivate their central complaint against deliberative theory by noting that "A key issue in game-theoretic models of policymaking is whether it is reasonable to expect those participants who possess valuable information to reveal it to others, and whether those others have good reasons to believe it" (431). Despite the implied contrast, however, we can also aptly render one of the key issues in deliberative conceptions of policymaking in *exactly* the same terms: Whether it is reasonable to expect those who possess valuable information to reveal it to others, and whether those others have good reasons to believe it. However, in the deliberative version, the significance of the key words in these sentences changes subtly from the way that game theorists typically use them: "Reasonable," "expect," "possess," "valuable", "information," "good," "reasons," and "believe."

For example, note the ambiguity between the predictive and the normative meanings of "reasonable" and "expect." I teach my daughters that it is "reasonable" (in the normative sense) to "expect" (in the normative sense) them to use good manners, even though it is not "reasonable" (in the evidentiary sense) to "expect" them (in the predictive sense) to do so consistently while they are still young. And yet, over time, it *is* reasonable to expect (in the predictive sense) that they will come to use good manners consistently, precisely *because* they will come to see that such behavior is a reasonable social expectation (in the normative sense). At first their motivations may be rooted in a desire to please me or to avoid sanctions. But unless something goes wrong, they will eventually come to recognize that they typically have good reasons to refrain from rude behavior, even when they feel a desire to engage in it and do not anticipate offsetting social sanctions.[11]

So it is emphatically not the case that normative theorists are unconcerned about game theorists' key issue regarding what it is reasonable to expect in political communication. Rather, normative theorists implicitly argue that the two senses of "reasonable" and "expect" are often internally related in a way that most extant game–theoretic models of political talk do not capture adequately. Indeed, for present purposes, I will define a *norm* as a pattern of action that is reasonable to expect of most people (in the predictive sense) largely *because* most people believe it to be a reasonable expectation (in the normative sense).[12]

---

[11] Though I will admit that one of the peculiarities of raising a child in the midst of "the terrible two's" is that it often seems all too plausible that they will never become socialized adults, despite the reassurances offered by low baseline rates of adult sociopathy. I should also note that the process can work in the other direction as well, when adults unlearn socialization to unjust norms. For example, adult males might subconsciously expect (in both senses) that a woman will defer to them in conversation because of implicit sexist norms common when they were socialized, and only somewhat less so now (Schegloff 2000). If so, then they may react more negatively to being interrupted by a woman than they would a man. Yet they may not be willing to defend those norms as reasonable if they are made consciously available to them through political thematization, and the unconscious reaction may lose its force *because* the gap in one's commitments makes it to conscious attention, or is subject to criticism via political articulation.

[12] This definition of norms is a bit more restrictive than one might want in that it cannot capture implicit norms, for example, about invasions of personal space. That said, it does a reasonable job capturing the main class of norms relevant for my discussion here, and highlights the cognitive, rather than just behavioral, dimension necessary to make sense of them in the context of deliberation. In another potential abuse of terminology, I include

To illustrate their point about reasonable expectations, Landa and Meirowitz note that, "In the game of poker, which has some strategic properties in common with the example of the decision process regarding the invasion of Iraq, expecting truthful revelation of someone's face-down cards is unreasonable" (431). Invoking the poker analogy here usefully illustrates one of the central problems with extant models. Far from serving as a sensible baseline for most social processes, poker is an aggressively limiting case that positively *inverts* otherwise ubiquitous norms and motivations. In the same way that a chess match would not count as chess if rooks could move diagonally, the Churchill anecdote illustrates how the meaningfulness of poker as a distinct social practice (i.e., a game) depends on excluding pervasive social norms and motivations.

Thus, arguing that poker shares "some strategic properties" with the Bush administration's putative deception about weapons of mass destruction in Iraq, while technically true, is quite misleading. When we failed to find such weapons (i.e., when "the cards were revealed"), opponents of the administration did not gamely congratulate them on "winning the hand" via deft strategic manipulation. Indeed, to this day, former members of the Bush Administration deny that it engaged in any deception, and describe the events as a mundane failure caused by human finitude (i.e., in a straight game of giving and asking for reasons). Perhaps their account is true, perhaps officials are sincere but self-deceived, or perhaps this episode is a case of the tribute that vice pays to virtue. The important point here is that a significant part of what makes game–theoretic models interesting is that their implications do not typically generalize in simple, foreseeable ways when games only share some properties. And if my argument about the ubiquity of deliberative buy-in, antes, and blind bets is right, then models that do not take account of them are liable to go wrong in important ways, both as explanatory accounts and for purposes of a normative theory of institutional design.[13]

---

under the term "game theory" (and, mutatis mutandis, its cognates) any mathematical model of rational choice or bounded rational choice. So, in addition to game theory proper, I mean to include social choice theory, mechanism design, implementation theory, evolutionary game theory, and computational and agent based models. Similarly, I use normative theorist, deliberative theorist, and deliberative democrat interchangeably here.

[13] Even a shift to implementation theory and mechanism design will not address this version of the sensitivity problem; the whole class of models will exclude norms. And even if the Iraq war example is a case of the tribute that vice pays to virtue, such tribute still points to the role of social norms. If the administration's opponents and the public were all just

Landa and Meirowitz do address themselves to one important facet of deliberative buy-in, and it is worth analyzing their response in some detail. They argue against the reasonableness of presuming that many people default to a basic normative commitment to honest deliberation in a wide variety of situations, arguing that "[I]n a complex environment with private moral values and noncommon veridicality, it must presuppose not simply abnegation of self-interest, but an extraordinarily high degree of abnegation of moral instrumental behavior as well" (2009: 441). On an inferentialist account, private moral values, noncommon veridicality (i.e., differing standards for judging the truth), and raw self-interest all end up looking structurally similar: They are all examples of an agent's proposed reasons for a collective choice that prove unpersuasive to others in deliberation. What makes private moral values private is that they cannot be justified on public grounds; what makes noncommon veridicality noncommon is that my standards of judgment cannot compel general assent; and what makes raw self-interest both raw and selfish is that it cannot claim grounds beyond my mere assertion of will. In the game of giving and asking for reasons, all three tend to be relatively weak reasons. Now, I grant that people typically act out of self-interest, but I also claim that they typically experience significant motivation to justify themselves to each other.

Landa and Meirowitz's more pregnant claim, then, is about "moral instrumental behavior." What does it mean to say that a norm of honest deliberation presumes an extraordinarily high degree of abnegation of moral instrumental behavior? Contrary to what they suggest, I would argue that most social and political situations start with a rather strong presumption *against* "moral instrumental behavior," since that is just another term for a familiar concept – paternalism. I know what is best for you (or for society), and even though I cannot convince you, I do not hesitate to strategically manipulate the situation for your (or the public's) own good.

Sometimes, of course, we do behave paternalistically, and, on occasion, justifiably so. For example, I routinely find myself incapable of reaching an agreement with my two-year-old daughter. In some of those cases, I may withhold information or otherwise strategically manage our discussion out of instrumental altruism. But the set of circumstances in which I would think myself justified in doing the same to my wife or my fellow citizens is

---

playing their role in a larger strategic game without norms, then one of the key papers in this literature, Austen-Smith and Feddersen (2006), implies that if they are right, the pretense of deliberation would be odd and inexplicable, since deliberation would be uninformative (without, presumably, being completely costless).

much smaller and more peculiar. All of this is just to say that a defeasible presumption against paternalistic manipulation is a generic part of the buy-in to the game of giving and asking for reasons. If so, then it hardly presumes "extraordinary" restraint, and the burden of proof runs in exactly the opposite direction. We need specific reasons to think ourselves reasonable in acting paternalistically, and most of us default to not doing so in a wide variety of situations. If so, insisting that we must always "earn the sincerity by reconstructing it as equilibrium behavior rather than assuming it by default" will tend to lead us to *less* accurate models by sending us on a search for deep, structural explanations that do not track the real dynamics commonly at play, thereby generating misleading "normative argument[s] for institutional design" (442).

To see why, consider one of Landa and Meirowitz's more engaging examples. They astutely point out that, "One of the central issues of contention among deliberative democrats is the expectation of consensus following deliberation," concluding with an ironic twist that "the very fact that the scholars of deliberative democracy disagree on this point strongly suggests that the assumption of common values is untenable" (435–6). But as we saw earlier, the word "expectation" is ambiguous, even in ordinary language. Recall that Habermas referred to the one right answer thesis as a "pragmatic presupposition." He certainly intends "expectation" in the normative rather than the predictive sense. Just as poker is no longer poker if we are not trying to win, rational discussion is no longer rational discussion if we are not trying to find the right answer. The "expectation of consensus" is not an empirical claim about the distribution of agreement after deliberation, but rather a conceptual claim about how to define different phenomena properly. The fact that scholars of deliberative democracy disagree about that claim is, therefore, hardly dispositive for their point.

For example, Dennis Thompson, an eminent deliberative theorist, strongly disagrees with Habermas' analysis of the consensus criterion (Gutmann and Thompson 2004). But what is the import of this fact for judging Thompson's future contributions to scholarly deliberation about deliberation. Suppose that he were asked to review a paper that develops some new bit of social–psychological research suggesting that the consensus criterion may be better supported than we previously thought.[14]

---

[14] To be clear, this example is entirely hypothetical, and intended to illustrate how jarring it is for us to have to consider such scenarios. Thompson has authored a book on professional ethics, and has an impeccable professional reputation.

In this hypothetical scenario, his judgment is that the research is sound, but he also expects that the broader scholarly community will give the new evidence more weight than he believes is appropriate, persuading more people to Habermas' (for Thompson, importantly mistaken) view. Would he write a dishonest review so that the evidence is suppressed or appears in a less prominent venue? Would he knowingly misrepresent Habermas' position about the philosophical grounds and meaning of the consensus argument so as to confuse the issue among non-experts?

It seems quite reasonable to expect (in both the normative and predictive senses) that Thompson would not manipulate the review. Moreover, those expectations are not grounded merely in thinking that he might worry about getting caught and paying a steep price in his professional reputation. Instead, I expect that he would not lie in his review because I believe both that he *should* not do it, and that he would *recognize* that he should not do it. This shared expectation articulates a professional norm against such behavior in doing academic reviews – one that is rooted partly in a presumption against paternalism. So I do not think that his restraint would evince any extraordinary abnegation of moral instrumental behavior.

On the contrary, it would be quite ordinary. The academic enterprise relies on individuals exercising their own judgment within a community of scholars. Paternalism subverts the process by which others form their judgments, and substitutes one's own judgment for the community's via strategic manipulation. The game of giving and asking for reasons, as played in the academy, would implode if such restraint was anything but mundane – which is not to say that it is perfectly realized. To the extent that I think that the answer to many important questions is procedurally defined (at least in part) – for example, whether justice was served by "good" jury deliberations in a liability case – strategic manipulation can be logically self-defeating. I cannot promote some good via means that subvert the original logic of what I use to judge that good.

Yet a very large swath of the formal critique of deliberative democracy implies that Thompson's (presumed) candor should not be mundane – that his restraint would be mysterious, if not irrational (Austen-Smith 1990; Austen-Smith and Banks 1996; Austen-Smith and Feddersen 2006, 2009; Calvert 2006; Feddersen and Pessendorfer 1998, 1999a, 1999b; Gerardi and Yariv 2007; Meirowitz 2006, 2007). Even if we are purely altruistic (or we all want the same thing), by this view, whatever our best assessment of the public good is, we should be expected (in both senses) to pursue it with full paternalistic abandon. Austen-Smith and Banks (1996), for example, rely on a setup that is nearly identical to the situation in which I imagined Thompson, since journal reviewers can be conceived of as a kind of jury. Positing a simple taste for the truth or against paternalism – adding a constant to people's utility functions – will not really resolve the issue, since we would then just act with "meta-paternalistic" abandon on the new assessment of utility, with no way out of a regress.

Of course, the logic of such a regress is part of why game theorists believe that the problem is harder than deliberative theorists have recognized. But the problem is rooted in the same kind of consequentialist biases that led Mutz into mistaken conclusions in her analysis of empirical research on deliberation. Landa and Meirowitz argue that "the existing game-theoretic analysis of deliberation" should influence "the development of deliberative democratic theory" and guide institutional design (428). Yet I cannot imagine that they or any of these authors actually teach (or expect, in either sense) their graduate students to make a habit of writing journal reviews in a way that is consistent with the deliberative logic of the models: Strategically withholding key information, consciously distorting assessments, voting "as if pivotal," and so on. To the extent that scholars do engage in such behavior (which, I grant, may be substantial), it seems much more likely that they do so out of simple self-interest rather than out of a desire to serve the greater good of the scholarly community. If so, nearly all of these papers emerged out of a deliberative process ill captured by the models that they contain.[15]

Existing models cannot make sense of deliberative democrats' concern over legitimate procedures. Landa and Meirowitz foresee this objection, and try to pre-empt it:

[I]n order for the argument [from legitimacy] to have bite, it must effectively endorse the following two claims: (1) interest in the perception of the outcome as legitimate overrides whatever interest [the actor] may have in revealing less information; and (2) perception of the outcome as legitimate is responsive to how

[15] Indeed, I take it as a corollary of Austen-Smith and Feddersen (2006) that peer review would unravel if their model *did* capture its dynamics. *None of this is to deny that reviewers can be biased, venal, lazy, self-interested, and paternalistic.* But if such considerations completely swamped a basic tendency to report our candid assessments, the entire academic enterprise would collapse. Since I do not think that the enterprise has collapsed, it is hardly naïve to believe that basic academic norms play too important a role in deliberation to be ignored. In my view, bias is probably the most important issue, and paternalism the least important in peer review, whereas these formal results on deliberation focus mostly on the latter.

much information [the actor] reveals...[and] that it is known when [the actor] has relevant information and refuses to share it. (441)

They argue that the first claim runs into their objection regarding "moral instrumental behavior." But, as we have seen, there is nothing extraordinary in believing that people regard paternalistic manipulation as a costly and, in this context, even a logically incoherent mode of default behavior. Indeed, the burden of proof may run in the other direction for a large range of cases.

Regarding the second claim, they argue that we will not typically know whether someone has acted strategically, and thus it is implausible to think that acting paternalistically will decisively affect perceptions of legitimacy. This response evinces a deep misunderstanding of the argument from legitimacy. The idea is not merely that we want outcomes to be *perceived* as legitimate (whether or not the perceptions are rooted in lies and manipulation). Instead, we want the outcomes to be perceived as legitimate *because* they *really are* legitimate. Again, we seek an internal connection between the two senses of our "expectation" of legitimacy. And we regard the test of that legitimacy as largely procedural.

If this all seems too abstract, consider the following example. As part of my research, I sometimes observe deliberative field experiments, silently sitting in on small group discussions. Toward the end of one session, the group could not reach consensus, and decided to vote instead. A somewhat cantankerous participant who had been defending the minority position ended up voting with the majority, much to everyone's surprise. The group member who had argued the most with him during the discussion asked why he ended up supporting the group's position. He explained: "If I were king, I would still choose [the other policy]. But I'm glad not to have that responsibility...[pause]...And after spending the day together I bet you're all glad I'm not king too!" Everyone laughed, but he was making a serious and important point. He was not the sort to be bullied easily into mere conformity, but neither was he the sort to think that his individual judgment, removed from the context of the larger deliberative process, should be the relevant standard of social choice. If so, then paternalism – even if an actor can secure *perceived* legitimacy – will rarely appear as a sensible (or perhaps even coherent) principle of action.[16]

---

[16] In my experience, the sort of behavior and the rationale offered for it by this participant is quite common in deliberative forums among regular citizens. After pressing their cases vigorously, participants routinely exhibit a kind of humility about their own judgments

This fundamental tendency to conflate legitimacy and perceived legitimacy is common in formal literature. For example, Patty (2008) develops an "argument based" theory of collective choice that connects preferences over outcomes to rationales for those outcomes. The argument is novel, ingenious, and generative. And at first glance, the theory appears to be a promising way to formalize the way that deliberative democrats seek to promote legitimate outcomes by connecting them to processes of public reasoning. Yet, rather than developing a theory of deliberative choice, the model really amounts to a pure theory of sophistry.[17] In the model, actors choose their rationales with no regard at all to their internal persuasive force or logical entailments to the outcomes, but only because they prove effective in helping them achieve fixed, pre-given goals. This setup is practically the definition of sophistry, in that sophists actually practiced switching sides in an argument, and otherwise training their skills at manipulating arguments to serve external goals (Jacquette 2007). To the extent that there is any inferential articulation in this setup, its goal is purely formal and predetermined. In a related project, Patty and Penn (2010) use structurally similar logic to develop "a social choice theory of legitimacy." Principles "legitimate" the processes by which social choices are made, except the connection between principles and processes is purely formal, rather than operating in any substantively "principled" way. This setup threatens to equivocate on the meaning of "legitimate" as deliberative theorists use the term. It is hard to see why legitimacy so defined would be anything more than mere legitimation (achieving the *perception* of legitimacy by any means). Indeed, it is not clear how the process would even generate perceptions of legitimacy: Why should I feel respected by a process that offers me public rationales that I know are always mere rationalizations?

(or perhaps trust or investment in the procedures) for purposes of making a group decision that seems quite different than mere social conformity. Fishkin's deliberative opinion polls do not provide as much scope for the phenomenon to emerge, because his small groups are never called on to make group decisions per se. In my view, this phenomenon is of enormous potential significance, and deserves greater theoretical and empirical scrutiny. In preliminary work, I have proposed linking it to the ancient cardinal virtue of *sophrosyne*, which is often translated as "temperance" or "sound-mindedness," though the concept really does not have a clear modern referent (Neblo 2011a).

[17] To be clear, I do not think that Patty's paper *engages* in sophistry at all, only that the model really ends up capturing the heart of what the sophists were doing, rather than deliberation in either its Socratic or modern form.

WHY RULES ARE RULES

Much of this might seem familiar by now, but it is important to appreciate fully both the complications that mundane normative processes cause for extant formal models of deliberation, and the way that words and concepts fundamentally shift meaning when we move back and forth between the two literatures (Steiner 2008). Within standard models, one could, of course, just stipulate that agents have an aversion to lying, and build a large cost for doing so into games with communication. But in addition to the regress problem discussed earlier, we would not have "earned" sincerity, which was supposed to be the whole point in modeling deliberation. As the great game theorist John von Neumann quipped: "With four parameters I can fit an elephant, and with five I can make him wiggle his trunk," which he intended not as a boast, but as a methodological caution (Dyson 2004: 297).[18]

Even if we decided that building in some fixed cost to lying that was not circular and worth the loss of parsimony, doing so would not take account of the shifting contexts in which norms of truthfulness get activated across and even within games. Positing a fixed cost to lying does not explain why we have wildly different expectations about truthfulness in a poker tournament, in a confessional, in talking to our children about Santa Claus, in writing referee reports, or in contract negotiations. On an inferentialist account, most norms are not merely behavioral ticks, but *reasons* for action subject to dynamic social application and articulation.[19]

---

[18] The context of the quote is a bit complicated, but all the more interesting for it. As a young physicist, Freeman Dyson went to meet with the older and more eminent Enrico Fermi to show him results from Dyson's lab that connected a novel theory to measurements close to those that Fermi had observed independently. Fermi asked him how many arbitrary parameters he had used to get his calculations. When Dyson reported "four," Fermi replied with the elephant quote, prefacing it with, "I remember my friend Johnny von Neumann used to say..." Dyson recounts that the quip was a hard blow and a conversation stopper at the time, but that it ultimately "saved us from several more years of fruitless wandering along a road that was leading nowhere" (297).

[19] This is not to say that all norms have a rational basis. The test would be whether the implicit rationale for some norm (as well as instances of its application) can be rendered explicit in a way that stands up to coherence and deontic score-keeping criteria if challenged. Over time some norms (e.g., African–Americans stepping off of side-walks to let white people pass) have withered under critical scrutiny, while others (e.g., presumptions of innocence in legal proceedings) have stood up relatively well under challenge.

Reasons (as opposed to mere information) are offered with a specifically articulated set of suggested connections for their significance, rather than merely leaving the listener to figure out their relevance, or to apply the information in a way different from the speaker's intention, which is not to say that reasons cannot trigger different articulation. *Public reasons* do the same thing, but via paths that are regarded as articulable in common for the polity. Part of the distinction between reasons and information can be captured by the distinction between "hard" and "soft" information, as those terms are used in game theory. Hard information is something that is intrinsically verified upon inspection – say some mathematical proposition. Soft information relies more upon the credibility of the speaker and the institutional environment for its persuasive force. Cheap talk models mostly operate along the limiting case of soft information, whereas, if the inferentialist account is right, much deliberation effectively deals with various grades of "harder" information.[20]

But why should normative talk ever be anything but cheap? In the face of countervailing desires, norms and reasons can retain some motivational traction in much the same way that our other beliefs and commitments do. Note that having true factual beliefs is not always strategically beneficial on a standard rational choice account. For example, we might derive both direct psychic benefits as well as strategic advantages from being overly optimistic in some situations. Yet we (and most game-theoretic models) consider it the exception, rather than the rule, to credibly maintain to ourselves and convey to others false belief and irrational intent in the face of evidence and common knowledge. All of us have had the familiar experience of "not wanting to believe" something, but feeling compelled to do so by new evidence. Similarly, we have all experienced not wanting to *do* something, but feeling compelled to do it by recognizing some obligation or responsibility. Just as we cannot trivially turn on and off our responsiveness to the evidence of our senses and the laws of logic (norms of reasoning) as local expedience suggests, neither can we

---

[20] In practice, the distinction is probably more of a spectrum than a dichotomy, and varies by actor, context, and resource constraints. In principle, I could learn to assess climate science in a way that made it "hard" for me, but as a practical matter, I cannot take years to get a PhD in climatology. One might be tempted to think that "hard" information is necessarily factual, but on inferentialist terms, a norm or any other reliable inference can be "hard." Or rather, it is something whose support, once placed in an articulated context, is such that it compels acceptance, at least as a reason. Normative claims can have that property as well.

trivially turn on and off our responsiveness to social norms, roles, and meanings, nor accountability via public articulation. Our larger normative buy-in is not globally optional as a practical matter, and is locally "sticky" in most cases as well.[21]

Thus, the call to be "reasonable" and meet those expectations will at least sometimes be experienced as "good reasons" by all but sociopaths. Whether or not they end up being decisive, they become at least *a* motive for action, without necessarily becoming a desire in the strict sense. Again, we may feel obligated to do things that we do not really want to do in any straightforward sense. This distinction between a desire and a normative reason for action is difficult to capture in extant game–theoretic models, and doubly so without sacrificing the perspicuity and tractability that make them valuable in the first place. Yet the peculiar properties of norms vis-à-vis other kinds of motives reside in this distinction.

Now I hasten to emphasize that I do *not* believe that self-interest, private (though perhaps not selfish) values, different standards for judgment, and even paternalism are typically marginal in political discussion or politics more generally. Clearly there *are* fundamental incentive problems with which any adequate theory of deliberation must grapple. Moreover, some of the very social processes that I have been discussing (e.g., norms and procedural accountability to each other) can actually complicate the incentive problems. Just as Truman's game continued to look like poker after it stopped really being a game of poker, political discussion about going to war in Iraq may have looked something like rational public deliberation without actually meeting its minimal presuppositions.

Indeed, regular citizens routinely articulate their frustration with elected officials and other elites by accusing them of "playing politics"

---

[21] It is important to distinguish between motivated reasoning per se, which is quite common, and strategically *choosing* to engage in motivated reasoning in a way that is credible to others or to ourselves (Elster 1983). Moreover, while motivated reasoning is quite common indeed, nearly all of the evidence for it is based on deviations from a baseline. That is, we do not typically process reasons and evidence with utter impunity, but rather a certain degree of bias. And accountability to others, the hallmark of deliberation, tends to constraint that bias even further (Mercier and Sperber 2011). Standard game–theoretic models create a sharp distinction between beliefs and desires (especially with respect to being subject to articulation) by methodological fiat. Minozzi (2013) proposes a model allowing beliefs to be motivated by preferences, loosening the distinction in a way that comes from the opposite direction of what I am discussing here. One might think of schizophrenia and sociopathy as representing the limiting cases of beliefs and desires being unconstrained by physical facts and social norms, respectively.

with public discourse – allowing their behavior to be dominated by sophistic rhetoric, phony posturing, and veiled self-interest. The implicit contrast is with political deliberation understood as playing the game of giving and asking for reasons. Democratic citizens express frustration because they expect better of their public officials. But here, again, we run up against the ambiguity in the word "expect" in its normative and predictive senses. In effect, realist critics of deliberative democracy – Schumpeter, Riker, Schattschneider, Disch, and many others – claim that we should jettison the normative sense of our expectations about playing politics. "Expecting better" in either sense is unrealistic and immature, and will only lead to frustration when those expectations go consistently unmet.

Realist critics make this claim either because they deny that the game of giving and asking for reasons can be usefully distinguished from playing politics, or because they think that any internal connection between the two senses of expectation is so weak as to be ignorable. Unlike expecting my daughters to behave politely, expecting more of politicians will not lead to better deliberation or policy in the short run or over time. As I have argued earlier, though, if there is truly no useful distinction between the games, then we are back in something very much like Hobbes' world, however much it might look like we are playing at something more appealing on the surface. And the empirical claim seems wildly unsupported if for no other reason than that we have no relevant evidence for the counterfactual. Even authoritarian regimes maintain the pretense of public justification. And a cursory glance across cases suggests that there are hardly obvious benefits to regimes where the population has accommodated itself more thoroughly to mere pretense.

I agree with Landa and Meirowitz that the relative lack of fruitful interaction between game theorists and deliberative theorists is both unfortunate and unnecessary. But the main reason that deliberative democrats have not taken much account of the existing game–theoretic literature has little to do with its accessibility to a less technical readership. Some theorists understand the math just fine, and many others can grasp the intuitions well enough to interpret the results. Nor is the disconnection rooted in Panglossian disregard for incentive problems among deliberativists. Habermas, for example, is nigh unto obsessed with what he calls "systematically distorted communication" (1976). Rather, the key problem is that most extant models have taken essentially no account of the fundamental considerations that motivate the deliberative project. It is true that "deviations from the deliberative ideal are inevitable," but it is also true that deviations from the ideal of instrumental rationality – at least as conceived in anything like these models – are similarly inevitable.

All models, of course, simplify reality greatly. But if existing models of deliberation cannot account for essential elements of deliberative theory, and the implications of formal models do not typically generalize in simple, foreseeable ways as complexly interacting features are added and removed, then deliberative theorists have little reason to think that existing models will deliver any of the distinctive benefits of good formal theories. They are not likely to predict deliberative behavior successfully, explain the mechanisms behind deliberative phenomena, elucidate non-obvious theoretical connections, or, as a consequence of these, serve as reliable (or even non-perverse) guides for a normative theory of institutional design. Indeed, if my arguments regarding proceduralism are correct, some of the models may not even be logically coherent, at least as interpretations of deliberation per se.[22]

All of that said, I actually do think that existing models are more valuable for deliberative theory than their uptake would suggest. First, some of the theoretical knowledge produced by these models is intrinsically interesting. For example, Austen-Smith and Banks (1996) show that the logic of the Condorcet jury theorem lacks any straightforward foundation in a canonical theory of rational choice, a finding of significant philosophical importance. Second, these models are likely to capture the dynamics of some (apparent) instances of deliberation reasonably well, even if they will tend to be limiting cases. Surely there are quite a few cases of effectively pure sophistry, for example. And Patty's (2008) model can not only help us understand them, it can help us *identify* them, which may otherwise be difficult, precisely because deliberative norms do not allow

---

[22] Very little of this literature has been brought to data, and when it has, the findings have tended to be falsifying or weak. For an interesting exception, see Dickson, Hafer, and Landa (2008), though they, too, find substantially more "deliberative" behavior than their model predicts. Goeree and Yariv (2011) find results difficult to square with extant models, but highly consistent with a deliberative interpretation. To see how relying on pure theory to design institutions can be perverse, consider the behavioral literature on trust games as a cautionary tale. The canonical analyses of the "investment game" and many variations have been spectacularly falsified in the lab. Ben-Ner et al. (2010) describe "lavish returns on cheap talk," that current models of deliberation cannot make sense of. Similarly, Fehr and Rockenbach (2003) show that formally sensible institutional provisions for enforcement "crowd out" trust, and actually lead to socially inefficient results. As they stand, most extant models of deliberation would likely prove similarly perverse as guides to institutional design. And the most obvious ad hoc fixes threaten to send us into Ptolemaic epicycles of explanation that are unlikely to prove reliable in novel situations.

speakers to openly admit to their sophistry. Third, in other cases, the missing deliberative elements may not interact in confounding ways with basic strategic dynamics, so that the models will at least capture part of the story in mixed motives cases. Fourth, even in cases where the inter-actions are more complex and we do not have adequate accounts, the negative results can keep deliberativists vigilant in avoiding the other extreme position, and falling into wishful optimism. Staying clear about our knowledge of what we do not know can be valuable. Finally, many of these models can be informative in the breach, testifying to the contours of the things that must be missing from them given that they do not adequately capture the phenomena at hand.

In the past few years, there have been a few proposals for expanding the rational choice framework to include more distinctly social and cognitive processes. For example, Frohlich and Oppenheimer (2006) and Margolis (2007) significantly revise the standard model. Heath (2001) suggests a fairly simple "accounting" procedure for separating out distinctly normative considerations in a way that can help avoid the regress problem described earlier. And with collaborators, I have begun a project to develop a computational formal model of deliberation as a game of giving and asking for reasons that hews closely to Brandom's theoretical setup (Minozzi, Neblo, and Siegel 2012). It remains to be seen whether any of these approaches will prove empirically generative or manage to integrate with more canonical accounts of rational choice. But it seems clear that progress on developing formal models of delibera-tive rationality will require either significant extensions of canonical models of rational choice, or a partnering theory to help account for the structure of the games that we actually end up playing.

CONCLUSION

Despite the recurring analogy, most regular citizens do not regard politics as properly analogous to a high stakes game of poker. Indeed, they disdain politicians whom they perceive to be playing a game more like poker than the game of giving and asking for reasons. But even if they have bought-in to the game of giving and asking for reasons broadly, they may nevertheless choose to "sit out" hands in what they perceive to be a rigged political game. Many citizens feel alienated and overwhelmed by mass democratic politics, and so might reasonably choose to focus on tending their own gardens. For example, only about half of the eligible population in the U.S. bothers to vote in presidential elections. So it may seem fanciful to think that they would be willing to deliberate about matters of public policy. Thus, we might expect that the micro politics of the home, church, or office will be tempered by broad normative buy-in, while leaving large-scale politics to be dominated to a greater degree by the rough and tumble of struggles for power among directly interested parties. If so, then even if buy-in means that most people are motivated to try to speak in common voices, mass politics may yet not be held accountable to the voices of common citizens. Thus, deliberative legitimacy hinges crucially on who is willing to deliberate.

5

Who Wants to Deliberate?

In a monarchy, the king and his family are the country; in a republic it is the common voice of the people. Each of you, for himself, by himself and on his own responsibility, must speak. And it is a solemn and weighty responsibility, and not lightly to be flung aside at the bullying of pulpit, press, government, or the empty catch-phrases of politicians.

Mark Twain (1962: 109)

Every two years I stumble into one the few professional hazards of working in political science, as friends, family, and new acquaintances ask me to forecast the upcoming election, comment on details of the horse race, and give my professional opinion about policy proposals or the relative merits of candidates. I often try to sidestep the question by explaining that I am not an expert on campaigns and elections, perhaps throwing in a tepid opinion here or there. Strangely, many people simply ignore my professions of incompetence, and ask follow-up questions, at which point I usually oblige, and engage on whatever topic seems to be animating my conversation partner. At this point, something even more peculiar happens. In the large majority of cases where my prediction, analysis, or opinion diverges from my interlocutor's, he or she will contradict me, often forcefully. People seem very eager to talk to an expert about politics, but very reluctant to acknowledge that expertise when it contradicts their own views.

I will admit to occasionally finding such exchanges irksome, especially when I have tried to avoid expressing my views, or when I actually do have some professional competence on the question at hand. The deliberative democrat in me, however, admires that many people seem to be trying to live up to Twain's admonition regarding our weighty responsibility to speak – a responsibility which is "not lightly to be flung aside at the bullying of" experts and political elites. By locating the substance of the republic in our "common voice," Twain calls all of us as individuals – not just elites – to contribute to the common project of constructing that republic.

Many scholars, however, argue that most people deeply dislike politics and that such calls to speak up amount to a paternalistic imposition. Twain and his condescending intellectual inheritors can hector us all they want, but many people reasonably dislike talking about politics. Any apparent enthusiasm for political involvement is rooted in people's loathing of corruption, not in a deep sense of duty or desire to have their voices heard. As a result, deliberation would serve as, at best, yet another opportunity for the small number of people who are already deeply involved in politics to press their advantages. At worst, it would waste social resources, deepen inequality, and aggravate mass cynicism.

Many deliberative democrats, however, disagree, arguing that disaffection with politics manifests not apathy to politics *per se* but frustration with the political *status quo*, where politics is too often seen as ineffective blood sport. Given the significant resources being poured into both applied deliberative institutions (e.g., deliberative opinion polls, or the British Columbia Citizens Assembly) and research on them, the stakes in determining who is right are high, both in political science and political practice.

In this chapter, we[1] begin by reviewing the current state of the debate about deliberative participation (Section 5.1), concluding that the debate has been clouded by trying to extrapolate from current, naturally occurring patterns of political participation to conclusions about latent demand for deliberative opportunities. The confusion is manifest in the question that has driven much research in this area: "Who deliberates?" This question has a blind spot; it fails to address the contention of deliberative democrats that people would deliberate more if they were offered better opportunities for such interaction. When the research question is

---

[1] This chapter draws heavily on Neblo et al. (2010). I acknowledge and thank my co-authors on that paper: Kevin Esterling, Ryan Kennedy, David Lazer, and Anand Sokhey. In most cases, my use of "we" in this chapter is meant to acknowledge my debt to them, rather than signifying the *pluralis modestiae*. For more extensive technical details on the analyses in this chapter, see Neblo et al. (2010) and its supplementary materials.

reformulated so as to clarify the debate, the pertinent question becomes "Who is *willing* to deliberate?"[2]

Next, we address a basic disagreement between deliberative democrats and their critics (Section 5.2). Do citizens reluctantly mobilize in the face of perceived corruption as a way of chastening elites, or do otherwise enthusiastic citizens demobilize out of feelings of disgust and despair? We find much stronger evidence for the demobilization thesis of deliberative democrats than for the "stealth democracy" thesis of their critics. Next we investigate people's *hypothetical* willingness to deliberate (Section 5.3) conditioned on the institutional features of the deliberative forum. While the results are favorable for the demobilization thesis, it is plausibly noted that some citizens may not really know their own minds, or they may wish to appear more civically oriented than they really are. So, we also discuss the findings of a second study, which sought to identify the determinants of people's *actual* participation in a novel deliberative forum (Section 5.4). The results indicate that people's willingness to deliberate is much more widespread than expected and that it is precisely people who are less likely to participate in traditional partisan politics who are most interested in deliberative participation. People are attracted to such participation as a partial alternative to "politics as usual" (Section 5.5), rather than reluctantly participating merely to chasten corrupt elites. Taken together, these findings suggest that average citizens do not regard deliberative opportunities as filigree on "real" politics or as an indulgence for political activists and intellectuals (Section 5.6). We conclude with some brief notes on the consequences of deliberation (Section 5.7) among the participants in the Congressional deliberation study.

BEYOND SKEPTICISM AND OPTIMISM ABOUT DELIBERATIVE PARTICIPATION

Critics of deliberative democracy have good reasons to be skeptical of the fact that more deliberative opportunities will make a positive difference. Barely half of the U.S. population bothers to show up and vote, even in Presidential elections. Why should we think that they will be lining up for more costly and demanding forms of deliberative participation? Posner (2003:107), for example, argues that deliberative democracy is "purely aspirational and unrealistic...with ordinary people having as little

---

[2] Cook et al. (2007: 33), for example, found that "85% of those who said they had not attended a meeting to discuss public issues reported they had never been invited to do so."

interest in complex policy issues as they have aptitude for them." Less polemically, Mutz (2002) finds that mere exposure to political disagreement demobilizes people out of even non-deliberative participation. Eliasoph (1998) argues that otherwise concerned and involved citizens may avoid group deliberation because group dynamics narrowly delineate acceptable forms of political talk. Even major deliberative democrats express similar concerns. Jane Mansbridge's classic (1980) study of deliberation finds that the sometimes adversarial nature of deliberation may have a chilling effect on speech in situations where deliberators have repeat interactions. Sunstein (2009) goes further, arguing that people's natural proclivity is to avoid exposing themselves to ideas and viewpoints with which they disagree. Delli Carpini et al. (2004: 321) sum up this line of concern: "[D]eliberation is so infrequent [and] unrepresentative...as to make it at best an impractical mechanism for determining the public will, and at worst misleading or dangerous."

If the deliberative thesis is correct, however, then existing patterns of deliberation do not necessarily reflect how citizens would participate given more attractive opportunities. Thus, settling the real disagreement here requires broadening our focus beyond current levels of deliberation in the mass public, and the characteristics of those who already engage in it without being offered novel opportunities. Given the recent proliferation of applied deliberative forums and research on them, surprisingly little work has focused on who is willing to participate. This gap is a missed opportunity to understand a crucial component of deliberative politics. To the extent that deliberative theory is procedural, the composition of the deliberating body looms as a major question (Gutmann and Thompson 1996). Most studies do report on the characteristics of those who engage in deliberation, and many contrast these individuals with those who do not participate. Luskin and Fishkin (2005), for example, report one hundred and fourteen difference-of-means (or distributions) tests on a great range of demographic, attitudinal, behavioral, and other variables. Such analyses are crucial for showing that the sample of participants in the National Issues Convention was representative enough to warrant the normative benefits ascribed to deliberative opinion polls. However, their applied concerns lead Luskin and Fishkin to treat potential selection mechanisms as, in effect, nuisance variables. To get beyond the stalemate between skeptics and optimists about deliberation, we need a different analytical strategy that focuses on selection mechanisms as theoretically and substantively important phenomena in themselves.

Once we understand the basic psychology and sociology of deliberative participation, we can link up with normative theory to think more systematically about which selection processes really threaten the goals of deliberation, and perhaps devise remediation strategies. Many critics reasonably worry that deliberation in practice could be perverse, magnifying political inequality if the people who go in for deliberation are already privileged (Sanders 1997). Other critics are concerned that racial dynamics produce less than representative deliberative groups, with ensuing negative outcomes for underrepresented minorities (Mendelberg and Oleske 2000). Some sources of variation in willingness to deliberate may be normatively benign, and others that are less benign might be ameliorated in practice if we understood how they worked. But we cannot know until we sort out such selection processes. Alternately, it may be that inequalities in deliberative participation run so unavoidably deep that deliberative reforms would be hopelessly perverse from the outset.

The best known study to address the putative desire for greater deliberation came to a resoundingly negative conclusion that should give potential reformers pause. In their important and influential book, *Stealth Democracy*, John Hibbing and Elizabeth Theiss-Morse (2002) argue that most Americans want nothing to do with a more deliberative democracy, that such reticence is reasonable, and moreover that their unwillingness is a very good thing, because the average citizen is ill equipped to discharge the duties that deliberative theorists would assign to them. In effect, Hibbing and Theiss-Morse argue that people's apparent desire for more participatory democracy is actually a misleading artifact of what Lacy (2001) has called "non-separable preferences." The idea behind non-separable preferences is simple: People often condition their preference on a given question on the status of some other question. For example, if citizens prefer a divided government, they may condition their vote for Senator on the party of the sitting President. In the present context, the claim is that most people hate politics, but the only thing that they hate more than being involved in politics is the thought that corrupt politicians might feather their own nests at the expense of the public good. So citizens condition their choices to participate on their perceptions of corruption. Far from participation being attractive in itself, citizens reluctantly consent to being involved only to prevent their *summum malum*. If the political process could be made less corrupt, they would eagerly withdraw, and prefer that it operate quietly in the background. Deliberative reforms predicated on the contrary "are unlikely to improve the system and may very well damage it" (162).

The stealth democracy thesis thus runs precisely counter to one of deliberative theory's central claims – that a significant amount of citizen apathy is actually a *consequence* of frustration with and disempowerment in the current political system. This claim is also a matter of "non-separable" preferences, though in the opposite direction. Citizens still condition their choices to participate on their perceptions of corruption: If the political process could be rendered more rational and responsive in their eyes, they would be *more* inclined to engage it robustly. The disagreement between the stealth thesis and the deliberative thesis could hardly be clearer, and the stakes on which is right could hardly be higher.

Hibbing and Theiss-Morse are among the most unequivocal critics of the deliberative project, but they are hardly alone (Eliasoph 1998; Bartels 2003). Fair minded reviews of the relevant social–psychological literature reinforce similar worries (Mendelberg 2002). Posner (2004) does not even think that new data are necessary to make the case against deliberation. He mounts an argument from revealed preferences, denying any distinction between "who eliberates?" and "who wants to deliberate?" *a priori*. Dismissing Ackerman and Fishkin's (2004) proposal for "deliberation day", he argues that "If spending a day talking about the issues were a worthwhile activity, you wouldn't have to pay voters to do it" (41). Synthesizing the various strands from this larger literature, Hibbing and Theiss-Morse conclude that "pushing people to be more involved in politics and political decision making will not lead to better decisions, better people, or a more legitimate political system. Theorists are misguided if they think otherwise" (161–2).

At least three lines of response to the claims of such skeptics have emerged so far. First, Thompson (2008) has pointed out that deliberative democracy is a normative theory that is supposed to challenge the status quo, so arguing that American politics as it stands does not meet this normative standard hardly disposes of the normative claims.[3] Muhlberger (n.d.) combines a similarly normative response with empirical evidence that antideliberative attitudes are part of a larger syndrome of anti-

---

[3] Though I focus on empirical arguments here, I acknowledge both the normative categories motivating the empirical research and its normative implications. In Neblo (2005), I argue that deliberative freedom does not consist in somehow acting outside of the causal nexus, but in being responsive to reasons. Such responsiveness is likely to generate detectable patterns in behavior. Moreover, even if social forces are acting *on* rather than *through* citizens, knowledge of those forces is typically a pre-condition of negating them. So I see no contradiction in doing scientific research on deliberative democracy, even if it is understood as an emancipatory ideal.

democratic attitudes (e.g., authoritarianism) that cannot be dismissed as a simple matter of citizen preferences.[4] Finally, Dryzek (2005) levels a more fundamental attack on standard survey methods, arguing that they cannot capture the inherently holistic, social, and dynamic aspects of deliberative opinion formation.

All three lines of critique have merit, though they also risk being seen as overly dismissive. In the following sections, we show that a different strategy, one that confronts the claims of deliberation's critics on their own terms generates a more robust response. We begin by conceding that Hibbing and Theiss-Morse, as the most sophisticated and recent of such critics, make a strong *circumstantial* case given their evidence. We then more *directly* test people's willingness to deliberate. These direct tests both reverse Hibbing and Theiss-Morse's findings and explain how their circumstantial evidence led them to mistaken conclusions. While it is true that many people find standard partisan politics and interest group liberalism distasteful, these people tend to see deliberation as a partial alternative to standard forms of participation, and are thus much more open to deliberating than expected. Critics may have a case against theories of *direct* or *participatory* democracy if they simply call for a larger volume of standard forms of political participation.[5] Many critics assume that deliberative democracy is simply an extension of participatory democracy. But the theory does not conceive of deliberation as merely "voting plus" – an activity for political junkies akin to attending rallies or donating to an issue advocacy group. Nor do average citizens regard it this way, as we shall see. Thus, it would be hasty to dismiss deliberative reforms as hopelessly utopian or perverse merely because many citizens do not vote,

---

[4] Thompson and Muhlberger are careful to avoid flat-footed inferences from their arguments. This general line of argument, though, can easily lead to claims of false consciousness: The masses have not thought things through, so they do not understand how important deliberation is. Thus, for their own good, we might have reason to proceed with deliberative reforms even in the face of disinterest or resistance. Whatever the merits of this particular case, the history of reforms predicated on false consciousness suggests that they are at least morally and politically risky. The findings in this chapter lower the normative burden of proof for deliberative reform by obviating the need to invoke false consciousness. If many citizens express interest in these events, and almost all of those who participate in them want to do more, then it becomes harder to dismiss them as a paternalistic imposition on the public.

[5] In practice, there is no strict dichotomy between partisan politics and interest group liberalism and deliberation. That said, the distinction between, for example, participating in a deliberative opinion poll and a partisan rally is sufficiently robust to warrant contrasting the terms. I leave to the side whether non-deliberative participatory democrats might have their own rejoinders to skepticism about participation (e.g., see Pateman 1970).

or find much about status quo politics distasteful. Deliberative democracy cannot (and should not) do without voting and much of the machinery of status quo politics. Quite the contrary. But rather than thinking of deliberation as, at best, a nice frill to add onto interest group liberalism (Walzer 1999), we might better think of the deliberative character of a political system as conditioning the legitimacy of standard democratic practices.

CONDITIONAL PREFERENCES ABOUT DELIBERATIVE PARTICIPATION

As noted above, deliberative democrats and their critics make starkly contrasting claims about why people would or would not want to participate more in politics, and thus about the prospects for various democratic reforms. Hibbing and Theiss-Morse, for example, aim to resolve the question of why citizens, who purportedly hate politics, would nonetheless want more direct forms of democracy. They answer that the only thing that most citizens hate more than participating in politics is for corrupt politicians to subvert the process: "Ironically, the more the public trusts elected officials to make unbiased decisions, the less the public participates in politics" (159). They state their broader thesis in stark terms:

Americans do not even want to be placed in a position where they feel obliged to provide input to those who are making political decisions...People often view their political involvement as medicine they must take in order to keep the disease of greedy politicians and special interests from getting further out of hand...This form of latent representation, stealth democracy, is not just what people would settle for; it is what they prefer, since it frees them from the need to follow politics...This desire for empathetic, unbiased, other-regarding, but uninstructed public officials is about as distinct as possible from the claim that people want to provide decision makers with more input than is currently done. (131–132)

We agree that citizens want empathetic, unbiased, and other-regarding public officials. Once we acknowledge the need for elected representatives, no sensible person would prefer alienated, biased, and selfish public officials. The real disagreement thus hinges on whether people want "*uninstructed*" public officials.[6] On this point, deliberative democrats and their critics do indeed disagree.

---

[6] The term "uninstructed" is misleading here because it conjures the old Burkean distinction between delegates and trustees that deliberative theories cut across. Most deliberativists would leave representatives "uninstructed" in the strong sense, but none would be willing to leave them *unadvised* by a vigorously deliberative public sphere.

Deliberative democrats argue that much disaffection with modern mass democracy stems from feelings of disempowerment and disillusionment. If citizens thought that the system were less rigged and corrupt, they would be more willing to contribute their voices to the process. The contest between these two claims can be usefully framed as a question of "non-separable preferences" (Lacy 2001). That is, are people's preferences about political participation conditioned on their sense of the extent to which the political system is corrupt and irrational?

Recent public opinion research gives us a simple framework for testing the competing accounts of non-separable preferences. In a nationally representative survey, respondents were each asked two versions of a question about the conditions under which they would be more or less interested in getting involved in politics. Both versions frame the question with reference to the conditions Hibbing and Theiss-Morse (158) see as underpinning stealth motivated participation. The first version posits that those conditions get better, and the second version posits that they get worse.

If politics were [1:less/2:more] influenced by self-serving officials and powerful special interests do you think that you would be more or less interested in getting involved in politics? [1:Definitely more interested; 2: Probably more interested; 3: Probably less interested; 4: Definitely less interested][7]

Subjects were then sorted into three categories to test for conditioning. Those subjects who give the same response to both questions have "separable preferences" because their attitudes toward involvement in politics remained the same whether we stipulated more or less influence by self-serving officials and special interests. "Positive complements" (Lacy 2001) are subjects who would want to participate *less* under the condition of less corruption (consistent with the stealth thesis, the two processes move in the same direction, with less perceived corruption leading to less participation, and more perceived corruption leading to

---

[7] These items were administered by Knowledge Networks (KN) to a sample of 404 subjects from September 9, 2008 to September 19, 2008. This sample was separate from the larger KN sample that we report on later. KN administers web-based surveys, and maintains a national probability sample panel. If those who remain on the KN panel have a relatively high propensity to participate, the marginals for participation we report would be too high, but the effects of the determinants of participation we report here would be biased toward zero. The two versions of the question were presented successively on the same screen. The order was not randomized. The following pair of questions specifically about deliberative participation appeared on the following screen.

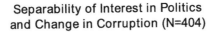

Separability of Interest in Politics
and Change in Corruption (N=404)

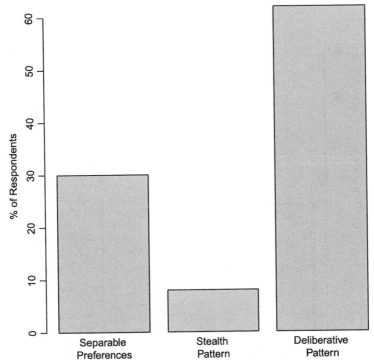

FIGURE 5.1 Separablility of interest in politics and change in corruption.

more participation). "Negative complements" are subjects who would want to participate *more* under the condition of less corruption (consistent with the deliberative thesis, the processes would move in opposite directions).

Figure 5.1 demonstrates considerable attitude dependence (non-separability), with only 30 percent of respondents exhibiting separable preferences. The results do uncover some evidence for the stealth thesis – that is, that some people participate in politics only as a form of taking their medicine and that they would happily withdraw if they could. However, such "positive" complements were relatively rare, comprising only 8 percent of respondents – many fewer than one would have predicted, given the circumstantial evidence, for the stealth thesis presented in Hibbing and Theiss-Morse. On the other hand, the test found vastly more evidence in favor of the deliberative thesis – that is, that

Separability of Interest in Deliberation
and Change in Corruption (N=404)

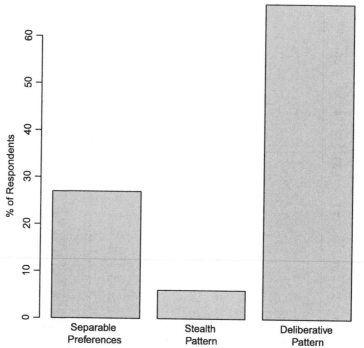

FIGURE 5.2 Separablility of interest in deliberation and change in corruption.

people would participate more if they thought that the system were less corrupt (and would be further de-mobilized if it became even more corrupt). A solid majority, 62 percent of respondents, were "negative" complements, dwarfing the rate of the stealth pattern. For every respondent who fit the stealth thesis, another *eight* fit the deliberative thesis.

The same respondents were also asked a similar – but more specific – pair of questions about *deliberative* forms of participation:

"Recently there has been interest in helping regular citizens get more input into the policy process. For example, some organizations run sessions where citizens discuss important issues with their Members of Congress. If politics were [less/ more] influenced by self-serving officials and powerful special interests do you think that you would be more or less interested in participating in such a session?" [1: *Definitely more interested; 2: Probably more interested; 3: Probably less interested; 4: Definitely less interested*]

As Figure 5.2 illustrates, the results were even more skewed in favor of the deliberative thesis: More than *eleven* times as many subjects fit the deliberative pattern as did the stealth pattern. This test showed even more enthusiasm for specifically deliberative opportunities than for more general political participation. Admittedly, the stealth thesis is "distinct from the claim that people want to provide decision makers with more input than is currently done" (132). However, on this matter, the stealth thesis applies to only a small portion of the public, whereas the deliberative thesis applies to a wide swath.

In order to understand what went wrong with the stealth thesis, we need to revisit another claim made by its proponents; they assert that "stealth democracy, is not just what people would settle for; it is what they prefer" (131). Hibbing and Theiss-Morse provide very strong evidence that many people do hold stealth beliefs. It is true that many people would settle for stealth democracy *given a restricted range of choices*. However, as we shall see, this is *not* what they would ultimately prefer if they believe that effective republican consultation might be available.[8] The following analyses will demonstrate that most people with stealth attitudes also have highly conditional attitudes regarding participation, and that their frustration with status quo politics is not the same as apathy or dislike of political involvement per se. Hibbing and Theiss-Morse (among others) miss this conditioning and so end up overextending their otherwise insightful analysis of stealth attitudes. In order to substantiate this claim, we now shift gears and turn to a more detailed discussion of who is willing to deliberate.

THEORY AND DATA ON DELIBERATIVE PARTICIPATION

As we have seen, the terms "deliberation" and "deliberative democracy" encompass a range of phenomena and mean somewhat different things to different people (Neblo 2007). The discussion here focuses on direct, real-time deliberation among citizens and direct, real-time deliberation between citizens and their elected representatives. To investigate citizens' interest in these two deliberative processes, two surveys were conducted in the summer of 2006. The first investigates citizens' *attitudes toward hypothetical* opportunities for deliberation, as did Hibbing and Theiss-

---

[8] Here "republican consultation" does not indicate delegate instructions but rather communication between citizens and their representatives in which the representatives seek input from their constituents in forming agendas, and in advance of their formal votes, as well as efforts to explain their votes to constituents post hoc. See Lazer et al. (2011b)

Morse's study. The second survey investigates citizens' expressed interest in and *behavioral response to a real opportunity to deliberate* in online forums with their Member of the U.S. House of Representatives.

In the Polimetrics survey concerning hypothetical opportunities to engage in political talk, the characteristics of the hypothetical deliberative session were randomized and data on the attitudes and attributes of respondents were collected.[9] These deliberative sessions were hypothetical in the sense that there was no promise or suggestion that the respondent's answer would lead to an invitation to participate in an actual political conversation. These experimental variables and individual covariates were included in our statistical models to clarify the conditions that motivate citizens' participation in deliberative sessions. We specified the models drawing on four broad currents of theoretical work: Sociological, psychological, "philosophical," and institutional.

First, we drew on the well-established literature on socio-demographic processes to identify the *individual level characteristics* that prompt civic volunteerism. In their landmark study of participation, Verba, Schlozman, and Brady (1995) find that resources, recruitment, and engagement drive traditional political participation. Burns, Schlozman, and Verba (2001) extend that general account, reaching further back into "the private roots of public action." Starting from this base, we included a broad array of demographic and political variables known to influence traditional political participation. It might be expected that many of the same factors that drive one's willingness to attend a rally (for example, time, money, and education) may also drive deliberative participation since they are fairly general resources. On the other hand, deliberative theorists conceive of deliberation as a partial alternative to traditional partisan politics and interest group liberalism (or, perhaps, a condition enhancing the legitimacy of traditional politics). Conceived as such an alternative, deliberation may be especially motivating to precisely those people for whom traditional participation (under status quo conditions) is

---

[9] The survey was part of the 2006 Cooperative Congressional Election Study (CCES), conducted by Polimetrix Inc. Polimetrix obtains interviews from a very large number of opt-in subjects, and then draws a weighted sample from this large pool via sample matching. Our questions were asked of more than 3000 subjects, even though the matched sample contains only 1000 observations. For the following analyses whose inferences rely on marginal distributions, we use the smaller, matched sample. For regression analyses on the deliberative conditions experiment, we use the larger, raw sample. It is important to note that even the smaller matched sample has limitations vis a vis generalizability because of the intense skew in the original sample on interest in politics.

relatively unattractive. We thus have conflicting theoretical expectations, and have reason to regard it as an open question, prima facie, as to how such factors will play out.

Second, deliberation differs theoretically from standard forms of participation in that it is especially cognitively effortful. Thus, in addition to standard demographic, resource, and engagement predictors, we also include a set of psychological *antecedents of motivation* that have strong theoretical links to the kinds of demands that may be particular to deliberative participation. Mutz (2006) argues that many people are *conflict avoidant*, and so will be especially keen to avoid the inherently contentious give and take of deliberation. Cacioppo and Petty (1982) describe the personality variable *need for cognition* as the extent to which people enjoy effortful cognitive activities. Bizer et al. (2004) develop the *need to evaluate* as a disposition to make judgments or take sides. Because several studies show that both the need for cognition and the need to evaluate play an important role in forming and changing attitudes, they are good theoretical candidates for increasing one's willingness to deliberate. As with some of the other standard participation predictors, we have competing theoretical expectations about how *political efficacy* might relate to willingness to deliberate. Several studies have shown, unsurprisingly, that feeling confused and powerless in the face of politics is de-motivating. However, deliberative forums are designed to be opportunities to remediate confusion and to provide an alternate channel for involving oneself in politics. Citizens could therefore regard deliberative opportunities as a chance to become more empowered. Again, how these competing mechanisms will play against each other is an open question a priori.

Third, we have seen that deliberative democracy aspires to go beyond participation in status quo, power politics. As a result, we also include measures of people's preferences over *democratic practice and processes*, a facet of the social psychology of procedural justice (Lind and Tyler 1988). The idea here is that citizens have implicit folk "philosophies" about how democracy is supposed to work and beliefs about how various political processes measure up to those folk philosophies. Because Hibbing and Theiss-Morse's original four *stealth* items were intended to tap such folk intuitions, they were included as measures in this statistical model. An index of people's *trust in government* is also included under this rubric, because critics of deliberation claim that any apparent interest in more direct democracy is predicated on a lack of trust in current decision makers. Thus we should observe a significant negative interaction between stealth and trust – those high on the stealth index but low on trust will want to participate, but those high on both will opt out at higher rates. An index labeled *sunshine* democracy – a positive rewording of the stealth items was also included. The rationale behind the inclusion of the sunshine items was to make the stealth index more reliable and balanced in coding, and to assess acquiescence bias in the marginal distribution of the original items, which were all coded such that agreement indicated higher stealth. Toward that end, we included a "neither agree nor disagree" response option, and wrote four new items (in italics) similar in content to the original stealth items (no italics), but reverse coded so that agreement indicated lower stealth:

[Stealth 1] Elected officials would help the country more if they would stop talking and just take action on important problems.

[Sunshine 1] It is important for elected officials to discuss and debate things thoroughly before making major policy changes.

[Stealth 2] What people call "compromise" in politics is really just selling out one's principles.

[Sunshine 2] Openness to other people's views, and a willingness to compromise are important for politics in a country as diverse as ours.

[Stealth 3] Our government would run better if decisions were left up to successful business people.

[Sunshine 3] In a democracy like ours, there are some important differences between how government should be run and how a business should be managed.

[Stealth 4] Our government would run better if decisions were left up to non-elected, independent experts rather than politicians or the people.

[Sunshine 4] It is important for the people and their elected representatives to have the final say in running government, rather than leaving it up to unelected experts.

Despite the rather direct content overlap, the Sunshine items correlated well with each other, but not with the original stealth items, resulting in two separate factors. Surprisingly, the two scales are nearly orthogonal, correlating at only $r = -0.07$. Next, we shall argue at greater length that this counterintuitive finding indicates contextual conditioning on the part of many citizens when it comes to stealth/sunshine beliefs.[10] The *sunshine*

---

[10] Alternatively, it may be that asking respondents these reworded questions prompts them to examine implicit biases about democratic politics, a kind of deliberative interaction within the survey itself (Sanders 1999). The weak connection between scales is not a

items tap how they think that representative democracy should work in principle, whereas the stealth items tap what they would settle for as a step away from the corrupt status quo.

Finally, a person's willingness to deliberate is likely to vary according to the institutional characteristics of the deliberative events themselves. There are many ways to construct a deliberative forum, even if we restrict them to direct, real-time events. To get a sense of how willingness to deliberate varies according to several dimensions relevant to both theory and applied deliberative institutions, we embedded an experiment permuting the following variations in the CCES survey:

Recently there has been interest in helping regular citizens get more input into the policy process. For example, many organizations run [*one day / one hour*] sessions where citizens [*come together / use the Internet*] to discuss [*important issues / immigration policy*] [*<none>; with local officials; with their Member of Congress*].[*<none>; Participants get $25 as thanks for their involvement.*] If you had the chance to participate in such a session, how interested do you think you would be in doing so: (5) Extremely interested; (4) Quite interested; (3) Somewhat interested; (2) Not too interested; (1) Not at all interested.

In sum, the experiment's permutations allowed for variations along five dimensions relating to deliberative institutions, dimensions relating to: (1) The length of the deliberative session, (2) its medium, (3) its agenda, (4) its participants, and (5) its external incentives.

Each of the manipulations has the potential to encourage or discourage people's participation in a deliberative event. Varying sessions in terms of their length, for example, is a fairly obvious way to test for people's sensitivity to the amount of time necessary to participate in a deliberative event. After all, people are often busy, being already engaged in or committed to a range of other activities, tasks, and responsibilities. Indirectly, session length as a variable is also a way to test for people's sensitivity to monetary incentives in so far as participating in a deliberative event in all likelihood comes with some opportunity cost. Moreover, by varying session length, we can clarify the conditions in and extent to which traditional cost–benefit considerations influence and shape people's willingness to deliberate, as opposed to – or in conjunction with – competing norms, habits, and notions of duty. Similar to the dimension of session length, varying the medium of the deliberative session may also plausibly

matter of acquiescence bias; including a methods factor in the measurement model (Podsakoff et al. 2003) increases the strength of the relationship only to $r = -0.12$.

tap into people's cost sensitivities. Computer-mediated deliberation is generally more convenient (for those who have access to the Internet) and greatly reduces travel and logistical costs. But varying between face-to-face and computer-mediated deliberations also taps into other characteristics that varying session length cannot do itself. Moreover, it accommodates geographically disparate participants, which is especially crucial for deliberation within sub-publics that might not be geographically concentrated. For example, the relative buffer of computer-mediated deliberation may, on the one hand, mitigate reluctance to deliberate among those who dislike conflict or prefer partial anonymity. Alternatively, it may exacerbate people's reluctance to deliberate in so far as the medium permits or fails to discourage certain forms of incivility. Other pertinent sensitivities may concern such things as people's comfort with "digital" media or their preference for/dependence on non-verbal communication channels.

Varying agendas between general and specific topics was a way to investigate the extent to which marginal rates of interest in deliberation are predicated on people imagining the one topic that most interests them as opposed to people's more general interest in talking about important issues of the day. Much political behavior research shows that most people have a very narrow range of issues that they care about enough to be mobilized to participate around. Under an interest-group liberalism frame, we should not be surprised to find that participation is linked to particular interests. Deliberative theory, however, predicts somewhat weaker such effects for deliberative participation because we have reasons to participate deliberatively even when we do not have a large, direct stake in some particular outcome.

Finally, there are both theoretical and practical differences between deliberation among fellow citizens (i.e., horizontal deliberation), versus citizens and their elected representatives (i.e., vertical deliberation). By randomizing the type of session accordingly, we can tap into relative taste for direct democratic deliberation and more traditionally representative models.

Before explaining variation in expressed willingness to deliberate, we should note that absolute levels of interest in deliberative participation were quite high. A large majority of people (83 percent) expressed at least some interest in participating in a deliberative session. Combining across the various conditions, 27 percent said that they would be "extremely" interested in participating, another 27 percent said they would be "quite" interested, and 29 percent "somewhat" interested. Twelve percent said they were "not too interested," and only 5 percent said that they were "not at all" interested. Since this sample's stealth attitudes were comparable to what Hibbing and Theiss-Morse (2002) report, there is little reason to believe that peculiarities of the sample can account for such a high level of general interest in deliberation.

The desire to "get more input into the policy process" by discussing one or more issues with an official and/or other "regular citizens" appears to differ in its predictors from participation in partisan politics and interest group liberalism. Of the seven demographic characteristics from the literature, only education even has the sign usually associated with greater participation in partisan politics or interest group liberalism (and unlike its function in predicting voting, etc., it is not statistically significant here).[11] See Table 5.1. Younger people, racial minorities, and lower income people expressed significantly *more* willingness to deliberate, all of which are reversals from traditional participation patterns. Women, less partisan people, and non-church goers were also slightly more likely to want to deliberate, though not to a statistically significant degree. On these criteria, it would appear that the kinds of people attracted to the deliberative opportunities offered are fairly distinct from those drawn to partisan politics and interest group liberalism. These results are consistent with deliberative democracy's claim of providing an outlet for those frustrated with status quo politics.[12]

There were fewer surprises with the effect estimates for the cognitive antecedents of motivation. General political interest, need for cognition, need for evaluation, and conflict avoidance all had significant effects in the expected direction (i.e., positive for the first three and negative for the last). Efficacy had a small, negative coefficient but was not statistically significant. Similarly, the insignificant interaction between conflict

---

[11] These reversals in demographic effects were not driven by some peculiarity in our sample. Using the same sample, we specified models of voter turnout and an index of traditional participation, finding a pattern in these variables much like that in previous research, suggesting that there really is something different about deliberative participation.

[12] These findings suggest that some deliberative forums may not face the difficult trade-off between deliberation and participation that Mutz (2006) identifies with naturally occurring, cross-cutting political talk. Similarly, we found no such de-mobilization in our experiments involving actual deliberation between members of Congress and their constituents. These findings do not contradict Mutz's argument, but suggest possible ways to soften the effect of her findings in practice.

TABLE 5.1 *Hypothetical willingness to deliberate (CCES respondents)(OLS regression estimates)*

	B (SE)
Individual characteristics	
Strength of partisanship	−0.025 (0.022)
Church attendance	−0.015 (0.018)
Education	0.019 (0.018)
Income	−0.012 (0.007)*
White	−0.202 (0.071)***
Full time employment	0.045 (0.053)
Age	−0.008 (0.002)****
Male	−0.006 (0.047)
Motivation	
Political interest	0.296 (0.033)****
Conflict avoidance	−0.051 (0.027)*
Efficacy	−0.016 (0.024)
Need for cognition	0.136 (0.027)****
Need for judgment	0.048 (0.027)*
Democratic practice	
Sunshine democracy	0.021 (0.025)
Stealth democracy	0.026 (0.029)
Trust in government	0.040 (0.042)
Deliberative conditions (treatments)	
Member of Congress	0.144(0.047)***
Length of session (hour/day)	0.013 (0.044)
Place of session	0.010 (0.044)
Topic of session	0.038 (0.044)
Incentive for participation	0.124 (0.044)***
Interactions	
Congress condition × Stealth democracy	−0.131 (0.047)***
Place condition × Conflict avoidance	−0.024 (0.036)
Constant	3.74 (0.093)****
Number of observations	2242
R^2	0.135
Adj. R^2	0.126

*$p<0.1$; **$p<0.05$; ***$p<0.01$; ****$p<0.001$
Note: All covariates – except the level 1 dummies and treatment dummies – have been centered.

avoidance and the face-to-face versus online condition suggests that the distance provided by online discussion does not ameliorate conflict avoidant people's relative distaste for deliberation.

Presenting the results from the variables in people's attitudes toward democratic processes is a bit more complicated. None of the main effects for stealth, sunshine, or trust is significant. However, the interaction between stealth and the experimental "Congress" condition was negative and highly significant, indicating that, with the other variables controlled, people high on *stealth* were not as attracted as were others by the *hypothetical* prospect of talking with their (presumptively corrupt) Members of Congress.

The main effect for the Congress condition was positive and significant. Most people were motivated by the thought of talking with a high ranking government official, so there seems to be somewhat more enthusiasm for vertical (i.e., republican) deliberation than horizontal deliberation. Unsurprisingly, people were also attracted by a monetary incentive. More surprisingly, people did not seem sensitive to the length or mode of the deliberative session.

These findings merit further attention since they may indicate a theoretically interesting insensitivity to certain kinds of participation costs (akin to some findings in the voting literature), or they may reflect an inability to vividly imagine the logistical costs of participation at the time of response. There was also no significant effect on general, unspecified issues versus a specific issue of the day (immigration policy). This last finding suggests that, contrary to an interest-group politics frame, people are not especially parochial in their willingness to deliberate.

When taken together, the five manipulations in the question wording experiment constitute a $2 \times 2 \times 2 \times 3 \times 2$ experimental design, yielding forty-eight conditions. There are good theoretical reasons to include the main effects in the model, but we had no theoretical expectations about interactions among the conditions. It is possible, however, that some of the manipulations jointly explain willingness to participate in deliberative sessions. When we test for this more complex conditioning in a fully factorial ANOVA, however, none of the interactions between experimental conditions had significant effects in a saturated model (even with an "n" over 3000). So the main dimensions on which deliberative forums vary do not seem to interact much at all. One could spin a large number of hypotheses about how they might have interacted (e.g., that those getting to talk to a member of Congress would be less sensitive to financial incentives, or that people would be more sensitive to the topic when investing a full day). So by ruling all such hypotheses out, this negative result is of considerable interest in itself.

Overall, these findings present quite a different picture of willingness to deliberate than what we might have expected if we thought of deliberation as just another form of traditional political participation. I now turn to comparing these results on interest in hypothetical deliberation with those on actual behavior in response to a concrete invitation to deliberate.

DELIBERATING WITH MEMBERS OF CONGRESS

In the summer and early fall of 2006, my colleagues and I conducted a series of field experiments in which random samples of citizens from thirteen congressional districts were offered an opportunity to participate in an online deliberative forum with their Member of Congress to discuss immigration policy.[13] Sixty-five percent of respondents agreed to participate in principle. Subjects who agreed to participate in principle were randomized into treatment and control groups. Of those assigned to the treatment condition, 34 percent showed up on the specified date and time for the discussion with their Member of Congress. Given typical response rates to surveys, and the relatively burdensome requirements of this invitation (four surveys, reading background materials, plus an hour-long commitment at a specific date and time), these participation rates are reasonably high.

Since actual participation was conditional on agreeing to participate initially, we first estimated both stages simultaneously as a Heckman selection model. However, *rho* was not significant ($p = 0.428$), indicating that patterns in the determinants of the actual turnout were not conditioned on patterns in the initial agreement to participate. We report the determinants of people's willingness to participate in the first column of Table 5.2. As with the varying deliberative conditions experiment

---

[13] The Congressional Management Foundation, a non-profit, non-partisan organization recruited the Members of Congress to participate in the study. Five of the members were Republican and seven Democrats, spread across all four major geographical regions. The members themselves were diverse ideologically, including one member from each party who voted against their party on recent immigration legislation. As a kind of level two control condition, two sessions were conducted in which citizens were invited to deliberate with an immigration policy expert. Knowledge Networks conducted this survey in the summer of 2006. Participants were informed that indicating a willingness to participate made them eligible for an invitation to a session involving their Member of Congress.

TABLE 5.2 *Participation in deliberative sessions with Members of Congress (Knowledge Networks)*

	(Model 1) Expressing willingness to participate	(Model 2) Showing up for session *if* willing	(Model 3) Participants vs. non-participants	(Model 4) Participants vs. unwilling to participate
Individual characteristics				
Strength of	−0.033	−0.062	−0.090	−0.129
partisanship	(0.061)	(0.080)	(0.071)	(0.087)
Education	0.090	0.087	0.107	0.223*
	(0.079)	(0.106)	(0.096)	(0.119)
Income	−0.034**	0.015	−0.004	−0.044**
	(0.015)	(0.019)	(0.017)	(0.022)
White	−0.198	0.315*	0.242	0.076
	(0.144)	(0.184)	(0.170)	(0.208)
Children (<12)	0.180***	0.092	0.141*	0.231**
in household	(0.069)	(0.080)	(0.075)	(0.098)
Employment	−0.761****	−0.208	−0.513****	−0.931****
	(0.121)	(0.153)	(0.136)	(0.171)
Age	−0.013	−0.018	−0.014	−0.006
	(0.015)	(0.030)	(0.023)	(0.025)
Male	−0.057	−0.053	−0.048	−0.115
	(0.122)	(0.163)	(0.143)	(0.174)
Motivation				
Conflict	−0.163**	−0.026	−0.075	−0.146
avoidance	(0.066)	(0.085)	(0.077)	(0.095)
Efficacy	0.130*	0.228***	0.260****	0.332***
	(0.067)	(0.088)	(0.078)	(0.096)
Civil society	0.128***	−0.032	0.034	0.142**
	(0.046)	(0.051)	(0.047)	(0.063)
Attention to	0.161*	0.172	0.270***	0.363***
issue	(0.092)	(0.124)	(0.111)	(0.135)
Need for	0.049	0.073	0.085	0.124
cognition	(0.069)	(0.095)	(0.085)	(0.107)
Need for	0.108	0.026	0.098	0.189*
judgment	(0.069)	(0.095)	(0.084)	(0.101)
Democratic practice				
Sunshine	0.144***	0.156*	0.193**	0.304***
democracy	(0.053)	(0.084)	(0.076)	(0.091)
Stealth	0.160***	−0.032	0.054	0.180**
democracy	(0.059)	(0.075)	(0.068)	(0.087)
Trust in	0.186***	−0.032	0.045	0.116
government	(0.057)	(0.074)	(0.067)	(0.082)

(*continued*)

Table 5.2 (*continued*)

	(Model 1) Expressing willingness to participate	(Model 2) Showing up for session *if* willing	(Model 3) Participants vs. non-participants	(Model 4) Participants vs. unwilling to participate
Other model parameters				
Panel	2 Controls	2 Controls	2 Controls	2 Controls
District	12 Controls	12 Controls	12 Controls	12 Controls
Constant	0.460	−1.150	−2.621	−2.204
	(0.468)	(0.741)	(0.606)	(0.714)

*Call those who said they were unwilling to participate 0s, those who said they were willing but did not show, 1s, and those who said they were willing and did show, 2s. Model 1 is a binary logit comparing {0} to {1,2}. Model 2 compares {1} to {2}. Model 3 compares {0,1} to {2}. And Model 4 compares {0} to {2}.

described earlier, willingness to deliberate in this field experiment did not follow the standard pattern from previous research on participation in traditional partisan politics and interest group liberalism.[14] Again, the coefficients for age, race, gender, strength of partisanship, and income were all the reverse sign of models predicting standard participation, although of these variables, only income was statistically significant in predicting willingness to participate. Being white predicted a slightly higher rate of actually showing up for the session. Unlike the hypothetical experiment, in this specification, traditional employment dampened willingness to deliberate, probably as a proxy for constraints on specific dates and times. However, having young children in the household was positive and significant.

Included in the four surveys was a battery of questions (*civil society*) about participation in non-political forms of civic engagement. Consistent with Putnam (2000) and contrary to Hibbing and Theiss-Morse (2002: 184–9), an index of such engagement powerfully predicts willingness to

---

[14] Some previous research suggests that participation in standard "open" public hearings and face-to-face town halls, often show the same socio-economic status (SES) biases as voting (though it is not clear whether the difference is a matter of differing control variables). If the effects here are indeed reversed, then it may be that the reversal is driven by an *interaction* between the form of participation and the method of recruitment – i.e., identifying a broad sample and randomly inviting participation. This question is worth pursuing in future research, since it has important implications for institutional design regarding open forums and outreach efforts. We thank Archon Fung for raising this point.

deliberate.[15] The motivational factors all had the expected sign. *Conflict avoidant* people were significantly less likely to want to deliberate, whereas efficacious people and those paying attention to the issue were slightly more likely to express willingness.

Some of the most powerful and most interesting results hinge on citizen's attitudes toward democratic practice. Recall that *sunshine* attitudes and *trust* in government were not significant in the hypothetical deliberation model. In the current model, however, both of them are substantively large, statistically significant, and positive. This finding regarding *trust* fits uncomfortably with the stealth democracy story, since in that theory, those who trust government should be willing to withdraw and let it operate in the background. Instead, respondents seem more willing to participate in deliberation with a government in which they have more trust – a behavioral result reinforcing the findings reported here regarding non-separable attitudes toward deliberative participation. Because the sunshine index was designed to mirror the content of stealth with the opposite valence, it is not too surprising that it should positively predict willingness to deliberate. Indeed, as reported in column 2 of Table 5.2, *sunshine* is one of the few factors with a significant effect in driving turnout for the session among those who report a willingness to participate.

Things become even more interesting when we consider the results for *stealth*. In the hypothetical model, *stealth* had large, negative, and significant effects in the Congress condition. Yet here we get a complete reversal. *Stealth* has substantively large, statistically significant, and *positive* effects on willingness to deliberate. Given Hibbing and Theiss-Morse's (2002) interpretation of stealth attitudes, this stark reversal is difficult to explain. Indeed, that the *sunshine* and *stealth* indexes should point powerfully in the same direction is, in itself, perplexing at first blush. The items for the scales were explicitly designed to point in opposite directions in their content. However, if we question the standard interpretation of *stealth*, the results become less perplexing. If many or most people expressing stealth beliefs have conditional attitudes about the content of the items, then a different interpretation of the meaning of *stealth* offers itself. On the standard interpretation, most people dislike politics

---

[15] Again, sample differences do not seem to be driving demographic and other differences. We specified another set of models of voter turnout and an index of traditional participation, using the same Knowledge Networks sample. And again, those models yield a pattern on variables much more in keeping with previous research, suggesting that there really is something different about deliberative participation.

intrinsically, do not want to be more involved, but reluctantly agree to more direct democracy as a hedge against the corrupt status quo. They would most prefer a non-democratic technocracy that operates in the background. Recognizing that this model might not be achievable, they settle for more referenda and other forms of direct democratic control.

We agree with Hibbing and Theiss-Morse that most citizens prefer stealth democracy to direct democracy, and more direct democracy to the status quo. However, whereas Hibbing and Theiss-Morse see the preference for stealth democracy as an authentic/intrinsic preference of people, the results shown here indicate that it is a conditional preference. Just as Hibbing and Theiss-Morse showed that there was a reluctant desire for more direct democracy, a desire conditioned on the limited range of options people thought available to them, the results here show/suggest that the preference for stealth democracy is itself a conditional one; it is a first preference only given a certain limited range of options. To put it simply, people will settle for stealth democracy if the civics textbook version of deliberative representative democracy is not achievable.[16]

With an expanded menu in view, we can see why the *stealth* index reverses its effect between the hypothetical and actual offer to deliberate. The actual offer from their Member communicates new information about that Member that runs counter to their stereotypes of politicians. Constituents might believe that most Members of Congress are corrupt politicians who do not really care about what average citizens think. But when their Member, in effect, says *"No, really, I do want to talk with you. Will two weeks from Tuesday at 7pm work?"*, they update and reason that their Member must be one of the (perhaps few) good ones. The frustration and desire for reform evinced by stealth attitudes indicate motivation for change, rather than apathy or aversion. On this reading, those high on stealth order their preferences thus:

Status quo→more direct democracy→stealth democracy→
more deliberative representative democracy

These preferences are not single-peaked with respect to Hibbing and Theiss-Morse's notion of "process space" (2002: 47), so it makes sense

---

[16] The relationship between direct democracy and deliberative democracy is admittedly complex. On most accounts, legitimate direct democracy would have to include a mass deliberative component, whereas the issue is less acute on a representative account. That said, what I have called deliberative republicanism, over time, may well foster interest among citizens in more direct and participatory forms of democracy.

that the stealth index might behave non-monotonically when new options enter the perceived choice set.

Perhaps people high on *stealth* might want to participate in deliberation with their Member of Congress at higher rates for entirely different reasons. For example, they might consider it a golden opportunity to hold their presumptively corrupt Member's feet to the fire. But this explanation would not account for why the effect should *reverse* itself so dramatically between the hypothetical version of talking to one's Member of Congress and the actual version. Any proffered alternative explanation must make sense of how the new information being conveyed by the Member's concrete offer leads to the reversed effects of stealth beliefs specifically.

The model in the second column of Table 5.2 tests for the determinants of actually participating in a deliberative session, conditional on having reported willingness to participate. Once a participant expressed intent to attend a session, there are very few determinants of who actually shows up. This implies that the key to explaining participation is in understanding who expresses willingness to participate.

The third column reports an alternate way to code participation, where we group those who do not show up for a session (those who say they will not participate with those who say they will but do not). This column finds a few additional significant results compared to the second (attention to issue and young children in the household enhance participation, and employment suppresses participation). In addition, race is no longer net predictive of actual participation. We ran a series of Wald tests comparing the coefficients in Model 3 (net deliberative turnout) to a model with the same specification and the same subjects, predicting their voter turnout. Partisanship, education, income, employment, age, civil society, sunshine and stealth all showed significant differences in the expected direction, indicating that even variables that are not statistically significant in Model 3 may nevertheless differ significantly from their effect on more traditional forms of political participation – that is, several of these null results are a departure from the norm when it comes to voting. Put differently, on many criteria, actual deliberative participation in these sessions draws a significantly *less* biased population than voting. Again, these findings suggest that it is deeply misleading to think of deliberative participation as the provenance of activists and political junkies or any other proper subset of participants in "real" politics.

We conceptualize the propensity to actually participate as a continuous latent index, anchored at one end with those who have no interest at all in participating in such sessions, and at the other end, by those for whom participating in the sessions is their top priority; most respondents fall somewhere in between these two end points. Reporting an interest in participating (but not actually participating) indicates an intermediate level of interest in participating: something more than dismissing participating out of hand, but something less than actually committing the time to attend (perhaps by overcoming obstacles to do so). The results in columns one to three suggest that most of the consequential movement is at the low end of the latent index; once someone reports intent to show up, whether or not he or she does is largely random, perhaps due to exogenous conflicts with the meeting time.

Alternatively, one might worry that reporting intent to participate, but failing to show up, represents only a kind of social desirability. If one believed this counter interpretation, it might be tempting to say that, outside of the sunshine index and a few other variables, the significant findings in the first column of Table 5.2 are simply uncovering determinants of social desirability rather than determinants of actual participation. If it is the case, however, that those who express intent to participate are actually the type that are likely to actually show up, then the dependent variable in the third column combines two distinct types among the recoded zeroes: Those who certainly will not show up, and those who are likely to show up but do not for some exogenous reasons.

The fourth column of the table provides leverage to address the question of whether the determinants uncovered in the first column are actually predicting motivation toward behavior rather than simply social desirability, with a dependent variable that equals zero for those who are unwilling to attend and one for those who actually do attend (that is, this model discards those who report intent to show up but do not, or equivalently an unordered model with independent errors comparing these two categories). In the fourth column, note that there are quite a few determinants of who actually shows up, compared to those who are unwilling to participate. Indeed, most of the coefficients in this final model are of similar magnitude and precision to those reported in the first column: Only efficacy and sunshine show a statistically significant difference on a Wald test of equality across equations in Model 1 and Model 4, in both cases merely reinforcing the effect already present in model one. Thus, Models 2 and 4, together, provide fairly strong evidence for interpreting the respondents' expressed willingness to participate as an indicator of a genuine, if diffuse, interest in participating, rather than a mere expression of social desirability.

INTERPRETING ANTIDELIBERATIVE ATTITUDES

Deliberative democracy is rooted in the notion that legitimate political decisions typically must come with a rationale that does not merely restate the will of the decision maker, whether that decision maker is a dictator, a politburo, or even a democratic majority. In that sense, it is the antithesis of authoritarianism. Alas, much evidence suggests that authoritarian attitudes are not uncommon among citizens of even the most consolidated democracies (Altemeyer 1981). Indeed, certain "soft" authoritarian (Muhlberger n.d.) attitudes garner levels of support that would seem to make deliberative democracy a pipedream.

Take, for example, two of the items from the stealth scale:

Elected officials would help the country more if they would stop talking and just take action on important problems.

What people call "compromise" in politics is really just selling out one's principles.

As with previous studies, large portions of the public agree with these statements: Sixty-six percent agreed with the "talk versus action" item, and 43 percent agreed with the "compromise" item. Since compromise and especially debate are essential to deliberation, it would seem reasonable to infer that many members of the public have attitudes that would make it difficult for them to function in a deliberative public culture.

Yet, a different frame on very similar questions produces precisely the opposite conclusion, namely that average citizens evince a remarkably *favorable* disposition for deliberative participation. Along with the stealth scale, our field experiment's surveys included a sunshine scale, which positively framed the items included in the stealth scale. Consider the agreement rates generated by the positively framed versions of the two statements above:

It is important for elected officials to discuss and debate things thoroughly before making major policy changes. [92 percent agree]

Openness to other people's views, and a willingness to compromise are important for politics in a country as diverse as ours. [83 agree]

Even more people agree with these pro-deliberative attitudes than with the corresponding stealth statements. Given these competing results, it is worth exploring more closely what these results mean and how people's attitudes toward authority and compromise function in a broader view of public debate.

It is incorrect to infer that large majorities of the public have *unambiguously* negative attitudes about debate and compromise. We would be equally mistaken if we argue that large majorities of citizens have *unambiguously* positive attitudes about debate and compromise. Many of the citizens in our sample agreed with *both* the positive and negative versions of these questions. Either citizens are deeply confused about these issues (i.e., they exhibit rampant non-attitudes) or they are deeply conflicted.

Our many systematic findings regarding stealth and sunshine, indicate that the non-attitudes explanation is implausible here. If we were really dealing with random noise, the indices would not have so many interpretable causes and consequences. One is left to conclude that large portions of the public have complex and conditional attitudes about the role of debate and compromise in public discourse. In my view, such complexity is unsurprising and perhaps quite appropriate. The folk intuition that much elite political talk is a mix of reasonable debate and demagogic drivel seems entirely sensible. Similarly, some compromises are rightly regarded as reasonable, even noble, forms of mutual accommodation, while others are cynical or craven.

Hibbing and Theiss-Morse (2002) suggest that most citizens overreact to the negative parts of the mix and discount the positive. Quoting a participant in one of their focus groups as complaining that "Congress bickers all the time between the two parties, and they're always struggling for the power, rather than taking care of the issue", they argue that "people's impatience with deliberation and compromise is an important element of the American political system" (137). However, this inference assumes that there is little truth to this person's accusation about the quality of elite political discourse. The implication is that most people typically misperceive genuine deliberation as bickering, and reasonable compromise as the result only of power struggles. On the basis of this and other comments in their focus groups, Hibbing and Theiss-Morse infer that: "The notion that debating among elected officials may actually be necessitated by their responsibility to represent the interests of diverse constituencies across the country is rejected by most people" (142).

We doubt that most people are so simplistic and reductive in their views. Accordingly, we decided to test this claim more systematically. We asked a standard Likert agree/disagree question based on a close paraphrase of Hibbing and Theiss-Morse's inference, quoted earlier:

One of the main reasons that elected officials have to debate issues is that they are responsible to represent the interests of diverse constituencies across the country.

Far from most people rejecting this notion, only a small minority disagrees with it (6 percent). A large majority (84 percent) explicitly agrees with it. Most citizens seem quite willing to make room for debate and compromise, though (reasonably, in my view) they do not regard all debate as constructive or sincere, nor all compromise as principled. It is simply inaccurate to characterize all public frustration with partisan politics and interest group liberalism as rooted in naïve perfectionism. As we have seen, it is precisely those people who are high on stealth who *want* to deliberate when given a signal that they can actually have both rational debate and republican consultation at the same time. There is no contradiction between passionate support for democratic ideals and despair about the way status quo practices subvert them. Such attitudes can coexist in the same person, be activated by different stimuli, and interact in complex ways. Take for example, the other pair of questions from the stealth scale:

Our government would run better if decisions were left up to successful business people.

Our government would run better if decisions were left up to nonelected, independent experts rather than politicians or the people.

Hibbing and Theiss-Morse choose a negative frame for their data on these questions. Having found that 32 percent of citizens agreed with the "business people" statement and 31 percent with the "experts" statement, they infer from these numbers that the public likes "decision-making structures that are not democratic, and not even republican" (138). Simply turning around the frame provides a more optimistic interpretation though: Each of these statements was rejected by more than two-thirds of the public, so it seems gratuitously pessimistic to describe the public as having a broad fondness for non-democratic decision-making structures.

That said, it does seem troubling that a substantial minority of the public appears so frustrated with the status quo that it would forgo even the minimal autonomy afforded by the institutions of representative democracy. However, in qualitative follow-up interviews on these questions, many respondents who agreed with the "successful business people" item interpreted it as implying that such people would make good *candidates* for public office (e.g., Ross Perot or Michael Bloomberg), rather than directly crafting policy qua business people. On this interpretation, there is nothing at all antidemocratic about such beliefs. Indeed, the other interpretation conjured up images of having energy policy crafted by oil executives – a prospect that was decidedly unpopular, even among those who initially agreed with the item.

Finally, as with the first pair of stealth questions, there was substantially more agreement with the reverse coded statements than with the original ones:

In a democracy like ours, there are some important differences between how government should be run and how a business should be managed. [73 percent agree]

It is important for the people and their elected representatives to have the final say in running government, rather than leaving it up to unelected experts. [80 percent agree]

Whereas significant minorities agreed with the stealth questions, large supermajorities agreed with the corresponding sunshine versions. Unlike the first pair of stealth items, most of the public is not even conflicted here – they simply reject the stealth attitudes and embrace the sunshine ones. We conclude that any picture of the American public as so desperate to avoid politics that they are willing to submit lightly to plutocratic or technocratic rule is deeply misleading.

WHY SOME PEOPLE ARE UNWILLING TO DELIBERATE

None of the foregoing is meant to suggest that the public is unambiguously and uniformly positive about the prospects of a more deliberative democracy. Even if critics overestimate the number, they are surely right that substantial numbers of people do not want to deliberate. Critics argue that the main reasons are that most people are uninterested in politics and that they consider deliberation unnecessary because everyone already knows what needs to be done. If the critics' correctly explain the unwillingness of some to deliberate, the prospects for such a project are bounded and deliberativist ambitions must be constrained accordingly. But if better explanations exist, the proper shape of the deliberative project and the proper reach of deliberativist ambitions ought to account for this.

In Section 5.3, one of the survey experiments concerned people's interest in participating in different kinds of deliberative sessions. Seventeen percent of the respondents indicated that they were "not too interested" or "not at all interested" in participating in a deliberative session. As part of the experiment, there was a follow-up survey, which solicited from these respondents their reasons for not wanting to participate. As shown in Table 5.3, the results of this part of the experiment reveal that the reasons offered by those unwilling to deliberate did not usually conform to the critics' explanations for people's unwillingness. Indeed, the critics' explanations were among the least cited reasons.

TABLE 5.3 *Percent citing reasons for not wanting to deliberate (Among those "not too" or "not at all" interested in deliberating)*

Don't know enough to participate	42%
Too busy	31%
Dislike conflict	29%
Will not lead to binding decision	26%
Impossible to discuss politics rationally	17%
Political views private	15%
No interest in politics	15%
Everyone already knows what to do	4%

As we have argued earlier, people seem to regard deliberation as a partial alternative to more standard partisan politics and interest group liberalism. As a result, a general lack of interest in politics as conventionally understood does not seem to drive people's unwillingness to participate in deliberation. Similarly, consistent with the finding that most Americans are well aware that debate and compromise are often necessary, very few people find deliberation pointless on the grounds that everyone already knows what needs to be done. On the contrary, the modal response to the question about why respondents did not want to deliberate indicates that many people are quite humble in the face of complex policies and do not feel that they know enough to participate meaningfully.

While Table 5.3 provides little support for the typical claims of critics, it does support the claim that conflict aversion is a substantial deterrent to people's willingness to deliberate. Indeed, the results of the follow-up survey were consistent with the results of the baseline survey, in which 32 percent agreed with the conflict aversion item. That said, many factors go into people's decision to do things, and it would be easy to overestimate the effect of conflict aversion. For example, 60 percent of those who were conflict avoidant on the baseline survey were nevertheless willing to deliberate with their Member of Congress. Thus, even though some aversion to conflict may be widespread, it is hardly decisive with respect to participating in deliberation.

If we multiply out the rate of people who were not interested in deliberating (17 percent) with the percentage of those who cite conflict aversion as the reason (29 percent), we get a predicted net decrease in willingness to deliberate due to conflict aversion of about 5 percent. As it happens, this estimate comports well with the behavior we observe in the model predicting willingness to deliberate with one's Member of Congress. Holding the other variables constant, moving from one standard deviation above the mean to one standard deviation below the mean on a conflict avoidance index predicts about a 6 percent decrease in one's willingness to deliberate. This level of suppression indicates that conflict aversion should be regarded as a significant, but not overwhelming, impediment to realizing a deliberative culture.

A NOTE ON THE CONSEQUENCES OF DELIBERATION

Many scholars worry that pushing deliberation upon reluctant citizens, beyond wasting time and resources, will cause actual harm by leading to even greater frustration with and aversion toward politics. Even some who are highly sympathetic to deliberative democracy echo such concerns (e.g., Mansbridge 1980) under some circumstances. This chapter focuses on who is willing to deliberate, not the content and consequences of deliberation, addressed in concurrent work. Here, we cannot fully develop my response to such worries, and for now we concede that caution in interpreting the policy implications of these results is warranted. But it is worth noting briefly that nothing like these negative consequences came to pass in our field experiments. Quite the contrary: Participants almost uniformly described the experience as positive: Ninety-five agreed (72 percent strongly agreed) that such sessions are "very valuable to our democracy" and 96 percent agreed (80 percent strongly agreed) that they would be interested in doing similar online sessions for other issues. Such positive reactions were nearly independent of whether the citizens were of the same party or agreed on the issue with their Member of Congress or the majority of the other citizens in the session. Open-ended responses to the sessions were also overwhelmingly positive, with participants remarking on various aspects of the sessions that fit quite well with the hopes and intentions of deliberative democrats. For example:

"It was great to have a member of Congress want to really hear the voices of the constituents." / "I believe we are experiencing the one way our elected representatives can hear our voice and do what we want." / "I thought he really tried to address the issues we were bringing up instead of steering the conversation in any particular direction, which was cool." / "I realized that there are A LOT more sides to this issue than I had originally thought."

In addition to these positive attitudes, we identified positive causal effects on people's issue-specific political knowledge, attention to politics beyond the issue under discussion, external political efficacy as a result of participation, and propensity to discuss politics with people in their social network (with many more potential benefits – and harms – of deliberation yet to be tested for).[17] Again, we acknowledge that it is entirely possible that these positive attitudes and effects are peculiar to something about these forums. All of the preliminary evidence, however, suggests that deliberation produced nothing like the perverse results critics worry would ensue.

CONCLUSION

Many scholars of political behavior (as well as many non-academics interested in politics) are inclined to be skeptical of the aspirations of deliberative democrats. The story goes that average citizens hate politics and cannot even get it right when they show up every four years (if they show up) to cast a vote on a simple binary choice between candidates who have been bombarding them with information for months. How can anyone seriously expect them to want to participate in more detailed discussion of policy, much less do so competently?

The intuition behind such skepticism is reasonable on its face. However, the aspirations of deliberative democrats do not seem so hopelessly utopian when we consider that many citizens are de-mobilized precisely by the peculiarities of partisan and interest-group politics that political sophisticates take as exclusively constitutive of political participation. The motivation to participate is not arranged in such an ordered way as to preclude a greater desire for alternative forms of participation. These findings suggest that willingness to deliberate is much higher than research in political behavior might suggest, and that those most willing to deliberate are precisely those turned off by standard partisan and interest group politics. If the standard forms of participation can be embedded in a more deliberative framework, the tension between the two may well lessen. Far from rendering deliberative democratic reforms ridiculous or perverse on their own terms, these findings suggest that the deliberative approach represents opportunities for new forms of participation quite congruent with the aspirations of normative political theorists and average citizens alike. Yet, even if citizens want to deliberate, whether they are competent to do so remains to be seen.

[17] For the results on knowledge and attention, see Esterling, Neblo, and Lazer (2011a). For the results on political efficacy, see Esterling, Neblo, and Lazer (2011b). For the results on network diffusion, see Lazer et al. (2015). For the results on persuasion see Minozzi et al. (2015) and Lazer et al. (2009)

6

A Few Days of Democracy Camp

Just tell'em you're gonna soak the fat boys and forget the rest of the tax stuff...Make'em cry, make'em laugh, make'em mad, even mad at you. Stir them up and they'll love it and come back for more, but, for heaven's sake, don't try to improve their minds.
Robert Penn Warren, All the King's Men

One must take men as they are, they tell us, and not as the world's uninformed pedants or good-natured dreamers fancy that they ought to be. But 'as they are' ought to read 'as we have made them.'
Immanuel Kant, Conflict of the Faculties

A few years ago, my father died after a long series of debilitating health problems. Toward the end, his quality of life was very poor by everyone's account, his own especially. Nevertheless, in the face of an acute episode, he was readmitted (we all lost track of how many times) to an intensive care unit. This time, however, the hospital offered us information on hospice and palliative care. Everyone agreed that moving to palliative care made sense. My father's transformation under such care was remarkable; the last few days of his life were among the best of the previous seven years. And the savings to our health care system were enormous. This may seem cold for a son to countenance, were it not for the fact that spending that small fortune would have done nothing but increase his suffering and rob our family of a peaceful parting.

This experience left a deep impression on me personally, but also professionally. I already had an interest in health policy, so I began to study end-of-life policy in particular, and came to the view that on these issues, the U.S. health care system often managed the sad feat of being gratuitously inhumane and grossly inefficient at the same time. I was pleased, then, when I learned that the health care bill being debated in 2009 contained a provision to reimburse doctors for counseling Medicaid patients about end-of-life options like hospice and palliative care. A few weeks later, however, Sarah Palin transformed that debate by posting the following message on her Facebook page:

> The America I know and love is not one in which my parents or my baby with Down Syndrome will have to stand in front of Obama's "death panel" so his bureaucrats can decide, based on a subjective judgment of their "level of productivity in society," whether they are worthy of health care. Such a system is downright evil.[1]

There are certainly legitimate political questions surrounding the morality of rationing and social pressures to forego care (to say nothing of the larger health reform bill). Palin's description, though, bore no resemblance to the counseling provision, and did not so much bother to make a slippery slope argument as baldly assert that the bill would immediately send us over a precipice. The distortion was so egregious that *PolitiFact*, a nonpartisan media watchdog, named it their 2009 "Lie of the Year."[2]

Yet, that summer, TV screens in the United States were awash in images of screaming (and sometimes armed) crowds at town-hall meetings denouncing death panels, and any Member of Congress who supported them. The end-of-life counseling provision was ultimately removed from the legislation. I had invested a lot of hope in town-hall meetings as a promising venue for deliberative democratic innovation. So it was a bitter pill to swallow, watching such egregious demagoguery kill a policy so important to me via one of my main hopes for deliberative reform. Palin denied that she was trying to "stir them up," as the populist Governor Willie Stark was advised to do in *All the King's Men*; indeed, she claimed that she was trying to do (and actually did) just the opposite – "improve their minds." She was gratified that she "got people thinking and researching" the issue.[3]

---

[1] www.facebook.com/note.php?note_id=113851103434. Posted July 8, 2009.

[2] "PolitiFact's Lie of the Year: 'Death Panels.'" December 19, 2009. Angie Drobnic Holan. *Politifact.com*. http://politifact.com/truth-o-meter/article/2009/dec/18/politifact-lie-year-death-panels/. FactCheck.org, another non-partisan clearing house, named it one of their "Whoppers of 2009." www.factcheck.org/2009/12/whoppers-of-2009/

[3] Quoted in an interview with Rich Lowry. "The Rogue on the Record," *National Review*. November 17, 2009. In the interview, Palin said that the term "death panels" "should not

I found it difficult to react with equanimity to this spectacle, until a colleague urged me to write an editorial contrasting what we found in the online town-hall experiments discussed in the previous chapter with what was going on in the face-to-face town-halls all over the country. I had been so frustrated with the death panels' debacle that the implications of its contrast with our findings had managed to elude me.

In a strange twist of fate, the health care and immigration town-halls became intertwined in ways that went beyond my personal perseverations. Around the same time, Sen. Tom Coburn began an effort to defund the political science budget of the National Science Foundation. He singled out our e-town-hall project for special opprobrium, sending out a separate press release denouncing it as a misuse of taxpayer dollars, and accusing us of abetting Democrats in avoiding the face-to-face confrontations that were on TV at the time (despite the fact that the study included Republican members and had been out of the field three years before the health care town-halls blew up). It also called on protesters to crash the briefing that we were planning with congressional staffers on how to implement e-town-halls. The story was picked up by Glenn Beck, the *Wall Street Journal*, and several blogs, leading to online calls for someone "to take out the academic vermin cooperating with those rats in Congress."

In any case, most town-hall meetings (whatever their other virtues) do little to promote reasoned discourse. Decades of research demonstrates that the people who show up are usually either nursing specific grievances or already love their representative. The first group is not really open to persuasion and the second group does not need to be persuaded. So members typically have little incentive to spend much time arguing the merits of a case. Instead, they merely try to reassure the aggrieved that they can be trusted to get it right the next time, or they "stir up" the people who already love them. Worse yet, there is a trend toward avoiding confrontation by creating carefully scripted encounters through controlling the questions, the participants, or both.

The attendees at standard town-halls, though, are wildly unrepresentative of the general population. In our electronic town-hall project, we invited a random sample of each member's constituents to participate in the discussions. The questions were uncensored, except for a provision for filtering out any that were deemed abusive, vulgar, or grossly

be taken literally," and compared her use to President Reagan's use of the term "evil empire" to describe the Soviet Union.

inappropriate by two facilitators unaffiliated with the member's staff. Yet, *not once*, in more than twenty sessions, with over eight hundred citizen participants, did we have to invoke this provision. There were no verbal equivalents of citizens wearing weapons in holsters to the sessions, no nuclear attacks on members' patriotism or humanity. Members had to answer challenging questions, but none had to call upon the Capitol Police for protection from their own constituents. Both the constituents' behavior and the members' were the opposite of what we have come to expect from standard town-halls. Yet the two issues debated in our events were scarcely less contentious than health care: Immigration reform (during the summer of 2006) and detainee policy (i.e., torture, rendition, etc., during the summer of 2008).

This utter divergence in behavior suggests that the average American, given the right setup, might be much more willing and able to talk about important policy issues in a reasonable and intelligent fashion than the scenes on TV would suggest. Perhaps even more striking, the politicians involved dramatically adapted their behavior in turn, offering much more substantive engagement.[4] Blanket generalizations about "politicians" and "the American public," then, risk running afoul of the fundamental attribution error – people's tendency to overrate dispositional factors relative to situational factors when we try to explain behavior. Since our events were experimental, though, one might wonder whether the generalizations hold well enough in the real world. If we cannot realistically expect much variation in situational factors, then there is a sense in which the fundamental attribution error is not an error. Everything, then, hinges on what we mean by invoking the "real" world.

"Real" cannot mean "under the status quo," since that would beg the question. The whole point of policy debate is to consider changes to the status quo – to assess what the real world *could* and *should* look like if we were to act to change the status quo. So the implicit criteria for "real" have to turn on things like hard limits to human nature, resource costs to realize changes within those limits, powerful structural impediments to change, and the like. In our forums, real members of Congress deliberated with real constituents about real legislation, and the results looked very different from the status quo. As noted in the previous chapter, the pool of

---

[4] Indeed, several of the members of Congress who participated in our study also engaged in standard town-hall meetings and "field hearings" about immigration around the same time, exhibiting the same striking inversion in the style and content of their interactions between the differing institutional contexts.

participants was *more* real than participants in standard town-halls, at least in the sense that they were more representative of the public. And participating did not take more time than face-to-face town-halls for either the citizens or the elected officials. In fact, reading the background materials likely took less time than traveling back and forth to a meeting site would for most participants, and the members of Congress only needed access to a telephone. So the necessary resources and logistics do not seem particularly unrealistic on their face.

When Kant bristled against admonitions to "take men as they are," he hardly meant to deny the frailty of human nature. In some ways, he was remarkably pessimistic about human nature. Rather, he meant to criticize the entrenched powers of his day for their complacency in failing to explore institutional strategies for *managing* those frailties. As we saw in Chapter 3, though, many critics regard deliberative democrats as just the latest example of "uninformed pedants or good-natured dreamers" and scoff at the idea that any institutional innovation, much less "a few days of democracy camp," could materially alter the parameters of mass democracy. I happen to agree with critics of deliberation that mass democracy imposes limits on the functional "competence" of citizens, and, moreover, that deliberative mini-publics (including my own e-town-halls) face irreducible impediments to fully resolve the problem of citizen competence. That said, I also believe that the debate so far has been miscast, and that with a better understanding of competence as well as the dilemmas facing mini-publics, we can better explore institutional responses to managing the problems endemic to mass democracy.

I begin (Section 6.1) by tracing the development of the concept of citizen competence as it emerged out of the aftermath of World War II, through Philip Converse's seminal contribution in the 1960s, up to John Zaller's extension of Converse (Section 6.2). I then analyze the main extant lines of response to the problem of competence (Section 6.3), including the use of heuristics, emotional regulation of attention, online processing, and aggregation. I go on to show that both Converse and his critics (Section 6.4) share an implicit assumption about citizen competence that is inimical to the deliberative democracy that is subtly built into Converse's setup. However, a more deliberative conception of competence (Section 6.5) does not solve the general problem, since deliberative democracy is subject to its own form of a "legitimation crisis," which can only be managed, not resolved. I then discuss promising institutional innovations for managing this dilemma sensibly (Section 6.6), and conclude by sketching systemic criteria for measuring the deliberative competence of citizens (Section 6.7) and showing how these criteria shed light on the relationship between public opinion as measured by standard polling and deliberative forums.

CITIZEN COMPETENCE AS A MORAL PROBLEM
FOR DEMOCRACY

In the summer of 1932, a large plurality of German citizens voted for the National Socialist German Workers' Party. The Nazis garnered more votes than the next two largest parties combined, and other extremist parties also fared well. Combining the votes for the Nazis, the Communists, and the like, a solid majority of citizens voted to elect representatives who were avowedly hostile to liberal democratic constitutionalism. Though the Nazis never formally replaced the Weimar constitution, soon after assuming office, they passed the Enabling Act, investing the Chancellor with temporary plenary power. In the ensuing years, the Reichstag dutifully renewed the Enabling Act at the appointed intervals, evincing a concern for democratic form that might seem quaint or comical were the context not so grotesque. A year later, Hindenburg, the German president, died, and the Reichstag called for a plebiscite to ratify a proposal to combine the powers of the Chancellor and the President under Hitler's leadership. With 95 percent of registered German voters turning out, the proposal won 90 percent approval. Over 38 million German citizens voted to invest Hitler with dictatorial power, with only 4 million dissenting. On paper, the Weimar constitution seemed like a reasonable blueprint for liberal democracy, but the democratic elements were mobilized to eviscerate the liberal elements, whose demise, in turn, destroyed democracy itself.

Given this context, it is not hard to appreciate why postwar social scientists regarded citizen competence as a topic of overwhelming importance. The initial catastrophic sequence of political events in Germany occurred with chilling rapidity and broad popular support in "what was once regarded as the citadel of Western civilization" (Adorno et al. 1950: vii). So it became a matter of real urgency to understand how it came to pass "that in a culture of law, order, and reason ... great masses of people [could] tolerate the mass extermination of their fellow citizens" (vii).

In their massive study, *The Authoritarian Personality*, Theodor Adorno and his colleagues sought "to develop and promote an understanding of social–psychological factors which have made it possible for the authoritarian type of man to threaten to replace the individualistic and democratic type prevalent in the past century and a half of our civilization, and of the factors by which this threat may be contained" (xii). The whole point of the project was to integrate normative, scientific, and practical concerns. The argument starts from an openly normative conception of good (democratic) and bad (authoritarian) citizenship, proceeds to develop operational measures of latent dispositions germane to those conceptions, their causal antecedents, and then to the prospects for remedy via policy interventions in educational and political institutions.

Adorno developed the "F scale" to measure people's dispositions toward authoritarian or democratic patterns of citizenship. The scale consisted of several factors: *Authoritarian submission* (being submissive and uncritical toward in-group authorities); *authoritarian aggression* (a tendency to see those who deviate from in-group ideology as enemies); *conventionalism* (rigid adherence to dominant in-group values and norms); *anti-intraception* (opposition to the subjective and imaginative, and thus an unwillingness to consider things from another's perspective); *stereotypy* (thinking in rigid categories, intolerance of ambiguity); *superstition* (mystical sense of causality and hostility to science); *hierarchical power* (thinking in terms of dominance–submission, strong–weak, leader–follower); *projectivity* (a tendency toward conspiracy theories and threat sensitivity).[5]

It is easy to see how most of these factors might work against good notions of democratic citizenship. For example, uncritical submission to in-group authorities is precisely the kind of democratic abdication that contributed to Weimar's fall. Similarly, being unable or unwilling to take up another's perspective on politics facilitates regarding those who disagree with us as threatening outsiders who should be marginalized. The whole syndrome might make peaceful co-existence in large pluralistic democracies more difficult. That said, some of the other criteria proved controversial, especially given the way that Adorno et al. operationalized them. Critics accused them of focusing exclusively on right-wing authoritarianism to the exclusion of left-wing authoritarianism. (Stalin's Russia was beginning to look scarcely less threatening than Nazi Germany had been.) Moreover, main-line conservatism was implicitly characterized as a soft form of authoritarianism on these measures. Milton Rokeach (1960),

---

[5] I have reorganized the factors a bit for purposes of my presentation. In the original, *superstition* and *stereotypy* are inexplicably combined. The original scale also contained a *sex* factor (exaggerated concern with sexual "goings-on") and *destructive cynicism* (generalized hostility; vilification of the human), both rooted in Freudian theory.

among others, tried to develop more general scales that did not run into these problems, and several of the ensuing controversies are still matters of active scholarly research today. But the debate became strangely detached from the question of civic competence, and another paradigmatic approach to citizen competence displaced the theoretical line initiated by Adorno and his colleagues.

CITIZEN COMPETENCE AS AN INFORMATIONAL PROBLEM FOR DEMOCRACY

Adorno thought of citizen competence in terms of adopting a peculiarly democratic political morality: Tolerance, intellectual independence, flexibility, openness to persuasion and fair compromise, and so on. In his seminal paper "The Nature of Belief Systems in Mass Publics", Philip Converse (1964) stepped back from this morally infused setup and focused on political knowledge as a precondition for *any* effective citizen action, whatever an individual's goals may be. Converse demonstrated that most citizens had remarkably low levels of political knowledge, and that the gulf in knowledge between nearly all citizens and political elites was vast.

Converse's analysis hinged on what he called "belief systems," a concept which, in turn, hinges on the notion of "constraint." Belief systems are systematic precisely insofar as the beliefs that they contain exhibit constraint; that is, they fit together in relations of entailment (whether as a matter of logic or convention). These relationships induce correlations between beliefs and opinions at any one time, and underwrite a degree of stability in individual beliefs and opinions over time. Converse argued that the knowledge gap between elites and citizens was so large that it was implausible to think that citizens could organize their political beliefs and opinions on their own terms. The best that they could hope to do was pick among the belief systems on offer from elites. Indeed, large swaths of the public appear to be too ignorant to manage even this modest task. They exhibit very little constraint in their beliefs, and end up expressing "non-attitudes" – effectively random guessing, which can serve no real democratic goal. In Converse's setup, then, constraint – understood largely in terms of committing to either a liberal or conservative ideology – became the touchstone for citizen competence.

At first glance, Converse's standard may seem like an obvious way to provide a more neutral conception of citizen competence by stepping back from the strong moral content built into Adorno's approach. Whatever goal citizens might want to pursue, they will at least need a rudimentary map to orient themselves in political space to achieve that goal. Faced with a forced choice between political illiterates and partisan ideologues, Converse chooses the ideologues, since they can at least make their preferences felt in democratic choice.

Upon reflection, though, this seemingly neutral choice ends up being much more substantive and objectionable than it might appear, since it defines citizen competence in a way that leaves citizens completely unaccountable to each other. In his celebrated book, *The Nature and Origin of Mass Opinion*, John Zaller extends Converse's empirical theory and draws out the normative implications of its elite-centered analysis with brutal frankness:

> [My theory] makes no allowance for citizens to think, reason, or deliberate about politics: If citizens are well informed, they react mechanically to political ideas on the basis of external cues about their partisan implications, and if they are too poorly informed to be aware of these cues, they tend to uncritically accept whatever ideas they encounter. As normatively unappealing as this implication of the model may be, it is consistent with a large body of theory and research concerning political persuasion. (1992: 5)

On this account, the normative content of Converse's conception of competence nearly dissolves into a descriptive category. And to the extent that it retains normative content, it comes close to turning Adorno on his head. For Adorno, mechanically accepting the exhortations of in-group elites and mechanically rejecting those of out-group elites is one of the foundations for authoritarian citizenship.

The rationale for preferring ideologues to political illiterates relies implicitly on an appeal to a market-model of democratic politics. If we accept this model, mechanical sorting on the basis of ideology need not seem so threatening. Indeed, it may drive efficiency. Preference satisfaction is the main goal, and partisan ideology is a decent proxy for individual preferences, so there is no real need for citizens to think, reason, or deliberate about politics independent of party elites. The "liberal" part of liberal democracy sets up institutional guard rails within which the "democratic" part can run its course without the need to worry about moralistic notions of citizen competence. Strong partisan ideology appears to help average citizens relate their preferences to the choices on offer from elites.

This implicit appeal to a populist interpretation of the market model explains why Converse's conception of democratic competence seemed so attractive. But it also reveals that his move is at least as substantive and contestable as Adorno's more openly normative conception. I have already discussed several reasons why deliberative democrats want to move beyond the minimalist, market conception of democracy. To those, we might add the reason that seemed so looming and urgent to social scientists in the aftermath of Weimar's rapid, unforeseen slide from parliamentary republic into authoritarian barbarism. In the end, liberal rights depend on the democratic practices that they structure. On a long view, it seems like whiggish speculation to be confident that institutional guard rails can do all of the work in containing inevitable crises. And even if one feels justified in being whiggish about liberal democratic institutions, the enormity of being wrong counsels against too easily accepting partisan ideologues as the only alternative to political illiterates for a realistic aspiration of democratic competence.[6]

ATTEMPTS TO REDEEM THE PUBLIC

Though the Converse–Zaller approach to citizen competence has exerted enormous influence, counterstreams of research rapidly emerged. Early responses attempted to rebut Converse's empirical conclusions, or at least his interpretation of them. For example, Achen (1975) and Erickson (1979) argued that measurement error could account for much of what seemed so troubling in Converse's account. More commonly, though, dissenters do not dispute the facts of the case (i.e., that average political information among citizens is low and its variance high), nor really the standards of competence (i.e., being able to translate one's personal preferences into left–right ideological space).[7] Rather, critics made the

---

[6] Berelson (1952: 317) actually argued for something like a mix of ideologues and illiterates: "A sizable group of less interested citizens is desirable as a 'cushion' to absorb the intense action of highly motivated partisans." Others have deployed revealed preference arguments to suggest that apathy, ignorance, and disengagement from politics are actually signs that most people are basically satisfied with political processes and outcomes.

[7] V. O. Key Jr. (1966) anticipated this line of research in *The Responsible Electorate: Rationality in Presidential Voting, 1936–1960*. The most important books that sparked the revival of interest in this theme are Page and Shapiro's *The Rational Public: Fifty Years of Trends in Americans' Policy Preferences* (1992); Sniderman, Brody and Tetlock's *Reasoning and Choice: Explorations in Political Psychology* (1991); Samuel Popkin's *The Reasoning Voter: Communication and Persuasion in Presidential Campaigns* (1991); and Erickson, MacKuen, and Stimson's *The Macro Polity* (2002). This empirical line of research was bolstered by rational choice theoretic explanations of why and how voters effectively use information short cuts. This has become a huge literature, but see, especially McKelvey and Ordershook, "Information, Electoral Equilibria, and the Democratic Ideal" (1986), Lupia and McCubbins, *The Democratic*

startling claim that democratic regimes do not necessarily need anything but the most minimally attentive, thoughtful, and knowledgeable citizenry to function well.[8]

These minimalist claims come in four major varieties. The first group points to the efficiency of decision *heuristics*, claiming that individual voters can use information shortcuts to arrive at the same decisions that they would make if they were more informed. The second group argues that average citizens process information *online* – that is, on the fly – storing its significance for choice affectively, and discarding the factual content itself. Thus, even though they do not "have" much political information, their choices are nonetheless based on much more information than Converse's analysis would suggest. The third group is somewhat less minimalist in that it purports to show how *emotional* processes can explain how we efficiently sort cases for which heuristics and online processes suffice, and those that require more concerted attention. Finally, the fourth group appeals to the logic of *aggregation*, claiming that the electorate can be collectively rational and informed, even if individual voters are not.

Heuristics

Arguments that appeal to the efficiency of decision heuristics are helpful but of limited use in redeeming a normatively satisfying picture of public opinion. By "decision heuristic" I mean any cognitive shortcut which allows a voter to form a relatively reliable judgment without full information. For example, if a voter is a life-long Republican and feels confident that his or her considered judgments on matters of policy are usually those supported by the Republican party, then he or she might reasonably vote for the Republican candidate in a race about which she or he has virtually no information. Political scientists have identified many such decision heuristics ranging from the obvious, such as partisan identification, to the odd but plausible case described by Samuel Popkin:

When President Ford tried to eat an unshucked tamale, he committed a *faux pas* far more serious than spilling mustard on his tie...To Hispanic voters in Texas, he betrayed an unfamiliarity with their food which suggested a lack of familiarity with

---

Dilemma: Can Citizens Learn What They Need to Know? (1998), and William Minozzi, "A Jamming Theory of Politics" (2011).

[8] For example, Lupia and McCubbins write: "In this book, we concede that people lack political information. We also concede that this ignorance can allow people of 'sinister designs' to deceive and betray the uninformed." (1998: 1). See also Erickson, MacKuen, and Stimson (2002: 428).

their whole culture. Further, tamales were a way of projecting from the personal to the political, of assuming that personal familiarity with a culture and the acceptability of a candidate's policies to a group were linked. (Popkin 1991: 111)

Whatever one's view on the reasonableness of such inferences, recourse to decision heuristics is often beneficial, and to some extent unavoidable. Nevertheless, there are at least three major reasons why a deliberative democrat ought not to lean on them too heavily. The first two arguments are practical, while the third is conceptual.

First, there is little hard evidence that in real political settings, decision heuristics work as well as they are purported to do. There is evidence that voters use *putative* decision heuristics, but the crucial question is whether by using the heuristics they efficiently approximate some deliberatively relevant standard (e.g., how they would have voted under "full deliberation") in a real electoral setting. The best studies to date that look into this question find substantial deviations from the outcome predicted under full *information* (which is usually operationalized in an individualistic way) both for specific individuals and when those individuals aggregate up (Althaus 2003; Bartels 1996).

Second, even if such deviations were small, pressing the most common class of decision heuristics, elite cues (e.g., party endorsement), too far would be problematic on a deliberative account. If the interests of certain elite factions happen to conform to those of certain factions in the broader public, the elite-driven model may be an adequate base for some theories of aggregative democracy, but it is still problematic for deliberative theory. As Disch points out, elites typically give priority to achieving policy and electoral goals, and it is a happy accident if high quality deliberative persuasion serves those goals. Even when elites are not nakedly self-interested or cynical, we can expect a certain degree of what they may regard as instrumental altruism in their behavior. That is, they sincerely believe that their cause will serve the common good, so they may feel more justified in manipulating us into sharing their view. More than average citizens, considerations of role morality may make elites feel less compunction against altruistic manipulation (of the kind discussed in Chapter 4). Even in his earliest writings, Habermas criticized this logic of benevolent democratic despotism which he believed was coming to dominate elite campaigns to influence public opinion:

[T]he offers made for the purposes of advertising psychology, no matter how much they may be objectively to the point, in such a case are not mediated by the will and consciousness but by the subconscious of the subjects. This kind of consensus formation would be more suited to the enlightened absolutism of an authoritarian welfare regime than to a democratic constitutional state committed to social rights: everything for the people, nothing by the people — not accidentally a statement stemming from the Prussia of Frederick II. (1989: 219)

Third, the ways that "full information" and "correct voting" get operationalized in the empirical literature typically bear a weak relationship to deliberatively relevant standards. One prominent method is to estimate how low information voters would behave if they were highly informed by comparing them to others like them in many ways other than their level of information. However, even relatively well-informed voters on a given issue may not know much compared to someone who has participated in a deliberative mini-public. Moreover, by Converse's own logic, those who are highly informed may be different from those who are less so on (typically) unmeasured characteristics — for example, the highly informed tend to be relatively dogmatic and have a tendency to avoid or resist information that does not reinforce their ex ante beliefs. Despite their greater information, then, it is hardly obvious that they should serve as role models and standards of citizen competence from a deliberative point of view.

In addition, such an approach assumes that people's reports of their higher order views, like partisan affiliation and ideological disposition, are both much more considered and properly antecedent to their policy choices. Yet one of Converse's major points is that most people simply do not really have such well-articulated abstract systems ready to hand in any reliable way. So, for example, the fact that someone's position on abortion does not match up well with her party identification suggests that the latter is at least as likely as the former to be "wrong" when measured against a deliberative standard of "full information." Allowing for the possibility of reflective equilibrium between our concrete policy judgments and our abstract commitments makes much more sense than treating party, ideology, and the like as fixed, prior, and error-free.

Alternate approaches to assessing the value of heuristics run into related problems. For example, experimental methods that rely on intrapersonal comparisons to emulate "full information" and "correct voting" (Lau and Redlawsk 1997) operate on an implicit market model and ignore the social component of deliberative justification.[9] They fail to

---

[9] Or at least they ignore evidence suggesting that we are poor at emulating such justification without interacting with others (Mercier and Sperber 2011). Lau and Redlawsk set up an experiment with hypothetical candidates and issue positions. Subjects make a choice under conditions that mimic the limited information environment of an election.

capture any sense of what Elster (1986) has felicitously described as the difference between "the market and the forum."[10]

Lau and Redlawsk write: "Who is to decide what is 'correct'? We are reluctant to define what is 'good' for everyone ... Instead, we begin by defining 'correctness' based on the values and beliefs of the individual voter" (586). In one sense, it is easy to appreciate the motivation behind this move. As social scientists, they wish to refrain from making controversial normative assumptions. But in avoiding one set of controversial assumptions, they implicitly commit to the correctness of the market model of political justification, which, from a deliberative point of view, is no less controversial (though it is less transparently so). And if they wish to deny this implicit normative commitment, then their results fail to bear on democratic theory in the way that this whole literature clearly aspires to do. Like many others, Lau and Redlawsk implicitly assume that the market model is normatively neutral in a way that begs the central question behind deliberative democracy. Either their setup amounts to a positive claim that we are not accountable to each other, or their measure of "correctness" is not a valid operational indicator of their concept.

These discussions of "full information" and "correctness" are peculiar species of what, in Chapter 3, I called "articulation" – that is, trying to more fully elaborate our judgments and render the set of them more coherent. The difference is that these approaches (a) (in Bartels' and Althaus' cases) operate by third-party proxy, rather than through the subjects, (b) minimize the social dimension of articulation, (c) focus only on discrete final judgments, rather than their chains of support, and (d) do not allow anything but the final judgment to be updated in order to achieve greater coherence. Here, new inferences rely on a kind of expanded notion of revealed preferences, with no genuine articulation and certainly none that is socially accountable.

Online Information Processing

Much of the evidence for the functional ignorance of democratic citizens works something like this – interview voters after an election, and ask who they voted for and why they voted the way that they did.

Later, they read a compact version of all the relevant facts and decide if they want to change their vote. If they do not, they are coded as having voted "correctly" the first time and "incorrectly" otherwise.

[10] Similarly, Lupia and McCubbins (1998) model democracy as a straightforward principal–agent problem between individuals and their elected representatives. On a deliberative account, though, we are all accountable to each other, and only then does the moment of "vertical" accountability come into play.

This may seem like a very reasonable way to proceed. However, developments in cognitive psychology suggest that it may not be so reasonable after all. The "Online model" of judgment (OLM) represents the process of how we typically come to an assessment of someone or something as follows: We are bombarded with so much information during the course of our daily lives that when we receive a piece of information, say that Candidate X is pro-life, we adjust our running assessment of Candidate X consistent with our stand on abortion, and then promptly forget why we have made the adjustment. This method economizes on our cognitive resources. But note that if this picture is correct, then voters may have received dozens of such messages and formed a reasonable and reliable assessment of Candidate X given his or her political beliefs, and yet he or she will appear to be thoroughly uninformed after the fact.

Thus, for democratic theory, the OLM represents a potentially redeeming alternative to so-called memory-salience models. Zaller himself admits that, "If there is a threat to my simplified top-of-the-head Response Axiom, it comes from recent psychological studies of 'on-line' information processing" (1992: 50). Indeed, experimental results strikingly favor the OLM over alternative explanations (Lodge, McGraw, and Stroh 1989). Once we control for the information that subjects have received but forgotten, what they can actually recall at the time of their vote has no bearing on their choice, while a summary of the forgotten information powerfully predicts their choice.

However, experimental control problems have blocked efforts to test the model in a real electoral setting. This is very problematic because advocates of the memory-salience model quite plausibly claim that the cognitive mechanism used to assess candidates in the highly artificial experimental setting differs from that used in the extended and stochastic information environment of a real campaign. Neblo (2000) mitigates the practical impediments to testing the OLM in a real election, finding that voters do use online considerations in their evaluations, even if voters give considerations that can be recalled greater weight in their online tally.[11]

On its own, though, the logic of the OLM can only take deliberative legitimation so far for at least two reasons. First, the OLM only shows that citizens are responsive to more information than memory-based models would have us believe. It says nothing about the quality of that

---

[11] Zaller actually conjectured that something like this was probably happening, speculating that people engaged in what he called "bounded on-line processing" (279), that would produce results consistent with my findings.

information, its range, rational coherence, and so on. Like the heuristics literature, the logic of OLM studies stays purely agnostic about whether some consideration or piece of information is a defensible reason for or against a policy or candidate, and so cannot speak to a core concern in deliberative democracy. For example, suppose a given citizen does not like black people. Nevertheless, according to the OLM, becoming aware of and negatively responding to a candidate's African–American heritage would make them more "competent," without some ad hoc emendation of the theory. Second, the logic of the OLM suggests that people may be very poor at deliberation, even if they are motivated and sincere in engaging in it. If people cannot generally recall why they support what they support, and oppose what they oppose, then all of that antecedent information processing is not only lost to deliberation, the gravitational pull of such "dark matter" may actually distort and confuse deliberative processes.

Emotional Regulation of Attention

Some political psychologists concede that heuristics and online processing leave a lot to be desired in redeeming democratic competence, since there are a wide range of circumstances in which they can misfire. However, a new line of research argues that we have evolved emotional regulatory systems that help us to efficiently sort cases wherein we can safely rely on old cues and summary impressions, and when we need to spend our limited cognitive resources to engage political problems more directly. Consider, for example, anxiety, one of the two key emotions for the affective intelligence research program in political psychology. MacKuen et al. (2007) theorize the function of anxiety in political choice:

> Increased anxiety tells us when we are entering the geography of uncertainty. Absence of anxiety tells us we are in the realm of the safe and familiar and that we can entrust ourselves to rely on past actions that will, as they have before, successfully manage our lives. And, in such circumstances people display habituated choice as their decision strategy. (127)

MacKuen et al. go on to provide strong evidence that anxiety is active in the functional realm that they hypothesize for it – that is, anxiety has robust effects on whether habituated dispositions (e.g., party heuristics) get deployed, and they trace out the myriad behavioral and macro structural ramifications of that finding. All of this constitutes a major advance.

However, the affective intelligence research program never moves beyond its functional analysis to evaluate whether some mechanism *serves its function well.* Doing so greatly limits how this line of research can speak to democratic theory. MacKuen et al. (2007) seem to imply that that a functional analysis directly implies success in serving the function well:

[W]e resolve the long-lived conflict between an attractive normative macro theory – rational choice – and a seemingly more accurate but normatively disappointing micro theory ... sustain[ing] a normative portrait of democracy that is more encouraging than has previously been thought plausible. (21)

Setting aside the question of whether rational choice (i.e., the market model) is really an attractive normative theory of democracy, what does it mean to say that anxiety, for example, serves the function of managing novelty and threat? In a retrospective, evolutionary context, serving a function and serving it well begin to collapse into each other. If an evolved trait can be accurately explained in terms of some function, this is really just another way of saying that it served that function well enough to enhance survival. Here, the notion of success is largely redundant to function.

However, the leap from a neurobiological, evolutionary account of anxiety's "function" to the "function" it serves in a modern political context makes the question of success anything but redundant. An evolved trait's adaptivity for genomic reproduction in evolutionary time says almost nothing about its normative relevance for contemporary politics. Through a lack of anxiety, we tell ourselves that we are safe and can rely on familiar patterns. Whether, in fact, we are safe and can properly rely on the familiar is quite another thing. I see no direct evidence for the idea that the emotional mechanisms in question are, in fact, even approximately utility maximizing for the individuals involved, never mind from a larger deliberative perspective.

It is more than possible that people's attention regulating system will be engaged, say, by a candidate with a colorful sexual history while remaining dormant for some other candidate who manages to couch a radical proposal in soothing language. Our neurological systems were evolved to assess threat from noises in the jungle, not the vastly more complex (and recent) phenomena of modern democratic politics. There is little reason to think that they would be well adapted to the task. Indeed, with the rise of scientifically precise political communication strategies, it is truly an open question as to whether anxiety's function has become more a convenient lever of political manipulation than an adaptive mode for managing our political environment. All of this is only to say that if we want to make strong normative claims about the efficiency or adequacy of a given emotional response, we will have to find some way to connect it back to deliberative quality.

Aggregation

Put informally, the logic of the aggregation argument is that even if most individual voters are uninformed and make many mistakes, in the aggregate, these mistakes will tend to cancel out. The argument comes in two basic varieties: Either most voters have at least some information so that on average, they can do better than if they picked strictly at random; or some voters have substantial information and that the great masses are so random that this small group of informed voters is able to get its signals through the noise. In the first case, if the votes are even only slightly better than random, with sufficient numbers, the group's decision will converge toward the right answer. In the case of the numbers involved in the national electorate, this "slightly better than random" can be slight indeed.

Page and Shapiro (1992), for example, persuasively demonstrate that aggregate public opinion is much more stable and less capricious than one might expect if we focused exclusively on the considerable instability and context dependence of individual opinions. In effect, they argue that democratic minimalists make a basic logical error by inferring the incompetence of the *citizenry* from the (putative) incompetence of most *citizens*. Doing so commits the fallacy of composition.

Erikson, MacKuen, and Stimson (2002) make a structurally similar argument. They develop a macrostructural model that treats electorates, politicians, and governments as unitary actors, and find that the electorate behaves in a fairly reliable, stable, and intuitively reasonable way, and that politicians and government respond in kind:

We concur with the usual empirical assessments regarding the bleak distribution of political awareness, interest, and sophistication within the American electorate ... Our claim instead is that the macro-level dynamics are driven by an electorate where, in the aggregate, the more politically capable citizens possess dominant influence ... The interactions between the ignorant and the knowledgeable ... make aggregation more exponential than additive. *As thoughtful argument meets the vacuous, in daily conversation and in elite debate, the thoughtfulness gains weight with each repetition. At the end of the day, the weight of sophistication gains enormous power* ... Thus, three aspects of macro politics, taken together, account for the disproportionate power of sparse political intelligence. First, to the degree that people are inattentive, their perceptions and behavior tend to cancel each other out, contributing to their disappearance from the macro-level picture. Second, to the degree people hold information, they use it rather than throw it away when making political judgments. Third, it requires only a small proportion of individuals to change in response to their political environment in order to create the macro-level dynamics. (429–32: emphasis added)

It is important to note, however, that all of the micro level explanations offered here for the macro outcomes are purely speculative. Erickson, MacKuen, and Stimson (EMS) have no explicit bridging theory between the micro and macro levels, nor any test of the connections they propose. Rather than evidence in support of their theory, these claims are actually abductive conjectures *from* their macro results. Obviously, deliberative democrats would be delighted to have evidence that the seemingly reasonable connection, for example, between the ideological "mood" of the electorate and the laws that get enacted exists because thoughtful argument triumphed over "the vacuous." Such triangulating evidence would powerfully warrant the belief that the deliberative system was working well. Erickson, MacKuen, and Stimson, however, do not really provide such evidence. Thus, we should be hesitant about inferring that the seemingly reasonable connections they demonstrate are anything more than plausible or reasonable *prima facie*.[12]

Indeed, Erickson, MacKuen, and Stimson's "more politically capable citizens [who] possess dominant influence" are also much more likely to be rich, educated, middle-aged, white, male, ideologues.[13] So it is hardly an unqualified good that less politically capable citizens find their failure to fall into these social categories correlating with "their disappearance from the macro-level picture." Althaus shows that the "miracle of aggregation" is seldom a free, democratic grace, since political knowledge is unequally distributed in the populace (2003: 17). Thus, we should be

---

[12] EMS show that changes in ideological "mood" drive policy changes, but whether those moods have some rational basis beyond the vague urge to slow down after change, we do not know. Similarly, they show that the public holds incumbents responsible for economic performance, but whether they really are responsible in some way that bears on the counterfactual of the vote choice is not clear (e.g., a supply side oil shock that would have hit any incumbent). The macro account makes a big leap in claiming that "errors" really are being cancelled out in anything but the most general sense, that people "use" their information in a rational way (see the discussion of heuristics earlier), or that being knowledgeable should yield "dominant influence" given the other things that knowledge tracks. Huckfeldt (2001) does find that people have some tendency to defer to the more informed among their trusted political discussants. Needless to say, though, we would need much more and much more direct evidence to confidently infer that the macro polity findings emerge from the deliberative and informational micro mechanisms claimed for them, and thus that they should be regarded as anything more than not obviously unreasonable.

[13] In the U.S., they also tend to be married, Republicans, from the coasts, and urban or suburban areas (Althaus 2003: 17).

especially cautious about assuming that the plausibly rational macro connections that EMS find emerge from high quality deliberation rather than the hydraulics of social power.[14]

Page and Shapiro (1992) make arguments that are structurally similar to Erickson, MacKuen, and Stimson, demonstrating the general stability of aggregate public opinion, and arguing for the prima facie plausibility of the larger changes. To their enormous credit, though, they recognize that they cannot cut to the heart of the matter without getting their scientific hands dirty with openly normative analysis. After enumerating the challenges inherent in cleanly distinguishing between instances of educating and manipulating the public, they write:

> Still, the subject is so important to any serious discussion of public opinion and democracy that the attempt is worth making. Accordingly, we have done our best...to assess the extent to which the public appears to have been educated, misled, or manipulated, and to uncover systematic ways in which helpful or misleading information and interpretations may be conveyed. (357)

The analysis that follows is very well executed and enormously valuable as an example of what, later on, I will call *procedural social criticism* (i.e., the critic does not try to make a direct contribution to a substantive debate, but rather criticizes the procedural conditions surrounding its deliberative quality). The only problems are that Page and Shapiro's approach (like EMS's) leaves the process of rational aggregation in a black box, and thus sets a very low bar for considering the public rational. In effect, if we can warrant that the public has not been grossly manipulated and we can generate some plausible rationale for a significant shift in public opinion, then the public is deemed presumptively rational. Combining standard opinion polls and historical case studies gives them leverage on some questions, but like Erickson, MacKuen, and Stimson, they can get no direct leverage on the micro mechanisms of deliberative opinion change, and thus cannot warrant its specifically deliberative character. The main limits to their analyses, then, do not lie in the essential contestability of normative analysis, but more crucially in resting

---

[14] Althaus finds that "After controlling for information effects, collective opinion tends to become less approving of presidents and Congress, more dovish and interventionist on foreign policy, less conservative on social, environmental, and equal rights issues, and more conservative on morality issues and questions about the proper limits of government activity" (24). He is quick to admit, though, that these corrections themselves do not necessarily reveal "enlightened" preferences in some deep deliberative sense. Rather, they represent something like a more equal notion of aggregative political preferences.

entirely on indirect, macro evidence judged in third-party terms. That is only to say that if we want to evaluate the specifically deliberative quality of public opinion, we shall have to include studies of deliberation per se.

SURVEYING DELIBERATIVE COMPETENCE

All of the extant strategies for redeeming the public hinge on cashing out its specifically deliberative potential. But Zaller claims to show that citizens are incapable of meaningful deliberation. As we saw earlier, his theory stipulates that they do not "think, reason, or deliberate about politics" – and that is just for purposes of answering simple survey questions. If he is even approximately right about the cognitive limitations that they display in performing such simple tasks, it might seem preposterous to think that they are capable of the deeper kind of deliberation that would warrant the macro–micro link discussed in the previous section. Indeed, the heuristics and OLM arguments do not really contradict the claim that citizens are incapable of much deliberation, and the emotions argument claims that they are capable of sustaining such attention only intermittently and individualistically (i.e., the normative theory is "rational choice").The aggregation arguments are ambiguous about mechanisms, and the claims that they make for deliberation are largely speculative. All four of these attempts to redeem the public have a role to play in the deliberative system. As with Mackie's defense of aggregative democracy in Chapter 4, however, their value in defending democracy hinge on redeeming the specifically deliberative quality of the public. Indeed, there is a sense in which all four share some of the assumptions that motivate Converse and Zaller, specifically in presuming that democratic competence is akin to consumer competence, and that reasoning consists in choosing within a partisan oligopoly.

To the extent that Zaller allows for anything that looks like reasoning, it is in mechanically responding to elite information in the manner of a partisan ideologue. In Chapter 5, however, we saw that very substantial portions of the citizenry become disaffected and de-mobilized by the very idea of politics as partisan tribalism or interest group markets. By failing to account for this source of disengagement and heterogeneity in contextual motives for participation, scholars fell prey to the fundamental attribution error. They mistakenly assumed that if citizens are not motivated to vote or work on a campaign, they are surely not the "type" to be motivated to deliberate. Instead, the opposite is true. As Kant warned us, the status quo can become a self-fulfilling prophecy, with unsatisfactory institutions actually *producing* the conditions that supposedly make changing those institutions impractical.

Something similar might be happening with Converse's notion of competence; many people may largely reject Converse's criteria for competent democratic citizenship, and think themselves reasonable and responsible in doing so. Of course, thinking does not necessarily make it so. But recall that in Chapter 5, expressing a desire for alternative forms of participation was not just self-rationalization or a case of respondents giving what they consider to be the socially desirable response. The hypothetical and real cases followed very similar patterns. If something similar is true here, many citizens may not be particularly invested in appearing competent on Converse's criteria – answering survey questions in a way that bespeaks partisan constraint – and yet prove competent on deliberative criteria. In Converse's criteria, expressing no opinion or responding "don't know," having moderate opinions (and hence making measurement error more likely to encompass both sides of an issue), and being open to contextual features of a policy rather than applying rigid ideological tests, all makes a citizen look incompetent. However, if competence consists in remaining intransigent on policy (i.e., opinion "stability") and being able to map one's ideological proximity to competitive elites, then ideologues will look more competent, if for no other reason than that their choices are easier and clearer in most cases as a consequence of being on the extremes. Such a definition risks circularity, or at least perverse normative logic. In a deliberative conception, on the other hand, remaining undecided on an issue in advance of deliberation, being willing to switch sides in light of deliberation, and exercising contextual judgment are often good things. Upon reflection, there is something very strange about a normative theory of democratic citizenship that renders such dispositions direct indicators of *in*competence.

For example, consider a Justice who only knows the basic outlines of the case to which she has granted a writ of certiorari. Now imagine that she has already made up her mind about how she is going to decide the case based on the ideology of the politician that appointed her. She completely skips reviewing the lower courts' decisions, reading briefs, hearing oral arguments, questioning counsel, and deliberating with her peers.[15] We

---

[15] Of course, some political scientists who study the Court suggest that something very much like this explains the vast majority of judicial behavior. Such phenomena rely heavily on massive selection pressures, and do not indicate that legal reasoning is ineffectual in the court system.

would consider that judge incompetent and unfit for her role. The fact that citizens do not necessarily come equipped with pre-debate snap judgments on all matters is not necessarily a bad thing if one believes that articulation, deliberation, process, and common standards matter.

That said, Chapter 5 only showed that those who are turned off by partisan politics selectively *wanted* to deliberate, not that they were actually capable of doing so. So Converse may still be right that competence in his sense is a precondition for any meaningful form of political thought or action. And Zaller may be right that citizens are incapable of deliberating in any distinctive sense of the term. So it is worth scrutinizing exactly what he means by that claim, and how he claims to establish it. Zaller argues that his theory:

[A]ctually reduces to two main ideas. The first is that individuals do not possess 'true attitudes,' in the usual technical sense of the term, on most political issues, but a series of considerations that are typically rather poorly integrated ... The other main idea in the RAS model is that an interaction between political awareness and political predispositions is fundamental to the process by which citizens use information from the political environment to form opinions. (308)

In itself, Zaller's first main idea is not only unembarrassing for deliberation; something very much like it is one of my principal points of departure. The inferentialist account developed in Chapters 3 and 4 agrees that people do not typically have 'true attitudes' in the 'usual technical sense.' Indeed, that is precisely why we deliberate. At least some people must have no opinion, be uncertain, or be persuadable for deliberation to have much point.

Translating into Zaller's terms, predispositions are akin to the various elements of people's webs of belief and the ex ante connections between them. And *articulation* is just the process of better integrating our "series of considerations." The scorekeeping interpretation of beliefs and desires avoids the overly literal notion that we "have" beliefs, as opposed to a compositionally infinite and flexible set that is entailed by a more manageable set: Anything that we have not thought about explicitly prior to having some discrete belief or attitude elicited. All of our beliefs and attitudes are subject to articulation, and hence to reverberating contextual influences and revisions. Indeed, a "true" attitude would be a limiting case – some belief that becomes so central and well integrated into our webs of beliefs that it is not likely to be affected by further articulation, even upon receiving new information. Nor is the lack of true attitudes in this sense necessarily troubling. Indeed, in many cases it would be troubling if people *did* have fixed ex ante attitudes.

Deliberative democracy with republican consultation means that, at least some of the time, people's attitudes, opinions, and preferences *should* be responsive to debate among political elites and deliberation among one's fellow citizens. But Zaller intends his point to be a bit more radical:

> If different frames or different question orders produce different results, it is not because one or the other has distorted the public's true feelings; it is rather because the public, having no fixed true opinion, implicitly relies on the particular question it has been asked to determine what exactly the issue is and what considerations are relevant to settling it. (95)

He can admit that people's opinion reports will move around in response to what I have been calling articulation, and still claim that without any stable notion of a 'true opinion' that representative democracy has no leverage point. Though he cares about normative issues of good democratic governance, Zaller is reluctant to engage them in a way that could help us differentiate between good and bad instances of articulation. For example, he criticizes Page and Shapiro (1992) for their willingness to engage normative issues that I had praised earlier: "The difficulty ... is that [their approach] requires independent knowledge of (or assumptions about) which interpretations and information are correct" (312).

Yet Zaller goes on to propose an alternative approach, "defin[ing] elite domination as a situation in which elites induce citizens to hold opinions that they would not hold if aware of the best available information and analysis" (313). He then uses this concept to discuss his "parable of purpleland" in which elite factions correspond to citizen factions in a way that allows a well-functioning media to help the populace avoid elite domination.

But notice three things about this argument: First, it relies on something very much like my concept of a latent (Chapter 3) in defining what citizens *would* believe were they "aware of the best available information and analysis." So, on the concept of "true opinions," he gives back with one hand what, he has just prominently taken away with the other. Second, his definition of that latent has obvious normative content insofar as it relies on the "best" available information and analysis. And third, his notion of avoiding elite domination is clearly offered in the service of a normative conception of good democratic governance – one that takes ex ante personal and partisan preferences for granted, and operates on something like the market model. So Zaller is not doing anything fundamentally different from the move that I made in Chapters 3 and 4. My normative criteria are different. I proceed from a deliberative conception of good democratic governance, rather than the market model; and, correspondingly, my notion of the latent counterfactual relies on social articulation, rather than completely individual criteria. I will defend my criteria over Zaller's later on, but for now, it is only important to note that the logical structure of our arguments is not fundamentally different.

One apparent advantage of Zaller's "purpleland" approach is that it does not really require that citizens "think, reason, or deliberate" in any substantive sense. As long as we can establish functional alignment between elite and citizen factions, it does not really matter how we get there. So Zaller's finding of "mechanical" responsiveness to elite cues is not necessarily problematic for his theory in the way that it seems to threaten deliberative theory. But it is clearly fallacious to infer a lack of thinking, reasoning, or deliberation merely from mechanical responsiveness to new information. On an inferentialist account, reasons can function as causes that are likely to produce highly patterned (i.e., apparently mechanical) responses. For example, imagine two groups of people (one good at math, the other bad) doing mathematical problems in which new information is revealed. The group that is good at math will appear to respond more mechanically to the new information (by all converging on the same answer), even though they are also thinking, reasoning, and deliberating about the new information *better* than the ones who are bad at math (who are making many different kinds of mistakes).

Deliberation does not require that we somehow operate outside of the causal nexus – indeed, it presumes the opposite. If socially articulating our webs of belief operates as advertised, we should observe patterns in responsiveness to such articulation. Indeed, we might expect something observationally similar to what Zaller finds: Those with the most elaborated webs of belief may be unlikely to have as much to render coherent in the face of new information, and those with the least elaborated webs may not have the density of connections that would allow a new piece of information to reverberate as powerfully through that web. So we might expect those in the middle to realize the largest changes in the typical case.

The more problematic issue emerging out of Zaller's findings is that the response patterns appear to be almost entirely partisan and elite driven in nature. On the "one right set" interpretation developed in Chapter 4, we might expect (and welcome) a partisan pattern, but only if we had reason to believe that antecedent deliberative processes had already reduced the set of alternatives to those that would be hard to further distinguish on deliberative grounds. For example, much has been made of ideological voting on the U.S. Supreme Court (Segal and Spaeth 1993). But there is massive selection on the kinds of cases that reach the Court, with the obviousness of decisive legal grounds declining as cases move up the chain. So it should not be terribly surprising or troubling that votes tend to track the ideological dispositions of the judges in such cases.[16]

Clearly there are less dramatic selection pressures on the sorts of issues that make it onto standard political surveys. Yet they may be substantial, and Zaller does not really attempt to address the issue, calling into question the worries over the apparently elite driven nature of public opinion. In the simple, temporal sense, he is clearly right that elites lead in disseminating information. But if political actors are acting in the shadow of anticipated latent public responses to the various policy proposals and information streams, there is an important sense in which Zaller's dramatic statements about citizens being incapable of thinking, reasoning, or deliberating are deeply misleading. He never tests the counterfactual in which elites are not heavily chastened ex ante, and so his results are observationally equivalent to the alternate scenario in which citizens are quite capable of independent thought. And if they are, his results cannot speak (without circularity) to the question of how much deliberative competence they are likely to evince outside of the context of an individual opinion survey – that is, in more elaborated deliberative mini-publics.

As Robert Dahl noted long ago, it would be easy to underestimate the enormous background consensus that provides structure for manifest political conflict in democracies:

[P]oliticians subject to elections must operate within the limits set both by their own values, as indoctrinated members of the society, and by their expectations about what policies they can adopt and still be re-elected. In a sense, what we ordinarily describe as democratic 'politics' is merely the chaff. It is the surface manifestation, representing superficial conflicts. (1956: 132)

The way that Dahl characterizes the common background of democratic politics is akin to the common social resources that drive Brandom's game of giving and asking for reasons. Those background resources allow deliberation to proceed without grinding to a halt every time citizens encounter differing premises, beliefs, values, or commitments since they are "prior to politics, beneath it, enveloping it, restricting it, conditioning it" (Dahl 1956: 132). Deliberation proceeds by exploring opportunities

---

[16] The Court generally does not grant cert if the matter of law is obvious and clear ex ante (they can only consider a very small number of cases). And yet, in 2010, 38 percent of cases were decided unanimously, though presumably some of those were pulled up to correct clear legal mistakes by lower level courts.

for further inferential articulation and greater coherence when we encounter such differences or need to incorporate new information. Since standard opinion surveys do not provide much scope for articulation (especially *social* articulation), it should not be surprising that ideological responsiveness should predominate among ideologues. This inferentialist interpretation illuminates both why Zaller's findings probably bespeak less elite domination than they might seem, and why his results hardly demonstrate that citizens are ill equipped to engage in more elaborated deliberation.[17]

In fact, Zaller never actually tests, in any direct way, the proposition that citizens think, reason, and deliberate. That they do not is *not* an "implication of the model." In one sense, it is an assumption of the model, but even putting the matter this way is misleading. It would be more accurate to say that his model remains agnostic about the matter. He does not explicitly model reasoning. But some of the processes that he leaves in a black box may or may not involve reasoning, and elites may or may not pre-emptively respond to what they perceive to be citizens' latent capacity for reasoning about politics (heavily biasing against directly observing that capacity in action). Thus, the "normatively unappealing" "implication" of his model is notably undersupported as a positive claim.

Indeed, Zaller comes close to acknowledging that he does not test for this crucial (putative) implication of the model. He notes his model's:

failure to provide any mechanism for integration of information that has been acquired...Some people, and probably most, surely do build up complexly differentiated cognitions that cannot be adequately captured by my simple notion of a consideration ... What would be most desirable, then, is not the RAS model I have proposed, but a Receive-Accept-*Integrate*-Sample Model. (280–81)

Yet Zaller almost immediately backs off of the enormous implications of this concession. His reasons for doing so make sense on their own terms,

---

[17] My argument here is not the same as Zaller's Purpleland argument because the latter relies on a happy functional accident versus gyroscopic, anticipatory, or retrospective/ evolutionary representation, which has different deliberative properties. The latter also allows us to assess change over time, between representation relationships, as well as institutional variance in how things are likely to work well. Nor does the inferentialist notion of constraint reduce back down to Converse. First, the inferentialist setup is coherentist, whereas Converse's is foundationalist. Second, Converse focuses on elite-like constraint, whereas on the inferentialist account, the masses can have shifting notions of constraint that do not track the main partisan ideologies. Finally, on the inferentialist account, constraint is a social–normative category, rather than a purely formal notion of individual constraint. Thanks to Lisa Disch for pressing me on this point.

but they highlight the gap between his specifically scientific contributions and the normative implications that are thought to flow from them:

> I doubt, however, that theoretical elaboration ... along these [*Integrate*] lines will become fruitful to analysts of public opinion until we learn how to measure ... among other things, the volume and complexity of discrete cognitions ... These sorts of improvements in measurement capacity *in mass surveys* are not ... immediately in prospect. So, although I readily acknowledge phenomena that the axioms of the RAS framework cannot presently accommodate ... I do not see any reason for opinion researchers to make these elaborations until the data necessary for their testing become available. (281)

When Zaller speaks of integrating discrete cognitions, he is basically talking about *reasoning*, and more specifically, what I have been calling *inferential articulation*. I agree that it would be difficult (though not impossible) to measure such processes in the context of mass surveys. But that fact speaks much more to the limitations of mass surveys than to the limitations of democratic citizens. Zaller does not appear to see that the "normatively unappealing" implications of his model do not hinge on the variation that we see in mass surveys responses, but rather on what this variation can tell us about less directly observable but more normatively relevant processes. As it turns out, on its own, his model can tell us remarkably little about democratic competence.

Again, unless we investigate the specifically deliberative processes that generate public opinion, we simply cannot claim to be able to assess citizen competence in the relevant sense. Over the last few decades, James Fishkin has developed and deployed the idea of deliberative opinion polls™ (DOPs) to remediate what he sees as the evident normative shortcomings of standard public opinion surveys. Fishkin argues that DOPs emulate what the mass public would decide were it able to deliberate adequately. On this view, the main remaining problem for mass democracy is not really epistemic, but rather technical and volitional. Can DOPs be leveraged to influence mass opinion, and thereby voting and policy outcomes? The analysis here seems to support that idea, but the issue turns out to be considerably more complicated.

DELIBERATIVE POLLING'S LEGITIMATION CRISIS

To see why deliberative polling and other mini-public forums cannot simply serve as presumptive substitutes for standard public opinion polls (or other "entry points" for deliberative fora, 2009), it is necessary to reexamine the problem that deliberative forums were originally designed to solve. Almost ninety years ago, Walter Lippmann (1922: 144) crisply articulated the first crucial component of the problem:

As congenital amateurs our quest for truth consists in stirring up the experts, and forcing them to answer any heresy that has the accent of conviction. In such a debate we can often judge who has won the dialectical victory, but we are virtually defenseless against a false premise that none of the debaters has challenged, or a neglected aspect that none of them has brought into the argument.

Relative to most status quo opinion formation, even minimally well-designed deliberative forums greatly subsidize our access to experts, "stir them up" in perspicuous ways, and provide us with highly augmented resources to judge who has won the dialectical victory. Bracketing Lippmann's admittedly crucial caveat (for the time being): In my view, existing deliberative research renders it implausible to think that deliberative opinion would not tend to be more informed, better informed, and more considered, at least on average.

Online processing of the background materials and information in the sessions, combined with most citizens' low baseline of information, practically guarantees that their judgments will be based on substantially more information on average (Neblo 2000). And that is to say nothing of the direct evidence for knowledge gains in terms of recall (e.g., Esterling et al. 2011a). The case for this being a "better informed" opinion is, of course, less straightforward since it hinges on one's definition of better. Again though, bracketing Lippmann's caveat for now, the average participant will have been exposed to a much wider range of information, arguments, and perspectives deemed relevant by experts *and their fellow citizens* than under status quo conditions. And if central versus peripheral processing is an important criterion for "more considered" opinions, then only the most determined skeptic would doubt that deliberative opinion is more considered vis-à-vis standard public opinion interviews. The average respondent to a phone poll has not devoted three minutes of central processing to many of the issues about which she or he will be asked. Countless tapes and transcripts of deliberative sessions show large numbers of participants routinely engaging in exchanges that could not be sustained via peripheral processing. And if one cares about the deliberative goals of forming and justifying public opinions in a distinctly public way, rather than merely aggregating private opinion, again, the prima facie evidence in favor of deliberative forums versus standard polling is overwhelming.

I readily admit that this précis of my reasoning is compressed and peremptory.[18] Here, however, I do not offer it mainly to settle the empirical questions, but rather to make a prima facie case for why they should get lower critical priority than the literature has given them. My primary goal is to facilitate more effective criticism by shifting attention to what I take to be a much more important and vastly weaker spot in the case for deliberative forums. If my sketch here is right, minimally well-designed deliberative forums will, in expectation, yield higher quality public opinion relative to relying on the ambient political culture. And this is likely true even when we reintroduce Lippmann's worry over false premises and neglected considerations among elites, since we have even more limited access and attention in our everyday political lives. However, within deliberative forums, the effects of being captured by false premises and neglected considerations are likely to be larger than under status quo opinion formation, since the denser set of common influences on participants will induce more highly correlated errors. In itself, this issue is significant only to the extent that we are risk averse, and even then, we would need to trade it off against the broader gains in expected opinion quality.

A more serious problem, though, becomes apparent when we recognize that correlated errors create powerful incentives for interest groups and partisan elites to try to manipulate deliberative forums. Their smaller scale and captive audience (i.e., their potential for correlated errors) make them an extremely high-leverage/low-cost way to try to influence policy, versus trying to move the broader political culture. And dramatically more so precisely to the extent that deliberative forums are more directly empowered or invested with the imprimatur of representing the authentic voice of the people. But if special interests could intervene to change the distribution of errors substantially, and we were not reliably able to know when they had succeeded, then the simple version of the argument for the presumptive superiority of deliberative opinion would collapse.

It is important to note how the elements of this critique combine in a way that is not merely additive. The potential for manipulation, in itself, is not a particularly powerful objection, since the ambient political culture is rife with manipulation. Similarly, the potential for correlated errors, in itself, is not a particularly powerful objection, since there are good reasons to think that the overall error rate typically goes down with

---

[18] I discuss these issues at greater length in Neblo (2000, 2007b, 2011b).

deliberation. And blanket objections to attributing some scientific and civic status to deliberative forums beg the question, since the claim is that DOPs *deserve* such status. It is only with the interaction of these factors that a truly major problem emerges. And even then, if public officials and members of the public can find a way to distinguish between rigged deliberation and high-quality forums, then the problem would become much less acute.

Presumably something like this last thought led Fishkin to trademark "Deliberative Opinion Polls," as well as to settle on a high degree of uniformity in their features, and rely on a relatively small set of trusted insiders to design, execute, and analyze them. He has been criticized for all of this, but tight, proprietary branding and a program for quality control linked to that brand are the obvious ways to distinguish DOPs from those who might want to hijack the process, or at least muddy the waters. The problem, though, is that proprietary branding and insularity end up displacing the locus of democratic worries onto the brand itself.

Anyone organizing a deliberative forum has a legitimate need to appropriately delimit the scope of the deliberations and insulate the background materials from manipulation and bias, for example. Yet we need some set of procedures for warranting that these goals have been adequately accomplished. Since the relevant procedural standards are *democratic* procedures, the whole idea of a proprietary brand starts to become functionally paradoxical if pressed too far. Technocratic responses to democratic problems cannot be technocratic all the way down, even (or perhaps especially) when they claim to be technologies *of* democracy.

In trying to fend off one set of problems, reformers can easily create another. Without carefully embedding deliberative forums in a larger system of transparent democratic contestation, practitioners are sure to induce a "legitimation crisis" in representations of deliberative public opinion *even if* they have all of the properties claimed for them (e.g., high-quality samples, insulation from special interests, a wide range of expert input, free and fair deliberative exchanges, etc.).[19]

---

[19] Habermas' (1975) book *Legitimation Crisis* revises standard Marxist theory by laying out what he sees as the distinct crisis tendencies in welfare-state capitalism. His discourse theory of law and democracy (1996) was developed as an alternative model of legitimation that tries to avoid these processes. Since his theory does not lean as heavily on organized deliberative forums as Fishkin's does, it is not clear that my critique here speaks to deliberative democracy more generally.

All deliberative forums, then, face a deep tension in application: They must remain democratically accountable to the broader political system without becoming assimilated to it. The danger of assimilation comes in three principal forms. First, as noted earlier, if specific deliberative forums are too democratically endogenous – if everything is up for grabs locally – then they may not be able to provide much distinctive value vis-à-vis the broader political system. For example, I once attended a forum about how best to manage the privacy of medical records while also promoting potentially life-saving research. One of the sessions evolved into a completely different discussion because one of the participants believed that the U.S. government had bioengineered the AIDS virus and deliberately introduced it into the African–American community as part of a eugenics initiative. Such arguments should be given a hearing in the broader political system. Some conspiracy theories turn out to be true (this man cited the Tuskegee experiment as precedent to motivate his argument), and some initially fringe ideas eventually become common wisdom. But in the context of specific deliberative forums, allowing every such issue that comes up to dominate the discussion, in effect, dissolves deliberative forums back into the larger political discourse. If so, then familiar problems of scale, complexity, motivation, and competence return. Deliberative opinion loses its focus and its distinct normative potential.

Thus, even as they try to remain democratically accountable, organizers must circumscribe the scope, form, content, and procedures of deliberative forums to maintain the forums' coherence and distinctive role in the larger political system. But doing so opens the door to the second principal form of becoming assimilated to the broader political system: Strategic cooptation by elites (and, less acutely, their inadvertent biases). So there are good reasons to worry about whether DOP experiments can serve as a reliable model for a more deliberatively empowered future.

However, the obvious way to remain democratically accountable while providing adequate resistance to bias and strategic manipulation is to expose every element of the process to public review and criticism. Critics' efforts at contestation are an essential part of *alleviating* the dialectical tendencies toward deliberative democracy's own version of a legitimation crisis. They play a crucial role by standing in for the demos, monitoring for strategic cooptation, inadvertent bias, and so on. Deliberative practitioners should welcome such critique, and even encourage it.

However, there remains at least one more dialectical turn of the screw. Even if vigorous public review and criticism can help prevent strategic actors from capturing deliberative forums (or exposing them when they do), those actors will still have strong incentives to prevent deliberative opinion from overcoming their advantage in the broader political system. That is, even if they cannot *add* to their power by coopting deliberative opinion, they will seek to neutralize any deliberative effects adverse to their interests. And, ironically, facilitating vigorous public review and criticism provide ideal means to do so. Precisely to the extent that public review and criticism is open and vigorous, interested actors can feign the role of the social critic to muddy the waters and "jam" any signals unfavorable to their position (Minozzi 2011).

In principle, such a process may be self-correcting. Perhaps the cure for the ills of democracy is more democracy. But then we are thrown back on a second-order version of the problems of scale, complexity, motivation, and citizen competence in mass democracy that deliberative forums were supposed to alleviate in the first place. Displacing those problems onto another level may attenuate them, but it hardly eliminates them.

So to summarize: This deliberative "legitimation crisis" emerges from an initial dilemma, one of the horns of which then branches off into a trilemma. Deliberative forums must remain democratically accountable to the larger political system without being assimilated to it. Democratic accountability pushes deliberative forums to become more internally democratic, but that risks making them too diffuse and chaotic, at which point they begin to dissolve back into the broader political discourse. So someone needs to make decisions about structure, content, and limits to the process, and such decisions risk cooptation, bias, and strategic manipulation (or a retreat from democratic accountability). Vigorous public review and criticism can help, but it opens the door to strategic jamming, which makes it difficult and costly for the public to differentiate between high-quality deliberation and manipulated opinion, thus recapitulating the first-order dilemmas of mass democratic politics. I see no general solution to this interlocking series of dilemmas, and on theoretical grounds, I doubt that one exists.

This argument is not meant as a counsel of despair. It is only intended to establish the claim that we cannot reasonably expect mini-public forums (DOPs or other versions) to serve as a miracle cure for what ails mass democracy. Doing so asks too much of them, but more importantly, it also misunderstands their role and real potential in the larger deliberative system of democracy.

Deliberative forums are the most promising institutional innovation in recent memory. However, by understanding the structure of the trade-offs that such forums face, we can make more sensible choices about how to embed them in the larger deliberative system of democracy, and about how to adapt them to various functions within that system. What I called a dilemma is not a true dilemma; or rather, it only appears as such in the abstract. In practice, some elements of the problem may be less acute or easier to ameliorate than others, so that we would have good reasons to favor concessions in one area rather than another.

PUBLIC OPINION AND MINI-PUBLICS FORUMS IN THE DELIBERATIVE SYSTEM

Indeed, we already know a fair bit about which problems are likely to be more acute in various circumstances, and how we might experiment with institutional variations to further realize the potential of deliberative forums. For example, the tension between democratic accountability and structure need not be resolved in one go. Organizers could distribute the burden of accountability across time and participants. Rather than moving from organizers and experts to citizen forums in one step, we could begin a project with very informal, unstructured brainstorming or focus-group style input from citizens, organize pilot forums designed to elicit feedback and criticism, and only then run the main forums in light of democratic input, accountability, and contestation along the way.

It is hardly fanciful to expect criticism and contestation from average citizens, if it is sincerely elicited by the organizers. I once helped organize a project in which groups within the pilot forums *unanimously* rejected the original set of policy choices that the experts and organizers had worked up, generating an entirely new and very attractive option that went on to win plurality support in the main forums (Damschroder et al. 2007). Moreover, forum participants and a fresh sample of citizens could be recruited to evaluate and criticize the process and organizer reports on the forums ex post as well. Thus, relatively simple procedures could be used to maintain robust democratic accountability throughout the process without the forums degenerating into a free-for-all.

The anecdote about participants in our pilot project resisting the original elite-determined set of choices raises an important caveat. While it is reasonable to worry about elite manipulation to a point, we should not sell citizen participants short. Participants can and do resist the information, frames, and other elements provided for them in deliberative forums. For example, progressive critics pre-emptively attacked a recent America Speaks forum on the federal budget deficit, accusing one of its sponsors of rigging the briefing materials and response formats. Yet the participants ended up moving sharply toward a package of policies favored by progressives. Whether one believes that this forum's design was an active attempt at manipulation, a case of inadvertent bias, or a reasonable choice among many in presenting the options, the frame and format here were hardly destiny. The social critic's reasonable concern over protecting citizens from elite manipulation can easily devolve into a well-intentioned elitism of its own, treating one's fellow citizens as dupes or children incapable of independent critical thought.[20]

Critics reasonably worry that biases in the background information presented in deliberative sessions may unduly influence participants. Yet there are good reasons to believe that participants are hardly passive receptacles, waiting for organizers to tell them what is true and what to do. A recent study (Esterling et al. 2011a), for example, found a distinct and substantial deliberative effect on gains in policy specific factual knowledge. That is, participating in deliberation induced knowledge gains beyond those realized by participants randomly selected to receive only the background materials. Crucially, however, those distinct knowledge gains were not driven by the content of the deliberative sessions themselves, but rather by living in their shadow. People who knew that they were going to confront experts and deliberate with their fellow citizens trained up in anticipation by seeking out more information about the topic (and politics more generally) on their own. Far from merely waiting to be told what was important about the topic, participants wanted to judge for themselves whether the information was balanced, and chose to talk to friends, consult trusted sources of information, and otherwise plug into the larger, less-regulated deliberative system. Such external preparation would make it much harder to distort deliberative opinion.

Finally, one particular institutional innovation for deliberative forums strikes me as having particular promise for helping with several facets of

---

[20] Some of the Internet and blog based attacks in this episode were, in my view, savagely unfair to the organizers and condescending to the citizen-participants, amounting to a pre-emptive attempt at "jamming" the results. Page and Jacobs (2010) released a much more temperate and scholarly white paper pressing similar arguments. I happen to disagree with some of their claims, but they did raise reasonable concerns. For example, one of the key survey questions about how much to cut the deficit started at zero and moved up from there, even though many reasonable people having been arguing that, in the context of the recession, we should actually be increasing deficit spending, at least temporarily (e.g., Paul Krugman has been pressing this argument for the last two years).

the problem simultaneously. Rather than asking deliberating groups or individuals to simply register a summary opinion after deliberating, the forums could be organized around producing more elaborated artifacts of the deliberative process, representing the rationales behind deliberative opinion. With colleagues I have begun experimenting with having deliberating groups use concept mapping and online visualization tools to register not only their group's policy recommendation, but also to create a record of the reasoning that led them to that recommendation.

This approach has several potential advantages for lessening the tensions that drive deliberation's legitimation crisis. First, it better represents some deliberative theorists' concern with making public the *reasons* for a democratic choice, rather than mere preferences, no matter how well-informed and publicly spirited their backroom origins may be. Second, it provides more direct evidence that deliberative opinion is more considered (and may actually encourage more and better consideration). Third, it creates an artifact of the decision-making process that is more substantive, transparent, and subject to review and criticism. Fourth, such opportunities for review and criticism might engender greater trust in the results among those who were not able to participate simply because they *could* review the process in principle. Fifth, it might engender trust directly among those who choose to actually engage in such review (or allow them to appropriately discount deliberative opinion should it not earn their trust). Sixth, reviewing the process and reasoning allows citizens who could not participate directly to do so in a virtual way. Such forums could actually *subsidize* broader participation, rather than demotivating it by functioning as a black-boxed substitute. Seventh, they could facilitate uptake of deliberative opinion in the broader population by helping non-participants sort themselves more appropriately. Non-participants face an ecological inference problem in trying to decide how summary results from DOPs should affect *them*, as individuals, rather than aggregate opinion. This ecological inference problem represents a major theoretical and practical impediment to Fishkin's hope for deliberative to influence broader opinion. And finally, such "process output" forums would be more robust to jamming, since citizens who participate virtually would be less reliant on elites to review and criticize the process.

Even if suggestions like these work reasonably well, new problems with applied deliberation are sure to emerge. The tensions internal to deliberative legitimation admit to no general, permanent solution. So it is important to investigate the relationship between deliberative opinion and public opinion measured by other means, especially standard opinion polls. When both more or less converge, the strengths of each shore up the weaknesses in a way similar to triangulation between experimental and natural settings research. In such cases, we have a warrant for believing that heuristics, online processing, emotional regulation of attention, and the mechanisms of opinion aggregation are working in ways that are congruent with the normative goals of democratic theory, and for believing that the mini-public has not been captured or jammed in a way that compromises its deliberative content.[21] Althaus's research is particularly valuable here, since we might also compare deliberative opinion to his simulated standard opinion, which corrects for information effects driven by social inequality. If deliberative opinion converges with such corrected opinion estimates, then again, we have strong grounds for thinking that it represents something like the considered opinion of the public.

Some critics have complained that if deliberative opinion ends up converging with standard opinion, then we have wasted resources on a scale quite different than with standard polling. Yet the expense of deliberative consultation, while hardly trivial, is typically tiny compared to the potential costs and benefits implicated in the policies themselves. Moreover, deliberation can be quite valuable even if it is not decisive in altering policy. Policy makers can be more confident that they have enacted policies that have the informed support of their constituents, which is hardly of marginal value in a democracy. Those constituents, in turn, can be more confident that they *should* support the policies that have been enacted – that they have earned legitimacy. Moreover, there may be downstream benefits in terms of trust in government more generally, support for policies when fiscal or political conditions change, giving elected officials incentives to behave in more civics textbook like ways and an improved sense of efficacy among citizens, among many others. And these processes are the sort that may reinforce themselves over time.

The more difficult case is when deliberative opinion and standard opinion diverge. Fishkin has argued forcefully for preferring deliberative opinion, but as I have argued in the previous section, I do not think that his arguments go through as a general matter, but rather have to be

---

[21] Of course, convergence will not protect us against them being captured in ways similar to the distortions of the ambient political culture. Here, though we are in a situation of hegemonic domination, where the social critic and struggles for recognition are the only recourse over time.

argued on a case basis, in the face of external critique. Page and Jacobs (2011) invert Fishkin's argument, claiming that when deliberative and standard opinion diverge, we should almost always prefer opinion measured the traditional way. On standard deliberative grounds, I cannot agree: Public opinion with the strongest claim to serve its function in democratic legitimation will be formed and justified in a public way for the simple reason that majorities can tyrannize just as easily as much as any other person or group. Precisely to the extent that some public opinion scholars want more deference to democratic majorities (e.g., Jacobs and Shapiro 2000), it becomes all the more important for those majorities to meet the normative demands of public reason.

I see no reason to believe that the vagaries in the persuasion processes that exist in the ambient political culture are any less biased or problematic than those in a well-designed deliberative forum. So I see no general grounds for preferring one to the other without further inquiry. Perhaps social critics can persuade us that a given mini-public contained crucial biases, or conversely that interested parties have successfully "jammed" the signals from mini-publics, blocking them from influencing main stream opinion. Alternately, we may find that an easy–hard rationale dynamic has skewed standard public opinion away from solutions that rightly command the support of deliberative majorities, or that both policies belong in the "one right set." By consulting both deliberative and mass modes, however, we can realize huge efficiency gains through focusing critical attention and further public inquiry on those instances where they diverge.

CONCLUSION

In the aftermath of World War II, the problem of citizen competence assumed an urgency and substantive inflection that was qualitatively different from similar inquiries going back to Aristotle up through Mill, Tocqueville, and Dewey. In the United States and other Anglophone countries, however, the problem of citizen competence got transformed from a moral problem to one of information and efficiency. The general ignorance of mass publics raised anew questions about the fitness of the masses to rule, and underwrote retrenchment under the aegis of democratic minimalism and elitist theories of democracy. Deliberative theories appear especially naïve and aspirational from this perspective, pushing democratic expectations in precisely the wrong direction. But the case against the competence of the demos turned out to rest largely on the same question, begging presumptions about the market model and partisan ideology that confused matters on the motivation to deliberate as well. The public's input to the deliberative system cannot be assessed adequately without investigating deliberative quality directly. Yet neither is it the case that deliberative mini-publics can solve the problems of mass democracy on their own. The dialectics of deliberative legitimation mean that there are no closed, simple solutions apart from assessing the quality of deliberation in many forms throughout the deliberative system. Deliberative democracy is not an engineering problem to be solved once and for all, but rather an open-ended search for a better way to live together.

7

Conclusion: A Preface to Deliberative Democratic Theory

It would be easy to kill off political theory altogether in the name of empiricism and rigor. To do so would be of no service to the intellectual community. Political macroanalysis suffers from certain inherent difficulties; but we cannot afford to abandon it.

Robert Dahl

Why should there not be a patient confidence in the ultimate justice of the people? Is there any better, or equal, hope in the world?

Abraham Lincoln

How peculiar to a modern audience that Lincoln should have felt the need to justify democracy at his inaugural – the culminating toast at "democracy's feast." Perhaps even more striking is the sober, even somber, defense that he offers. We get no lofty encomium for democracy. Lincoln merely shifts the burden to those who would disdain what common citizens can accomplish, suggesting that we can hope for no more from the alternatives. He was realistic about the people and their capacities, yet he resolutely placed his hopes in their "virtue and vigilance," appealing to the better angels of our nature.

None of the arguments that I have developed in this book establish that citizens in mass democracies even remotely approximate some golden ideal of a deliberative democratic regime. Nor were those arguments meant to do so. Rather, I have argued that, whatever the "distance" to the ideal, deliberative democracy represents an ideal worth embracing; indeed, our practices and institutions bespeak the fact that we have already implicitly embraced it in large measure. That said, I have shown that there is surprisingly little reason to think that citizens in mass democracies fall so absurdly short of any meaningful deliberative democratic prerequisites as to render deliberative theories perversely utopian as guides to democratic *reform*.

Having removed these dismissive presumptions, we can get down to the task of assessing when and why elements of the deliberative system do and do not serve the functions assigned to them in democratic theory. That is to say, I hope to prompt and facilitate productive reengagement between political theory and empirical research. Democratic theory cannot responsibly ignore empirical and formal research relevant to its claims and premises. And empirical and formal research cannot responsibly reduce deliberative theory to a brittle simulacrum for purposes of more easily subjecting it to standard tools. Now that deliberative democracy's theoretical elaboration is relatively mature, our most urgent research questions center on adapting the theory to foreseeably favorable psychological, sociological, and institutional conditions – to address organizational questions going forward.

It is customary in conclusions to call for further research, and all the more so here because the book's main goal has been to remove barriers to cooperative research between theorists, empirical researchers, and deliberative practitioners. In a sense, the positive argument of the book sketches the outlines of a theory, with most of the answers to deliberative democracy's "organizational questions" to be developed by traveling along the path that has been opened up. But it is ambition enough if this book can serve as an envoy and under-laborer to theorists, social scientists, and deliberative reformers, clearing the ground a little and removing some of the impediments that have lain in the way of fruitful exchange between them. Those impediments have been substantial and costly.

Fifty years ago, Robert Dahl explained why it might be difficult to manage productive engagement in the aftermath of the behavioral revolution:

The empirical political scientist ... [now] finds it difficult and uncongenial to assume the historic burden of the political philosopher who attempted to determine, prescribe, elaborate, and employ ethical standards... The behaviorally minded student of politics is prepared to describe values as empirical data; but, qua 'scientist,' he seeks to avoid prescription or inquiry into the grounds on which judgments of value can properly be made. (1961: 771)

At best, we are left with a sharp division of labor, and at worst a push to kill off political theory altogether in the name of empiricism and rigor.

Dahl was far from comfortable with this historical transformation, and the epigraph makes clear that he did not want political theory to be killed off. Yet he was not sure how to move forward either. He subtitled his 1961 article on the behavioral movement an "epitaph for a monument to a successful protest." The protest had died out as a self-conscious protest movement precisely because of its overwhelming success, leaving behind an ambivalent legacy. There is more than a bit of "be careful what you ask for" about his discussion, even as he argues that the movement was generative and even necessary.

A few years earlier, Dahl had analyzed the flip side, claiming that, since the divorce, normative political theory had become unmoored from accountability to the realities of political practice. He did not necessarily hold political theory to the strict new standards of behavioral research, but he did argue that the widening gap made fruitful interaction difficult:

This is not to say that political theorists ... should necessarily prescribe and execute rigorous 'tests' for their key propositions or for the theory taken as a whole. But it would be interesting to see what would happen to the study of political theory if some such process were required as an intellectual exercise – if, in other words, the contemporary theorist regularly assumed the obligation to spell out for his reader what he would regard as an adequate test of the truth or falsity of his major empirical hypotheses, and at least present some survey of the evidence as he sees it ... Until political theorists take some such requirement rather more seriously than they typically do, it seems unlikely that political theory...will play the commanding role in political science, and indeed in social analysis generally, that it once did. The social sciences will move haltingly on, concerned often with a meticulous observation of the trivial, and political theory will take up permanent cohabitation with literary criticism. (1958: 97–98)

I have tried to take the obligation that Dahl presses on political theorists seriously, characterizing my view of the proper relationship between deliberative theory and empirical research, and surveying the evidence as I see it.

The current relationship between political theory and the social sciences is both better and worse than Dahl described. Certainly there has been some trend toward meticulously documenting and explaining the trivial. But laments to this effect are often overstated. Many empirically and formally oriented political scientists clearly continue to care about "big" questions, and consciously direct their talents and energies toward problems relevant to the concepts that occupy normative political theorists: Justice, freedom, order, equality, prosperity, democracy. The problems that emerge are not so much rooted in neglect as in sublimation. In

194 *Deliberative Democracy between Theory and Practice*

seeking both "to avoid prescription or inquiry into the grounds on which judgments of value can properly be made" and yet to remain relevant to those judgments of value, empirical scholars often end up defending normative positions on the basis of scientific expediency. The two orders are not fungible, and trying to make them so leads to confusions in both (Neblo 2004).

In an effort to sidestep the "inherent difficulties" in relating political theory to empirical research, many behavioral and formal scholars implicitly substitute a minimalist market model of democracy that appears to offer more empiricism and rigor by making democratic choice accountable only to the revealed (or at best, "fully informed") preferences of each individual citizen. But in avoiding one set of controversial assumptions, they commit to the correctness of a theory whose normative content is no less contestable and much more surreptitious. Recall that Zaller, for example, criticizes Page and Shapiro's method for assessing the quality of public discourse, and yet he builds normative criteria into his notion of what people would believe if they were aware of the "best" information and analysis available. It is not obvious that it is any easier to operationalize the concept of the "best" information and analysis than it is to measure deliberative quality.

But even if it were, Zaller's argument begs the question, since, from a deliberative perspective, he is conflating reliability and validity. Deliberativists claim that we must be able to hold each other to account because even well-informed majorities can tyrannize. If so, then reliably measuring what southerners under Jim Crow would have decided under "full information" is not entirely to the point, because it does not validly measure democratic legitimacy on the deliberative account. Even on strictly scientific grounds, we must subordinate the search for reliable measures of a concept to the search for *valid* measures of that concept. Anything else courts confusion and risks actively misleading us by giving us confidence in inferences that have no warrant. This is the sense in which the relationship between normative theory and the rest of the discipline is sometimes even worse than Dahl suggests.

Democratic minimalists and empiricists make a similar mistake in perseverating over the supposedly massive gap between deliberative ideals and realistic democratic aspirations. In Chapter 2, I argued that such criticisms missed their target in part because they do not take account of a system conception of deliberation, and in Chapters 5 and 6, I argued that mistaken assumptions about citizens' willingness and competence to participate in deliberation underwrite intuitions about the supposed utopianism of deliberative reform. But there is a deeper sense in which the "realism" objection goes awry both scientifically and normatively. The difference between deliberative and realist criteria of democracy is *not* the same as the difference between ideal and non-ideal theory. Rather the key difference hinges on the distinction between norm referenced and criterion referenced measurement. In measurement theory, "norm" is used in the descriptive or statistical sense – more like "typical" than "morally required." Schattschneider's "realist" view of democracy clarifies the problem as he sees it:

> The modern American does not look at democracy before he defines it; he defines it first and then is confused by what he sees ... We need to reexamine the chasm between theory and practice because it is at least as likely that the ideal is wrong as it is that the reality is bad. (1960: 127–128)

Thus, for Schattschneider, the criteria for a well-functioning democracy are inherently comparative given the status quo – we simply look to see how we measure up against the other cases that we currently categorize as democracies. Criterion referenced measurement, on the other hand, argues that we should clarify a regime type's explicit and implicit normative commitments first, and *then* judge cases against those criteria directly (and against other polities only derivatively). Depending on the nature of the measurement problem, both strategies have their advantages.

The great disadvantage of norm referenced measurement is that it is inherently conservative (in the sense of status quo bias), and very poor at managing changes in the distribution of cases over time. Thus, it is ill-suited as a measurement strategy if we aspire to evaluate efforts toward *reform*. The normative sample of democracies seventy years ago would be quite inapt for assessing democracies today, and so would not have served as a reliable guide to get us where we are today. Schattschneider claims that modern American citizens are confused by what they see when they look at their democracy. The evidence that I presented in Chapter 5 suggests that they are more dismayed than confused, and it is hardly clear that we should hope that their dismay turns to quiescence.

* * *

In Chapter 2, I argued that three crucial conceptual moves transformed the relationship between deliberative theory and empirical research. First, conceptualizing deliberation as a set of normative criteria, rather than as a set of talk-based political innovations means that we can assess a whole range of non-facially deliberative institutions and practices for their potential to serve deliberative ends. Thus, research on implementing possible deliberative reforms will be able to address itself to a much more flexible set of organizational questions. Second, by moving to a systemic view of deliberative democracy, we can better integrate deliberative theory with existing democratic institutions, and take normative pressure off of any given site of deliberation. Third, I introduced the inferentialist account of shared meaning as a bridge between normative and empirical meaning. Together, these three moves expand the deliberative research agenda considerably, making the theory much more flexible, but also more protean. I argued that scientific concerns over deliberative theory's flexibility were misplaced, and sketched various measurement strategies for deliberative quality.

In Chapter 3, I argued that the market model of politics was much less normatively attractive than it might appear. Without covert appeals to adequate deliberation, it reduces to something very much like Hobbesian decisiveness. Democratic minimalists rely on arguments that are similar enough to Hobbes that they end up having similar normative implications, without acknowledging the connection. Critics argue that citizens in mass democracies not only fail to form stable preferences, but that cognitive limitations and the vagaries of natural language mean that they *cannot* form stable preferences. I argued that the critics' argument was not well specified enough to even be evaluated, and developed an inferentialist account of deliberation to give the objection adequate specificity. But the switch to an inferentialist framework revealed that the problem that critics point to must be remediable in principle, and that thinking about democratic preferences as a kind of latent construct opens up the possibility of giving them enough substance to serve their function in the deliberative system. I conclude by showing how deliberative procedures are especially well suited to manage the context dependency problem that motivated the minimalist objection in the first place, and to provide some leverage in distinguishing between leadership and manipulation in the deliberative system.

In Chapter 4, I argued that minimalist critiques based on the formal results of social choice theory and game theory also led to a Hobbesian interpretation of democracy. I showed how previous attempts to defend the cogency of democratic voting from such critiques depend crucially on defending specifically deliberative processes from such critique as well. I deployed the inferentialist model of deliberation – the game of giving and asking for reasons – to explain how extant formal models of deliberation fail to capture the key concerns of deliberativists, and how the two paradigms might fruitfully engage going forward

In Chapter 5, I argued that critics of deliberative democracy mistakenly assume that motives for political participation are ordered in such a way as to make deliberative participation a pipedream. While it is true that citizens often dislike politics, for many, it is actually the presumptions of partisan politics and interest group liberalism that turns them off. Precisely those people who are demobilized by partisan politics selectively express a greater desire to deliberate, both hypothetically and in response to a real invitation to deliberate with their member of Congress.

In Chapter 6, I argued that citizens were not only more willing to deliberate than commonly thought, but that they were more competent as well. After World War II, the problem of citizen competence loomed large, but it was rapidly transformed from a substantive normative theory into an informational problem, with the market model as the unstated normative substitute. The main attempts to redeem public competence end up sharing the same normative presumptions of the theory that they criticize, and so do not address the fundamental issue for deliberative purposes. Deliberative opinion polls and other mini-public experiments are promising avenues of reform, but they are subject to dialectical tendencies toward a legitimation crisis of their own. Thus, they cannot serve as the lynchpin for democratic reforms, and must be integrated into a larger systemic perspective on deliberative democracy. There are many promising routes for doing so, but they highlight the need for further research and democratic experimentation in order to move forward.

* * *

As I write these words, my older daughter is finishing up her first week of kindergarten. She now has more formal education than my paternal grandfather had in his lifetime. Soon she will be able to read the newspaper on her own, and by the time she finishes high school and gets the right to vote, she will have knowledge and skills far beyond my grandfather's. College and anything after will only widen the gulf. Yet when my daughter Anna turns eighteen, she will get one vote, the same that my grandfather Stefano got a few years after he came to this country, poor, illiterate, and unaccustomed to the rights and responsibilities of democratic citizenship. Democracy is predicated on the conjecture – it is hardly obvious – that such equality is sensible and just, and that our institutions should reflect those commitments. Dewey went so far as to put this point in terms of faith:

Democracy is a way of personal life controlled not merely by faith in human nature in general but by faith in the capacity of human beings for intelligent judgment and action if proper conditions are furnished ... For what is the faith of democracy in the role of consultation, of conference, of persuasion, of discussion, in formation of public opinion, which in the long run is self-corrective, except faith in the capacity of the intelligence of *the common man* to respond with *common-sense* to the free play of facts and ideas which are secured by effective guarantees of free inquiry, free assembly and free communication? I am willing to leave to upholders of totalitarian states of the right and the left the view that faith in the capacities of intelligence is utopian. For the faith is so deeply embedded in the methods which are intrinsic to democracy that when a professed democrat denies the faith he convicts himself of treachery to his profession. (1939: 227)[1]

I certainly do not mean to suggest – and nor would Dewey – that formal education cannot contribute greatly to good democratic citizenship. This conjecture or "faith" hardly reduces to some gauzy version of "all I ever needed to know about democracy I learned in kindergarten." But it is to say that, strictly on knowledge criteria, all of us will be overwhelmed rapidly by the technical details of nearly every policy we consider in adequate detail. Beyond basic political literacy, we are congenital amateurs, and as such, our contributions to the deliberative process will not usually hinge centrally on the technical knowledge that we have at our disposal.

Rather, if Dewey's "proper conditions are furnished," our ability to discharge our roles ably will likely hinge most crucially on virtues and vigilance of a different sort. Our buy-in to the norms of the game of giving and asking for reasons will typically loom larger than the number of facts that we bring to the table. Our motivations to understand each other, to be understood, and to align our understandings with others emerge early in life, well before our formal education begins. Healthy political cultures must prevent cynicism from eroding and overwhelming these dispositions, and should perhaps even nurture and amplify them. At least some of the time, common people must make the effort to speak up about politics, to listen, and, on that basis, to speak with more common voices.

* * *

[1] I do not believe that by invoking "faith" Dewey meant to insulate democratic institutions and practices from social scientific critique, but rather that we should exhaust our search for "proper conditions" before concluding that democracy itself, rather than its current forms of organization, is irredeemable. It is a kind of strong, practical working theory. For Dewey, the social science of democracy was a kind of secular version of the traditional notion of *fides quaerens intellectum* – in this case, democratic faith seeking social scientific understanding.

Coincidentally, my older daughter's first attempt to involve herself in an adult conversation about politics, like the conversation at my father's tavern when I was a child, concerned unions. My wife is a public high school teacher, and the state of Ohio was considering legislation to restrict the collective bargaining rights of public unions. Members of the union canvassed their neighborhoods, distributing signs, placards, and stickers opposing the legislation, and my daughter overheard discussions about the campaign. Later she asked why anyone would want to be so "mean" to teachers, police officers, and firefighters. My wife took pains (it may have literally caused her pain) to represent her political opponents in a reasonable light, explaining the recession, budget deficits, and calls for shared sacrifice. She conveyed that people on the opposing sides of the issue disagreed about what would be fair and how the sharing should work. My daughter, echoing her teachers' standard admonition toward resolving conflicts, replied earnestly, "I hope that they will listen to each other's words."

References

Achen, C. H. (1975). "Mass Political Attitudes and the Survey Response." *American Political Science Review* 69(4): 1218–31.

Ackerman, B. and J. Fishkin. (2004). "Righting the Ship of Democracy." *Legal Affairs* January/February: 34–9.

Adorno, T. W., E. Frenkel-Brunswik, D. J. Levison, and R. N. Sanford. (1950). *The Authoritarian Personality*. New York: Norton.

Altemeyer, R. (1981). *Right-Wing Authoritarianism*. Winnipeg: University of Manitoba Press.

Althaus, S. L. (2003). *Collective Preferences in Democratic Politics*. Cambridge: Cambridge University Press.

Arrow, K. J. (1951). *Social Choice and Individual Values*. New York: John Wiley.

Austen-Smith, D. (1990). "Information Transmission in Debate." *American Journal of Political Science* 34(1): 124–52.

Austen-Smith, D. and J. S. Banks. (1996). "Information Aggregation, Rationality, and the Condorcet Jury Theorem." *American Political Science Review* 91(1): 34–45.

Austen-Smith, D. and T. J. Feddersen. (2006). "Deliberation, Preference Uncertainty, and Voting Rules." *American Political Science Review* 100(2): 209–17.

(2008). "In Response to Jurg Steiner's, 'Concept Stretching: The Case of Deliberation.'" *European Political Science* 7(2): 191–3.

(2009). "Information Aggregation and Communication in Committees." *Philosophical Transactions of the Royal Society of Biological Sciences* 364: 763–9.

Bächtiger, A., S. Niemeyer, M. A. Neblo, M. R. Steenbergen, and J. Steiner. (2010). "Disentangling Diversity in Deliberative Democracy: Competing Theories, Their Blind Spots and Complementarities." *Journal of Political Philosophy* 18(1): 32–63.

Barabas, J. (2004). "How Deliberation Affects Policy Opinions." *American Political Science Review* 98(4): 687–701.

Bartels, L. M. (1996). "Uninformed Votes: Information Effects in Presidential Elections." *American Journal of Political Science* 40(1): 194–230.

(2003). "Democracy with Attitudes." In *Electoral Democracy,* edited by Michael B. MacKuen and George Rabinowitz. Ann Arbor, MI: University of Michigan Press, 48–82.

Belzer, M. H. (2000). *Sweatshops on Wheels: Winners and Losers in Trucking Deregulation.* Oxford: Oxford University Press.

Ben-Ner, A., L. Putterman, and T. Ren. (2010). "Lavish Returns on Cheap Talk: Two-Way Communication in Trust Games." *The Journal of Socio-Economics* 40(1): 1–13.

Berelson, B. R. (1952). "Democratic Theory and Public Opinion." *Public Opinion Quarterly* 16: 313–30.

Bizer, G. Y., J. A. Krosnick, A. L. Holbrook, S. C. Wheeler, D. D. Rucker, and R. E. Petty. (2004). "The Impact of Personality on Cognitive Behavioral, and Affective Political Processes: The Effects of Need to Evaluate." *Journal of Personality* 72(5): 995–1027.

Blair, J., D. R. Mitchell, and K. Blair. (2005). *The Psychopath: Emotion and the Brain.* Malden, MA: Wiley-Blackwell.

Bohman, J. (1996). *Public Deliberation: Pluralism, Complexity, and Democracy.* Cambridge: The MIT Press.

(2007). "Political Communication and the Epistemic Value of Diversity: Deliberation and Legitimation in Media Societies." *Communication Theory* 17(4): 348–55.

Brady, D. W. and C. Volden. (2005). *Revolving Gridlock.* Boulder, CO: Westview Press.

Brandom, R. (1994). *Making It Explicit.* Cambridge, MA: Harvard University Press.

Brinkley, D. (1996). *11 Presidents, 4 Wars, 22 Political Conventions, 1 Moon Landing, 3 Assassinations, 2,000 Weeks of News and Other Stuff on Television and 18 Years of Growing Up in North Carolina.* New York: Ballantine Books.

Burden, C. T. Hysom, K. M. Esterling, D. Lazer, and M. A. Neblo. (2007). *2007 Gold Mouse Report: Lessons from the Best Web Sites on Capitol Hill.* Washington, DC: Congressional Management Foundation.

Burns, N., K. L. Schlozman, and S. Verba. (2001). *The Private Roots of Public Action: Gender, Equality, and Political Participation.* Cambridge, MA: Harvard University Press.

Cacioppo, J. T. and R. E. Petty. (1982). "The Need for Cognition." *Journal of Personality and Social Psychology* 42(1): 116–31.

Chambers, S. (2009). "Rhetoric and the Public Sphere: Has Deliberative Democracy Abandoned Mass Democracy." *Political Theory* 37(3): 323–50.

Cohen, J. (1999). "Habermas on Democracy." *Ratio Juris* 12(4): 385–416.

Converse, P. E. (1963). "Attitudes and Non-Attitudes: Continuation of a Dialogue." In *The Quantitative Analysis of Social Problems,* edited by E. R. Tufte. Reading, MA: Addison-Wesley.

(1964). "The Nature of Belief Systems in Mass Publics." In *Ideology and Discontent,* edited by D. E. Apter. New York: Free Press, 206–61.

Cook, F. L., M. X. Delli Carpini, and L. Jacobs. (2007). "Who Deliberates? Discursive Participation in America." In *Deliberation, Participation and Democracy: Can the People Govern?*, edited by Shawn W. Rosenberg. Hampshire: Palgrave Macmillan.

Dahl, R. A. (1956). *A Preface to Democratic Theory.* Chicago, IL: University of Chicago Press.

　(1958). "Political Theory: Truth and Consequences." *World Politics* 11(1): 89–102.

　(1961). "The Behavioral Approach in Political Science: Epitaph for a Monument to a Successful Protest." *American Political Science Review* 55(4): 763–72.

Dahlberg, L. (2005). "The Habermasian Public Sphere: Taking Difference Seriously?" *Theory and Society* 34(2): 111–36.

Delli Carpini, M. X. and S. Keeter. (1996). *What Americans Know about Politics and Why It Matters.* New Haven, CT: Yale University Press.

Delli Carpini, M. X., F. L. Cook, and L. R. Jacobs. (2004). "Public Deliberation, Discursive Participation, and Citizen Engagement: A Review of the Empirical Literature." *Annual Review of Political Science* 7: 315–44.

Dewey, J. (1927). *The Public and Its Problems.* Chicago, IL: Swallow.

Dickson, E. S., C. Hafer, and D. Landa. (2008). "Cognition and Strategy: A Deliberation Experiment." *The Journal of Politics* 70: 974–89.

Disch, L. (2011). "Toward a Mobilization Conception of Democratic Representation." *American Political Science Review* 105: 100–14.

Druckman, J. N. (2004). "Political Preference Formation: Competition, Deliberation, and the (Ir)relevance of Framing Effects." *American Political Science Review* 98(4): 671–86.

Dryzek, John S. (2005). "Handle with Care: The Deadly Hermeneutics of Deliberative Instrumentation." *Acta Politica* 40(2): 197–211.

Dyson, F. (2004). "A Meeting with Enrico Fermi." *Nature* 427: 297.

Eliasoph, N. (1998). *Avoiding Politics: How Americans Produce Apathy in Everyday Life.* Cambridge: Cambridge University Press.

Elster, J. (1983). *Sour Grapes: Studies in the Subversion of Rationality.* Paris: Cambridge University Press.

　(1986) "The Market and the Forum: Three Varieties of Political Theory." In *Foundations of Social Choice Theory*, edited by J. Elster and A. Hylland. Cambridge: Cambridge University Press.

　Ed. (1998). *Deliberative Democracy.* Cambridge: Cambridge University Press.

Erickson, R. S. (1979). "The SRC Panel Data and Mass Political Attitudes." *British Journal of Political Science* 2: 25–60.

Erickson, R. S., M. B. MacKuen, and J. A. Stimson. (2002). *The Macro Polity.* Cambridge: Cambridge University Press.

Esterling, K. M., M. A. Neblo, and D. Lazer. (2011a). "Means, Motive, and Opportunity in Becoming Informed about Politics: A Deliberative Field Experiment with Members of Congress and Their Constituents." *Public Opinion Quarterly* 75 (3): 483–503.

Esterling, K. M., D. Lazer, and M. A. Neblo. (2011b). "Representative Communication: Web Site Interactivity and Distributional Path Dependence in the US Congress." *Political Communication* 28(4): 409–39.

(2011c). "Estimating Treatment Effects in the Presence of Noncompliance and Nonresponse: The Generalized Endogenous Treatment Model." *Political Analysis* 19(2): 205–26.

Esterling, K. M., D. Lazer, and M. A. Neblo. (2013). "Connecting to Constituents: The Diffusion of Representation Practices among Congressional Website." *Political Research Quarterly* 66: 102.

Farrar, C., J. Fishkin, D. Green, C. List, R. Luskin, and E. Paluck. (2010). "Disaggregating Deliberation's Effects: An Experiment with a Deliberative Poll." *British Journal of Political Science* 40: 333–47.

Fehr, E. and B. Rockenbach. (2003). "Detrimental Effects of Sanctions on Human Altruism." *Nature* 422: 137–40.

Ferrell, R. H. (1994). *Harry S. Truman: A Life*. Columbia, MO: University of Missouri Press.

Fishkin, J. S. (2005). "Defending Deliberation: A Comment on Ian Shapiro's The State of Democratic Theory." *Critical Review of International Social and Political Philosophy* 8(1): 71–8.

(2009). *When the People Speak: Deliberative Democracy and Public Consultation*. Oxford: Oxford University Press.

Fishkin, J. S. and R. C. Luskin. (2005). "Experimenting With a Democratic Ideal: Deliberative Polling and Public Opinion." *Acta Politica* 40(3): 284–98.

Frohlich, N. and J. Oppenheimer. (2006). "Skating on Thin Ice: Cracks in the Public Choice Foundation." *Journal of Theoretical Politics* 18(3): 235–66.

Gastil, J., E. P. Deess, et al. (2002). "Civic Awakening in the Jury Room: A Test of the Connection between Jury Deliberation and Political Participation." *Journal of Politics* 64(2): 585–95.

Gerardi, D. and L. Yariv (2007). "Deliberative Voting." *Journal of Economic Theory* 134(1): 317–38.

Goeree, J. K. and L. Yariv. (2011). "An Experimental Study of Collective Deliberation." *Econometrica* 79(3): 893–921.

Gibbard, A. (1973). "Manipulation of Voting Schemes: A General Result." *Econometrica* 29(1): 33–43.

Goodin, R. E. (2000). "Democratic Deliberation Within." *Philosophy and Public Affairs* 29(1): 81–109.

(2003). *Reflective Democracy*. Oxford: Oxford University Press.

Gutmann, A. and D. Thompson. (1996). *Democracy and Disagreement*. Cambridge: Belknap Press / Harvard University Press.

Gutmann, A. and D. F. Thompson. (2004). *Why Deliberative Democracy?* Princeton, NJ: Princeton University Press.

Habermas, J. (2006). "Political Communication in Media Society: Does Democracy Still Enjoy an Epistemic Dimension? The Impact of Normative Theory on Empirical Research1." *Communication Theory* 16(4): 411–26.

(1996). *Between Facts and Norms: Contributions to a Discourse Theory of Law and Democracy*. Cambridge: The MIT Press.

(1993). *Justification and Application: Remarks on Discourse Ethics*. Cambridge: The MIT Press.

(1979). *Communication and the Evolution of Society*. Boston: Beacon Press.

(1976). *Legitimation Crisis*. Boston: Beacon Press.

(1989b [1962]). *The Structural Transformation of the Public Sphere: An Inquiry into a Category of Bourgeois Society*. Cambridge: The MIT Press.

Heath, J. (2001). *Communicative Action and Rational Choice*. Cambridge: The MIT Press.

(2008). *Following the Rules: Practical Reasoning and Deontic Constraint*. Oxford: Oxford University Press.

Herbst, S. (1998). *Reading Public Opinion: How Political Actors View the Democratic Process*. Chicago: University of Chicago Press.

Hibbing, J. R. and E. Theiss-Morse. (2002). *Stealth Democracy*. Cambridge: Cambridge University Press.

Hobbes, T. (1991 [1651]). *Leviathan*. Cambridge: Cambridge University Press.

Huckfeldt, R. (2007). "Unanimity, Discord, and the Communication of Public Opinion." *American Journal of Political Science* 51(4): 978–95.

Jacobs, L. R. and R. Y. Shapiro. (2000). *Politicians Don't Pander: Political Manipulation and the Loss of Democratic Responsiveness*. Chicago: University of Chicago Press.

Jacobs, L. R., F. L. Cook, and M. X. Delli Carpini. (2009). *Talking Together: Public Deliberation and Political Participation in America*. Chicago: University of Chicago Press.

Jacquette, D. (2007). "Two Sides of Any Issue." *Argumentation* 21(2): 115–27.

Jensen, J. L. (2003). "Public Spheres on the Internet: Anarchic or Government-Sponsored: A Comparison." *Scandinavian Political Studies* 26(4): 349–74.

Kahneman, D., P. Slovic, et al., Eds. (1982). *Judgement Under Uncertainty: Heuristics and Biases*. New York: Cambridge University Press.

Kant, Immanuel. (1979) [1798]. *The Conflict of the Faculties*. New York: Abaris Books.

Kelly, J. (2012). *Framing Democracy: A Behavioral Approach to Democratic Theory*. Princeton: Princeton University Press.

Key, V. O. J. (1966). *The Responsible Electorate: Rationality in Presidential Voting, 1936–1960*. Cambridge: Harvard University Press.

Knoke, D., F. U. Pappi, J. Broadbent, and Y. Tsujinaka. (1996). *Comparing Policy Networks: Labor Politics in the U.S., Germany, and Japan*. Cambridge: Cambridge University Press.

Kohlberg, L. (1971). *From Is to Ought: How to Commit the Naturalistic Fallacy and Get Away With it in the Study of Moral Development*. New York: Academic Press.

Krehbiel, K. (1998). *Pivotal Politics: A Theory of U.S. Lawmaking*. Chicago: University of Chicago Press.

Kühberger, A. (1998). "The Influence of Framing on Risky Decisions: A Meta-Analysis." *Organizational Behavior and Human Decision Processes* 75(1): 23–55.

Kuga, K. and H. Nagatani. (1974). "Voter Antagonism and the Paradox of Voting." *Econometrica* 42: 1045–67.

Lacy, D. (2001). "A Theory of Nonseparable Preferences in Survey Responses." *American Journal of Political Science* 45(2): 239–58.

Landa, D. and A. Meirowitz. (2009). "Game Theory, Information, and Deliberative Democracy." *American Journal of Political Science* 53(2): 427–44.

Lau, R. R. and D. P. Redlawsk. (1997). ""Voting Correctly"." *American Political Science Review* 91(3): 585–97.

Lazer, D., A. Sohkey, M. A. Neblo, R. Kennedy, and K. Esterling. (2015). "Expanding the Conversation: Multiplier Effects from a Deliberative Field Experiment." Forthcoming, Political Communication.

Lazer, D., M. A. Neblo, and K. Esterling. (2011). "The Internet and the Madisonian Cycle: Possibilities and Prospects for Consultative Representation". *Connecting Democracy: Online Consultation and the Flow of Political Communication*, pp. 265–85.

Lazer, D., I. Mergel, C. Ziniel, K. M. Esterling, and M. A. Neblo. (2011). "The Multiple Institutional Logics of Innovation." *International Public Management Journal* 14(3): 311–40.

Lazer, D., M. A. Neblo, K. Esterling, K. Goldschmidt. (2009). "Online Town Hall Meetings: Exploring Democracy in the 21st Century." Congressional Management Foundation.

Lind, E. A. and T. R. Tyler. (1988). *The Social Psychology of Procedural Justice.* New York: Plenum Press.

Lippmann, W. (1922). *Public Opinion.* New York: Harcourt, Brace.

Lodge, M., K. M. McGraw, and P. Stroh. (1989). "An Impression-Driven Model of Candidate Evaluation." *American Political Science Review* 87: 399–419.

Lupia, A. and M. D. McCubbins. (1998). *The Democratic Dilemma: Can Citizens Learn What They Need to Know?* Cambridge: Cambridge University Press.

Luskin, R. C. and J. S. Fishkin. (2002) "Deliberation and 'Better Citizens'." Paper presented at the Joint Sessions of Workshops of the ECPR, Turin, Italy, 3/2002.

Mackie, G. (2003). *Democracy Defended.* Cambridge: Cambridge University Press.

Madar, D. (2000). *Heavy Traffic: Deregulation, Trade, and Transformation in North American Trucking.* Vancouver: UBC Press.

Mansbridge, J. (1980). *Beyond Adversary Democracy.* New York: Basic Books.

(1999). "On the Idea that Participation Makes Better Citizens." In *Citizen Competence and Democratic Institutions*, edited by Elkin and Soltan. University Park, PA: Pennsylvania State University Press.

(2003). "Rethinking Representation." *American Political Science Review* 97(4): 515–27.

(2007). "Self-Interest in Deliberation." *Kettering Review* 25(1): 62–72.

Mansbridge, J., M. Amengual, J. Hartz-Karp, and J. Gastil. (2006). "Norms of Deliberation: An Inductive Study." *Journal of Public Deliberation* 2(1): 1–47.

Mansbridge, J., J. Bohman, S. Chambers, D. Estlund, A. Follesdal, A. Fung, C. Lafont, B. Manin, and J. L. Marti. (2010). "The Place of Self-Interest in Deliberative Democracy." *Journal of Political Philosophy* 18(1): 64–100.

Marcus, G. and M. MacKuen (1993). "Anxiety, Enthusiasm, and the Vote: The Emotional Underpinnings of Learning and Involvement during Presidential Campaigns." *American Political Science Review* 87: 672–86.

Margolis, H. (2007). *Cognition and Extended Rational Choice.* London: Routledge.

McKelvey, R. D. (1979). "General Conditions for Global Intransitivities in Formal Voting Models." *Econometrica* 47: 1085–112.

McKelvey, R. D. and P. C. Ordershook. (1986). "Information, Electoral Equilibria, and the Democratic Ideal." *The Journal of Politics* 48: 909–37.

McManus, J. (2009). *Cowboys Full: The Story of Poker*. New York: MacMillan.

Meirowitz, A. (2006). "Designing Institutions to Aggregate Preferences and Information." *Quarterly Journal of Political Science* 1: 373–92.

   (2007). "In Defense of Exclusionary Deliberation: Communication and Voting with Private Beliefs and Values." *Journal of Theoretical Politics* 19(3): 301.

Mendelberg, T. (2002). "The Deliberative Citizen: Theory and Evidence." *Research in Micropolitics* 6: 151–93.

Mendelberg, T. and J. Oleske. (2000). "Race and Public Deliberation." *Political Communication* 17: 169–91.

Mercier, H. and D. Sperber. (2011a). "Argumentation: It's Adaptiveness and Efficacy." *Behavioral and Brain Sciences* 34: 94–111.

   (2011b). "Why do Humans Reason? Arguments for an Argumentative Theory." *Brain Sciences* 34(2): 94–111.

Miller, D. (1992). "Deliberative Democracy and Social Choice." *Political Studies* 40(s1): 54–67.

Minozzi, W. (2011) "A Jamming Theory of Politics." *Journal of Politics* 73(2): 301-15.

   (2013). "Endogenous Beliefs in Models of Politics." *American Journal of Political Science* 57(3): 566–81.

Minozzi, W., M. A. Neblo, and D. A. Siegel. (2012). "A Theory of Deliberation as Interactive Reasoning." APSA Annual Meeting.

Minozzi, W., M. A. Neblo, K. M. Esterling, and D. M. Lazer. (2015). "Field experiment evidence of substantive, attributional, and behavioral persuasion by members of Congress in online town halls." *Proceedings of the National Academy of Sciences* 112(13): 3937-42.

Muhlberger, P. (n.d.) "Stealth Democracy: Authoritarianism, Parochial Citizens and Deliberation."

Mutz, D. (2006). *Hearing the Other Side: Deliberative versus Participatory Democracy*. Cambridge: Cambridge University Press.

Mutz, D. C. (2002). "The Consequences of Crosscutting Networks for Political Participation." *American Journal of Political Science* 46: 838–55.

   (2008). "Is Deliberative Democracy a Falsifiable Theory?" *Annual Review of Political Science* 11(1): 521–38.

Neblo, M. A. (2000). Thinking Through Democracy: Deliberative Politics in Theory and Practice. Dissertation, University of Chicago.

Neblo, M. A. (2003). Impassioned Democracy: The Role of Emotion in Deliberative Theory. In *Democracy Collaborative Affiliates Conference*.

   (2004). "Giving Hands and Feet to Morality." *Perspectives on Politics* 2(01): 99–100.

   (2005a). "Thinking Through Democracy: Between the Theory and Practice of Deliberative Politics." *Acta Politica* 40(2): 169–81.

   (2005b). "The Weight of Passion." In Annual Meeting of the Midwest Political Science Association, Chicago, IL.

(2007a). "Family Disputes: Diversity in Defining and Measuring Deliberation." *Swiss Political Science Review* 13(4): 527–57.

(2007b). "Change for the Better? Linking the Mechanisms of Deliberative Opinion Change to Normative Theory." Paper presented to the Midwest Political Science Association Annual Meeting, Chicago

(2007c). "Philosophical Psychology with Political Intent." *The Affect Effect: Dynamics of Emotion in Political Thinking and Behavior*, pp.25–47.

(2009a). "Three-Fifths a Racist: A Typology for Analyzing Public Opinion About Race." *Political Behavior* 31(1): 31–51.

(2009b). "Meaning and Measurement: Reorienting the Race Politics Debate." *Political Research Quarterly* 62(3): 474–84.

(2011a). "The Virtue of Deliberation: Sophrosyne and Epistemic Democracy." Annual Meeting of the American Political Science Association.

(2011b). "Deliberation's Legitmation Crisis." *Critical Review* 23(3): 405–19.

Neblo, M. A., K. Esterling, R. Kennedy, D. Lazer, and A. Sokhey. (2010). "Who Wants to Deliberate – and Why?" *American Political Science Review* 104(3): 566–83.

Neumann, J. von and O. Morgenstern. (1944). *Theory of Games and Economic Behavior*. New York: Wiley.

Page, B. I. (1996). *Who Deliberates?: Mass Media in Modern Democracy*. Chicago: The University of Chicago Press.

Page, B. I. and R. Y. Shapiro. (1992). *The Rational Public: Fifty Years of Trends in Americans' Policy Preferences*. Chicago: The University of Chicago Press.

Parkinson, J. (2003). "Legitimacy Problems in Deliberative Democracy." *Political Studies* 51(1): 180–196.

Parkinson, J., and J. Mansbridge, Eds. (2012). *Deliberative Systems: Deliberative Democracy at the Large Scale*. Cambridge: Cambridge University Press.

Pateman, C. (1970). *Participation and Democratic Theory*. Cambridge: Cambridge University Press.

Patty, J. W. (2008). "Arguments-Based Collective Choice." *Journal of Theoretical Politics* 20(4): 379–414.

Patty, J. W. and E. M. Penn. (2010). "A Social Choice Theory of Legitimacy." *Social Choice and Welfare* 36(3): 365–82.

Pettit, P. (2001). "Deliberative Democracy and the Discursive Dilemma." *Philosophical Issues* 11: 268–99.

(2003). "Discourse Theory and Republican Liberty." *Critical Review of International Social and Political Philosophy* 6: 72–95.

Pitkin, H. F. (1967). *The Concept of Representation*. Berkeley: University of California Press.

Podsakoff, P. M., S. B. MacKenzie, J. Lee, and N. P. Podsakoff. (2003). "Common Method Biases in Behavioral Research: A Critical Review of the Literature and Recommended Remedies." *Journal of Applied Psychology*. 88 (5): 879–903.

Posner, R. (2003). *Law, Pragmatism, and Democracy*. Cambridge, MA: Harvard University Press.

(2004). "Smooth Sailing." *Legal Affairs* January/February: 41–42.

Putnam, R. D. (2000). *Bowling Alone*. New York: Simon & Schuster.

Raskinski, K. A. (1989). "The Effect of Question Wording on Public Support for Government Spending." *Public Opinion Quarterly* 53: 388–94.

Riker, W. H. (1980). "Implications from the Disequilibrium of Majority Rule for the Study of Institutions." *American Political Science Review* 74(2): 432–46.

(1982). *Liberalism Against Populism: A Confrontation between the Theory of Democracy and the Theory of Social Choice*. Prospect Heights, IL: Waveland Press.

Rokeach, M. (1960). *The Open and Closed Mind*. New York: Basic Books.

Rorty, R. (1982). *Consequences of Pragmatism*. Minneapolis, MN: University of Minnesota Press.

Sanders, L. M. (1997). "Against Deliberation." *Political Theory* 25(3): 347–76.

(1999). "Democratic Politics and Survey Research." *Philosophy and the Social Sciences* 29 (2): 248–80.

Satterthwaite, M. A. (1975). "Strategy-Proofness and Arrow's Conditions: Existence and Correspondence Theorems for Voting Procedures and Social Welfare Functions." *Journal of Economic Theory* 10(April): 187–217.

Scargle, J. D. (2000). "Publication Bias: The 'File-Drawer Problem' in Scientific Inference." *Journal of Scientific Exploration* 14(2): 94–106.

Schattschneider, E. E. (1960). *The Semisovereign Public: A Realist's View of Democracy in America*. New York: Holt, Rinehart and Winston.

Schelling, T. (1960/2006). *The Strategy of Conflict*. Cambridge: Harvard University Press.

Schegloff, E. A. (2000). "Overlapping Talk and the Organization of Turn-Taking for Conversation." *Language in Society* 29: 1–63.

Schuman, H. and S. Presser. (1996). *Questions and Answers in Attitude Surveys: Experiments on Question Form, Wording and Context*. New York: Sage Publications.

Schumpeter, J. (1942/2008). *Capitalism, Socialism, and Democracy*. New York: Harper Perennial Modern Classics.

Searing, D. D., F. Solt, et al. (2007). "Public Discussion in the Deliberative System: Does It Make Better Citizens?" *British Journal of Political Science* 37(4): 587–618.

Shepsle, K. A. and B. R. Weingast. (1984). "Uncovered Sets and Sophisticated Voting Outcomes with Implications for Agenda Institutions." *American Journal of Political Science*, 28: 49–74.

Skinner, Q. (1974). "Some Problems in the Analysis of Political Thought and Action." *Political Theory* 2: 277–303.

Sniderman, P. M., R. A. Brody, and P. E. Tetlock. (1991). *Reasoning and Choice: Explorations in Political Psychology*. Cambridge: Cambridge University Press.

Steenbergen, M. R., A. Bächtiger, M. Spörndli, and J. Steiner. (2003). "Measuring Political Deliberation: A Discourse Quality Index." *Comparative European Politics* 1(1): 21–48.

Steiner, J. (2008). "Concept Stretching: The Case of Deliberation." *European Political Science* 7: 186–90.

Steiner, J., A. Bächtiger, M. Spörndli, M. R. Steenbergen. (2004). *Deliberative Politics in Action: Analyzing Parliamentary Discourse*. Cambridge: Cambridge University Press.

Sunstein, C. (2009). *Republic.com 2.0*. Princeton, NJ: Princeton University Press.

Taylor, Q. P. (2002). "Public Deliberation and Popular Government in Aristotle's 'Politics'." *Interpretation – A Journal of Political Philosophy* 29(3): 241–60.

Thompson, D. F. (2008). "Deliberative Democratic Theory and Empirical Political Science." *Annual Review of Political Science* 11(1): 497–520.

Tocqueville, A. D. ([1835/1840] 1969). *Democracy in America*. New York: Doubleday.

Tomasello, M., M. Carpenter, J. Call, T. Behne, and H. Moll. (2005). "Understanding and Sharing Intentions: The Origins of Cultural Cognition." *Behavioral and Brain Sciences* 28: 675–735.

Tversky, A. and D. Kahneman. (1981). "The Faming of Decisions and the Psychology of Choice." *Science* 211(4481): 453–58.

Verba, S., K. L. Schlozman, and H. Brady. (1995). *Voice and Equality: Civic Voluntarism in American Politics*. Cambridge, MA: Harvard University Press.

Von Neumann, J. and O. Morgenstern. (1944). *Theory of Games and Economic Behavior*. New York: Wiley.

Walzer, M. (1999). "Deliberation and What Else?" In *Deliberative Politics: Essays on Democracy and Disagreement,* edited by Stephen Macedo. New York: Oxford University Press.

Wanderer, J. (2008). *Robert Brandom*. Montreal: McGill-Queen's University Press.

Warren, M. (2007). "Institutionalizing Deliberative Democracy." In *Deliberation, Participation, and Democracy: Can the People Govern?* edited by S. Rosenberg. Baskingstoke: Palgrave.

Warren, R. P. (1946). *All the King's Men*. New York: Harcourt Brace and Company.

Zaller, J. (1992). *The Nature and Origins of Mass Opinion*. Cambridge: Cambridge University Press.

Index

Achen, Christopher H., 161
Ackerman, Bruce, 123
Adorno, Theodor, 157, 159–60
aggregating independently formed
    preferences, 66–7
aggregation. *see* under individuals
Althaus, Scott, 165, 170, 188
America Speaks forum, 185
arbitrary variation, 57, 69
Arrow, Kenneth, 81–2, 86
"Asian Disease" example, 54
attitudes, anti-deliberative, 145
attitudes: sunshine, trust or stealth,
    141–2
Austen-Smith, David, 33n. 10, 105n. 13,
    107, 108n. 15, 115
authoritarian attitudes. *see* attitudes,
    anti-deliberative

Banks, Jeffrey S., 107, 115
Bartels, Larry, 8n. 7, 55–7, 60, 165
Beck, Glen, 154
beliefs, factual and non-factual, 112–13
beneficial outcomes of deliberative
    democracy, 43–4
Ben-Ner, Avner, 115n. 22
Bizer, George Y., 131
"bonding" communicative capital. *see*
    communicative capital
Borda rule, 85
Brady, David W., 73
Brandom, Robert, 29–30, 89–90, 91n. 7,
    116, 177

"bridging" communicative capital. *see*
    communicative capital
Burns, Nancy, 130

Cacioppo, John, 131
Carter, Pres. Jimmy, 1, 15
Churchill, Winston, 48
citizen competence, 157, 159–61, 172,
    189–92
    heuristics or short-cuts, 162–5,
    172
    minimalist claims, 162, 194–6
citizens. *see* individuals
citizenship, authoritarian or democratic,
    157–9
civic organizations, 16, 20–1
Coburn, Sen. Tom, 154
coercion, 98
    and tyranny, 101
Cohen, Joshua, 43, 48n. 21, 64
communicative capital, 21
competence. *see* citizen competence
"concept stretching," 33
Condorcet, Marquis de, 72, 73,
    83–4
Condorcet Jury Theorem, 115
conflict aversion, 149
Congressional Management Foundation,
    138
consensus, 91–5, 100–2, 177–8
context dependency, 53
Converse, Philip, 53, 55, 156, 159–62, 164,
    172–4, 178n. 17

211

Made in the USA
Middletown, DE
16 January 2021